WITHDRAWN

D1055584

To the Victor . . .

To the Victor...

POLITICAL PATRONAGE
FROM THE CLUBHOUSE
TO THE WHITE HOUSE

Martin and Susan Tolchin

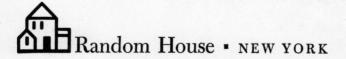

Random House · NEW YORK

Copyright © 1971 by Martin Tolchin and Susan Tolchin

All rights reserved under International and Pan-American Copyright Conventions. Published in the United States by Random House, Inc., New York, and simultaneously in Canada by Random House of Canada Limited, Toronto.

ISBN: 0–394–46036–7

Library of Congress Catalog Card Number: 70–140733

Acknowledgment is extended to *The New York Times* to reprint material which first appeared there. Copyright © 1968, 1970 by The New York Times Company.

Manufactured in the United States of America

Book design by Paula Wiener

9 8 7 6 5 4 3 2

329.024
To

To our parents

61.523

ACKNOWLEDGMENTS

This book is an attempt to unite two disciplines, journalism and political science, to explore a subject usually hidden in the shadows of the political process. We are indebted to colleagues in both fields for their insights and encouragement, and to the hundreds of politicians we interviewed across the country who took us behind the scenes as best they could.

We gratefully acknowledge the imagination and counsel of Jason Epstein, our editor at Random House, who conceived the idea for this book and guided it to fruition, and to Arthur Gelb, metropolitan editor of *The New York Times*, who guided the initial survey on which this study is based, for his encouragement and support. We also acknowledge the encouragement of A. M. Rosenthal, managing editor of the *Times*, and the insights offered by James Reston, a vice president of the newspaper.

Portions of the manuscript were read by Professor Dennis Palumbo, of the Political Science Department of Brooklyn College; Marvin Siegel, an assistant to the metropolitan editor of the *Times;* and Mildred Casson—to all of whom we are also grateful.

The themes of this study also were developed after prolonged discussions with the City Hall staff of the *Times* (Edward C. Burks, Maurice Carroll, Iver Peterson and Edward Ranzal), Sheldon Binn, William Luce, and Robert Alden of the *Times*, Joseph Schoener of the Associated Press, and other members of Room Nine, the reporters who cover New York city government; as well as with faculty members and students from the political science departments of Brooklyn College and New York University. We also acknowledge the help of Bill Sweet, political editor of *The Memphis Commercial Appeal*, Reg Murphy, editor of *The Atlanta Consti-*

tution, and Mike Royko and Lois Wille, of *The Chicago Daily News*.

For their immensely useful suggestions and criticisms, particularly with regard to the theoretical aspects of the manuscript, we owe special thanks to: Professors Rita Cooley and Louis Koenig, of the Department of Politics of New York University; Professor Charles Ascher, former chairman of the Political Science Department at Brooklyn College; Professor Erwin Wilkie Bard and Dr. Sara Silbiger, also of Brooklyn College; Professor Richard Spero of Howard University; Dr. Herbert E. Alexander of the Citizens' Research Foundation; Professor Roosevelt Ferguson, of the University of Illinois; Professor Stanley Kelley, Jr., of Princeton University's Department of Political Science; Vice-Chancellor Julius C. C. Edelstein of the City University of New York; Dr. Joyce Gelb, of the City College Department of Political Science; Professor Wallace Sayre of Columbia University; and D. B. Hardeman, Professor of Government at St. Francis College.

We also acknowledge an intellectual and personal debt to Professor Gertrude Leighton of Bryn Mawr College; Professor Duncan MacRae of the University of Chicago; Professor Ludwik Krzyzanowski of New York University; and the Rev. Ed Cunningham of the First Congregational Church, Eureka, California.

We would like to extend our special thanks to those participants in the political arena whose candor, accessibility and generosity with time were especially valuable to us: Charles B. Schultze, former Federal Budget Director; Senators William Proxmire and Jacob Javits; Congressmen Andrew Jacobs, Edward Koch, Ogden Reid and Thomas Rees; Lieutenant Governor Paul Simon; Kenneth Young, legislative aide to the AFL-CIO; Nicholas Kisburg, legislative representative for the Teamsters Union; former Secretary of the Interior, Stuart Udall; former presidential aides James L. Rowe and George Reedy; former U.S. Attorney Robert Morgenthau; State Senator Seymour Thaler; Dr. Winona Lipman, chairman of the Montclair, N.J., Democratic club; I. D. Robbins, past president of the City Club; Mayors John

V. Lindsay, Kevin White, Ivan Allen, Jerome Cavanagh; Joseph Alioto and Henry Maier; Deputy Mayor City Administrator Timothy Costello; Deputy Mayor Richard Aurelio; Thomas Morgan, press secretary to Mayor John V. Lindsay; Peter Tufo; Walter Diamond; Judge Dorothy Kenyon; Judge Daniel Gutman, formerly Dean of the New York Academy of the Judiciary at New York University; Ernest Friesen, of the administrative branch of the federal courts; Elizabeth Schack, of the Judiciary Committee of the New York State League of Women Voters; James Sayler; Jacob Arvey; Mary Hynes; Dr. Canute Bernard; Russell Hemenway of the National Committee for an Effective Congress; William Deane of the Citizens Union; Commissioner Beverly Moss Spatt; and Edwin Friedman and Edward Schwartzman, of the New York State Division of Planning Coordination.

We also acknowledge research assistance given us by Lois Weiss, a graduate student at Brooklyn College; Judith Greenfeld of *The New York Times;* and the librarians of the New York Public Library, the Institute of Judicial Administration, and the Montclair Public Library. Our thanks also to Sono Rosenberg, copy editor at Random House.

These are among the hundreds of persons who aided us with their research, insights, philosophies, and their concern for our project. The results, of course, are ours alone, for which we take full and sole responsibility.

Montclair, N.J.
August 1970

CONTENTS

To the Victor . . .

1

"I Seen My Opportunities": How Honest Graft Affects Political Decisions

"Politics is the art of putting people under obligation to you."
—Colonel Jacob L. Arvey

"Patronage is the root evil of politics. It keeps people in bondage."

—Arthur Telcser, Republican member of the Illinois House of Representatives

Mrs. Irwin Brownstein's credentials to help select a President of the United States at the 1968 Democratic National Convention in Chicago were simply put: she was a college-educated Brooklyn housewife and mother, in her mid-thirties, who maintained a lively interest in public affairs. More to the point, she was married to a Civil Court judge who aspired to become—and was subsequently nominated and elected—a State Supreme Court justice.

Both judgeships—and Mrs. Brownstein's nomination as a delegate—were part of the political patronage controlled by Stanley Steingut, Democratic Party minority leader of the New York State Assembly who was then Brooklyn Democratic leader. In fact, all 21 nominees of the Brooklyn Democratic organization to the Chicago con-

3

vention had long-standing ties with Mr. Steingut. There were officeholders and their relatives; lawyers who dreamed of judgeships while they received courthouse patronage; bankers whose banks received interest-free deposits of government funds—highly coveted in a tight-money market; insurance men who earned large premiums for insuring government property; holders of government franchises; and contractors and architects who built and designed government buildings.

Together with their counterparts across the nation, they wore campaign badges and straw boaters at both national conventions and caroused, paraded, and cheered in the quadrennial carnivals of American politics. They had little to do, however, with the real work of the conventions, and like most delegates, Mrs. Brownstein had no illusions about her role. "I just want somebody to make up my mind for me," she said in an outburst of candor. "This job is more an *aliyeh*—an honor—than anything else. You don't need any special skills." Partly because of her extraordinary candor—she had violated the rule of political *omerta* and lost her anonymity when the organization's opponents gave her statement wide distribution in her district—Mrs. Brownstein never made it to Chicago. She was defeated by a Eugene McCarthy delegate in the first Democratic primary in New York State for convention delegates to be contested in modern times, but her philosophy was nonetheless typical of convention delegates.

Edward Costikyan, a former leader of Tammany Hall, the New York City Democratic organization, put it succinctly: "The first thing a candidate who wants a nomination from a convention should realize is that the delegates are not free agents, nor are they subject to persuasion. The delegate is the property of his leader."

Paul O'Dwyer, twice a New York Democratic candidate for the United States Senate and a McCarthy delegate to the Chicago convention, observed that in the fight for delegates, "You don't even talk to the delegates, you talk to the chiefs." There are occasional defectors, he said, because "Every once in a while somebody becomes a delegate unexpectedly, and nobody is quite aware of him—a Pope John XXIII." A split delegation usually means that the leader has decided to divide his delegation, rather than have a real division in the ranks, he noted, although occasionally a split will occur because of the absence of a strong leader. Representative Shirley Chisholm of Brooklyn, the first black woman elected to the United States Congress, angrily told delegates to the 1970 gubernatorial convention of the New York Democratic Party, appropriately held in the never-never land of round-the-clock entertainment at Grossinger's, a resort hotel in the Catskills: "You delegates, you come to conventions consistently and persistently, and you're nothing but robots and automatons who can't even answer to the dictates of your own conscience." Nor was there a prospect for change, Mrs. Chisholm continued, because "Those who have been the beneficiaries of the status quo are not going to change anything."

The delegate becomes the property of his leader through patronage—the allocation of the discretionary favors of government in exchange for political support. Once thought of as consisting only of jobs, patronage includes the vast range of favors awarded by constantly expanding governments whose increased government spending [1]—much of it discretionary—has brought increased opportunities to political supporters. Non-officeholders

[1] The New York City budget alone is $7.8 billion, for example, nearly three times the $3 billion federal budget of the 1930s, which has now expanded to $192 billion.

receive construction contracts, defense contracts, banking and insurance funds, and specialized treatment by the discretionary agencies of government whose power continues to grow. Officeholders, in charge of the machinery of government, have more discretionary power to dispense. In addition to bringing home the dams, post-office buildings, military installations, and Model Cities programs that make them look good to constituents, they control the key committee assignments and judicial patronage that smooth their political futures. All these favors cement a politician's loyalty to his party leaders, to whom he is indebted for past favors and from whom he seeks future favors, while at the same time they help him earn the loyalty of those beneath him in the party structure who are in turn indebted to him for favors.

The 1968 Chicago convention was a classic demonstration of the two-step political process: first, control the patronage, and then control policy-and-decision-making. The convention was a confrontation between those who controlled patronage—the Johnson-Humphrey-Daley forces—and those who did not, the McCarthy and McGovern forces.[2] By controlling patronage, the Humphrey forces controlled the convention and its decisions. The McCarthy and McGovern forces lacked patronage power and therefore had scant power at the convention and relatively little power to effect change, even though changes were apparently desired by a majority of Democratic voters in the 15 presidential primaries.[3] It must be noted

[2] President Lyndon Johnson, Vice-President Hubert Humphrey, Chicago Mayor Richard J. Daley; Senators Eugene McCarthy (Minnesota) and George McGovern (South Dakota).

[3] Mr. Humphrey, who did not campaign in the primaries, received 3.3 percent of the vote in Oregon, 0.5 percent in Wisconsin, 7.4 percent in Nebraska, 22.8 percent in New Jersey. Johnson slates, representing the Democratic Establishment, won 49.4 percent of the New

that Senator McCarthy was personally unacceptable to many candidates who might have voted for Senator Kennedy, who was assassinated. Had Senator Kennedy lived, his popularity at the polls plus the past Kennedy favors, fears of future Kennedy reprisals, and the feeling that he would have made a better candidate against Nixon might have persuaded some of the Democratic leaders to support him. A better index of control of the convention was the vote on the peace plank, which was decisively defeated by a vote of 1,567-¾ to 1,041-¼, despite the fact that rank-and-file voters had indicated their opposition to the war in all 15 Democratic primaries. The balloting for the presidential nomination was Humphrey (1,760-¼), McCarthy (601), McGovern (146).[4]

Patronage powers explain why an incumbent President almost always controls his party's national convention. Usually vested in the party's elders, patronage powers also explain why national politics is oriented more to the past than to current movements, and more toward conservative than to innovative programs. The 79-year-old former Speaker of the House, John W. McCormack of Massachusetts, and the 73-year-old President pro tem of the Senate, Richard B. Russell of Georgia, are among the

Hampshire vote (their best showing), 34.6 percent in Wisconsin, and 30.1 percent in South Dakota. The combined McCarthy-Kennedy vote won every primary except in New Hampshire, indicating greater dissatisfaction than support for the Democratic leadership at the grass-roots level.

[4] One reform enacted at the 1968 Chicago convention was the abolition of the unit rule (under which the entire vote of a state delegation is cast as the majority of the delegation has voted), a device which many states retained to bind delegates by rule as well as in fact. The Republican national convention does not permit the unit rule; but nearly all state conventions still follow the unit rule. Without the unit rule, party leaders must rely even more heavily on patronage ties to enforce party discipline.

leaders of a congressional system that rewards longevity with power. Even those members motivated by ideological commitment quickly discover, in the words of the late Sam Rayburn of Texas, that "to get along, you have to go along." Mr. Rayburn never expected a congressman to vote against the interests of his constituents, but often advised members that "anyone should find a way to go along with his leaders 70 percent of the time." [5]

It is sometimes possible for those who seek change through persuasion to bypass the patronage system, and indeed an issue whose time has come may triumph over patronage commitments. Long-overdue drug-reform legislation championed by the late Senator Estes Kefauver finally reached fruition only after the thalidomide [6] scandal produced enough of a public outcry to push the law through its congressional obstacle course. Similarly, political conventions have been stampeded and delegations split by the sheer force of public pressure. The Republican National Convention of 1940 which nominated Wendell Willkie was a case in point. More typically, however, delegations are split by rival leaders, as the California delegation in 1960 was torn between John F. Kennedy and Adlai Stevenson because of the rivalry between the governor and lieutenant governor of California. In this case, past patronage and the promise of new patronage proved decisive, helping the Kennedy forces to victory.

[5] Of those vying for the posts of Majority Leader and Assistant Majority Leader, Morris Udall supported the party's leaders 85 percent of the time, Richard Bolling (Mo.), 64 percent; James G. O'Hara (Mich.), 93 percent; Edward Boland (Mass.), 70 percent; Hale Boggs (La.), 64 percent; John Moss (Calif.), 67 percent; Dan Rostenkowski (Ill.), 64 percent; Wayne Hays (Ohio), 62 percent. *Congressional Quarterly, Weekly Report*, May 29, 1970, p. 1451.

[6] The drug thalidomide was taken off the market by the Food and Drug Administration after it was discovered to have caused birth defects in fetuses when taken by pregnant women.

The patronage system thrives as one of the occupational hazards of our democracy. In a land where most men have some degree of freedom of choice, incentives are often required to bestir them to public action, or to persuade them to change a course of action. Hence, public officials who do not know how to use patronage are invariably poor administrators, from Governor Lester B. Maddox of Georgia to Mayor John V. Lindsay of New York in his early years in office. Presidents, governors, and mayors without patronage skills usually have great difficulty dealing with their legislatures, which are made up of representatives who are obliged to bring patronage rewards (highways, schools, health stations, jobs) home to their districts. Unable to dispense rewards effectively, these leaders lack tools with which to bargain their own programs into fruition. Many find that they can no longer recruit top-flight administrators who fear the difficulties presented by working with people who do not have the time, energy, or inclination to work hard without the promise of rewards.

The patronage system also ensures that ideology plays a relatively small role in the decisions of government because, as national political conventions indicate, political rhetoric often conceals the hard, cold, unemotional realities of men and their ambitions meshing into place. Not surprisingly, the ideological approach to politics and government is encouraged by the politicians themselves, who would much rather portray themselves as motivated by principle than by power or personal profit. The ideological approach to government also receives sustenance from the mass media, which find it easier, less costly, and infinitely safer to report campaign speeches or depict members of Congress standing toe-to-toe in angry debate on the floor of the House than to learn, for example, why a congressman changed his vote during a closed meeting of a congressional committee (43 percent of all House committee meetings in 1968 were closed).[7] The accent is on oratory—flowery, stentorian, and acerbic. Gone almost unnoticed—and frequently denied—is the crucial role of the patronage system of debts incurred and IOU's held, accompanied by the overriding theme of political ambition.

Patronage power is a necessary and legitimate extension of the power of elected officials. It is more humane, in one sense, than a meritocracy in which individuals advance solely on merit without regard to years of service or personal loyalties. But it can be cruel, too. In Illinois, for example, 10,000 state employees, including the lame, the halt, and some with less than a month to go for their pensions, were dismissed by a new Republican Governor, Richard B. Ogilvie, who had been a persistent critic of Mayor Richard Daley's patronage practices, but who felt that he needed these patronage jobs to firm up his own power base.

The major hazard of patronage, however, is not that it builds political empires or private fortunes, but that it encourages public officials to compromise the public interest for private gain, and to sacrifice the national interest for the needs of their regional constituencies. This begins with the selection of presidential candidates at national conventions, and includes every aspect of public policy and government funding. How much of the $80 billion defense budget is actually used to protect the country, for example, and how much is allocated for military installations and defense contracts intended to win the support of various legislators, anxious to obtain more jobs and money for their districts? "I am convinced that defense is only one of the factors that enter into our determinations for defense spending," charged Mississippi Representative

---

[7] *Congressional Quarterly Almanac,* 1968, p. 798.

Jamie L. Whitten. "The others are pump priming, spreading the immediate benefits of defense spending, taking care of all services, giving military bases to include all sections. . . . We see the effects in public and Congressional insistence on continuing contracts, or operating military bases, though the need has expired." [8] Patronage may not have been a major factor in our initial commitment to Vietnam, but it has certainly made withdrawal more difficult. Representative Andrew Jacobs, an Indiana Democrat, said of defense patronage: "Holy cows become spendthrift; other cows get slaughtered."

One wonders how long the Vietnam war would continue if it were *against* the patronage interests of our national political leaders, and if a reduction in military installations and defense spending enriched, rather than impoverished, their constituencies and themselves. Indeed, former Chief Justice Earl Warren couched his explanation of why the war protest was led by young people in these terms: ". . . so long as youth carry the burden of the war while their elders seem in no hurry to end it, and, indeed, seem to profit financially from it, they have a right to complain." [9] To what extent has tax reform been evaded because of the patronage needs of congressmen, and to what extent has pollution been ignored because the polluters had more favors to dispense than did those who opposed pollution? What would be the national commitment to the war on poverty if the principal recipients of antipoverty patronage were rich and influential, instead of poor and disenfranchised? And how is national policy affected by the 183 House members who have a financial or

[8] Testimony before the Joint Economic Committee's Defense Procurement Subcommittee, January 29, 1960.

[9] In a speech before a coalition of New York lawyers against the war, reported in *The New Yorker*, May 30, 1970, p. 24.

management interest in companies doing business with the federal government or subject to federal regulatory agencies? [10]

Patronage power also plays a crucial role in determining the quality of the nation's public officials, an interesting balancing act between the forces of obligation and the interests of professionalism. Perhaps the strongest evidence in the case against patronage can be seen in the current state of the judiciary; indeed, a spirited defense of mediocrity on the bench was advanced by Senator Roman L. Hruska, Nebraska Republican, who defended President Nixon's nomination of G. Harrold Carswell as a Supreme Court justice by arguing: "Even if he were mediocre, there are a lot of mediocre judges and people and lawyers. They are entitled to a little representation, aren't they, and a little chance." [11] Judicial patronage, by giving politicians the power to determine the caliber of the bench, also gives them the power to determine what kinds of decisions will be made.

Patronage powers also give politicians the power to determine the quality of law enforcement, one of the more oblique discretionary powers of government. "To put people in law enforcement for the purpose of non-enforcement is a very big attraction for politicians," said Alex Rose, head of New York's Liberal Party and adviser to Presidents Kennedy and Johnson. The discretionary aspects of law enforcement surface when a new administration vigorously prosecutes public officials who previously enjoyed immunity while their own party controlled the White House. The Nixon administration, for example, prosecuted Newark's Mayor Hugh J. Addonizio and his Democratic colleagues, whereas a similar investigation of Nel-

[10] *Congressional Quarterly, Weekly Report,* May 6, 1970, *passim.*

[11] *The New York Times,* March 17, 1970, p. 21.

son Gross, New Jersey Republican chairman and candidate for the Senate, was promptly quashed by Attorney General John N. Mitchell, according to U.S. Attorney Frederick B. Lacey.

Patronage vitally affects the nature of national and state legislation, and the quality of life in general, and like other forms of political power, is used for both public and private interests. Governor Nelson Rockefeller's threat to withhold "personal favors" from legislators led the New York State Legislature to reverse itself within a few hours and enact a $6 billion slum-clearance program—an example of patronage used in the public interest. In contrast, Governor Buford Ellington of Tennessee, a Democrat, acted to benefit private interests when he encouraged the state's six largest banks to endow their favors on legislators in the hopes of shoring up his party's power in the state legislature. The six banks divided up the legislature and made substantial campaign contributions to legislators shortly before the interest rate was increased from 6 to 8 percent. Environmental needs could not hope to compete with political considerations when New York's Mayor Lindsay allowed the rezoning of a Queens residential area for commercial uses in order to reinforce his flagging support within the Catholic church which owned the property in question. "We wanted to do something for the Catholic church," the mayor said, explaining the zoning change, which would have permitted the construction of a shopping center in a section that fronted two schools, a library, a hospital, and a post office. Although the value of the property was greatly enhanced by the zoning change, the quality of life affecting the area's residents (who took the case to court, where it is still pending) was unquestionably imperiled.

Even neighborhood projects, such as parks and traffic lights, which seem apolitical on the surface, can be used by enterprising politicians to appear as patronage rewards, intended to co-opt the grass-roots voter into the system. The political leader who understands how to use patronage can answer his community's needs by acting as a catalyst, prodding the bureaucracy toward speedily improving his district's services.

A voter who fails to vote his conscience in a general election out of gratitude to a party official for a personal favor or a traffic light or park can hardly be critical of the councilman, state legislator, or congressman who fails to vote his conscience in the legislature, but instead goes along with his party's leadership out of gratitude for favors he has received and hopes to receive. It may be argued, however, that a voter who supports a congressional candidate who has expedited the installation of a traffic light is at least acting on the basis of concrete performance, whereas a candidate's position on Vietnam or student uprisings may be a good deal less dependable.

The patronage system has a life of its own, developed and expanded over the years to function autonomously, regardless of who is in office or what party controls the legislature. The successful patronage seeker is well aware that government must bank its money, insure its property, and construct office buildings—all on a noncompetitive basis, because bank and insurance rates are uniform and there are no objective standards for architecture and construction.

Government buildings need furniture, stationery, plumbing, heating, wiring, and vending machines that dispense sandwiches, cigarettes, ice cream, and soda—franchises often worth millions of dollars to the recipient of this patronage. When the late Charles Buckley, Bronx Democratic leader, chaired the House Public Works Committee in Washington, he also was vice-president of the

Fidelity and Deposit Insurance Company in nearby Maryland. Beneficiaries of Public Works Committee projects were strongly encouraged to buy their own personal insurance from Mr. Buckley's company if they wished to continue doing business with the government. Other politicians own construction companies or form corporations to handle the contracts bestowed by government. Interior Secretary Walter Hickel, while governor of Alaska, was able to get a subcontract totaling $1 million for his plumbing and heating firm for Anchorage Airport, although his firm was not the low bidder. The setting up of a corporation by Representative Adam Clayton Powell and J. Raymond Jones to construct Esplanade Gardens in Harlem, under a Title I federal grant, led to a falling-out between the two black politicians, each fighting for control of the corporation. Still others parlay their favor power into courtroom patronage. Elected judges, who owe their nomination and election to the party, give the organization lucrative refereeships, trusteeships, and receiverships which often yield legal fees unjustified by the work required.

The cities provide some of the choicest patronage, spread across the board to party elites. The relationship between local patronage and national policy is illustrated by the career of Monroe Goldwater, the 84-year-old grand vizier of the New York City Democratic organization. Mr. Goldwater, a kindly and compassionate man, has been a delegate to every Democratic national convention since 1924, and was, expectedly, a Humphrey delegate to the 1968 Chicago convention. He has thus been helping to select presidents for nearly five decades. As the senior partner in the law firm of Goldwater & Flynn, a firm that he founded with the late Edward J. Flynn, former Bronx Democratic chairman, his patronage dates back to the nineteen-twenties when the city had a Chamberlain (Mr. Flynn) and Mr. Goldwater was counsel to the Chamberlain.

More recently, Goldwater & Flynn represented a successful applicant for a cable-television franchise. Richard Flynn, son of Ed Flynn, is now a partner in Goldwater & Flynn, and handled the CATV application. "Dick is politically able, and we are obtaining these permissions from a political body," said the applicant, Charles Dolan, president of Sterling Information Service. "But we rest totally on the merits." Even more blatant was the successful application of Teleprompter, whose counsel, Justin Feldman, withdrew saying that he lacked sufficient political influence to serve his client. Mr. Feldman was at that time a special counsel to the New York State Democratic Party. He was replaced by William Shea, an old friend of former Mayor Robert F. Wagner, whose administration awarded these franchises. Mr. Shea's law firm included Bernard Ruggieri, who had previously served as Mr. Wagner's legislative representative in Albany. "In dealing with any city, you have to go to the guys who know the guys," said Irving Kahn, Teleprompter's president. "There's no question that we put the heat on New York with Bill Shea. We're in 88 towns and we have 88 law firms, all politically connected."

Against this background of political influence, Morris Tarshis, director of New York City's Bureau of Franchises, told a Federal Communications Commission hearing that these franchises were awarded solely on the basis of merit. At the hearing, Mr. Tarshis strenuously opposed the introduction of competitive bidding for future CATV franchises, in keeping with the city's desire to keep its exclusive discretionary power over franchises safely locked up in its patronage collection. The 14 applicants, vying

for these franchises, included friends of Mayor Lindsay—
among them, Daniel Melnick, Andrew Heiskell, who is
board chairman of Time-Life,[12] and Heiskell's lawyer,
Bruce Bromley.

"What insurance is there that there would not be
some hanky-panky with city officials?" asked David I.
Kraushaar, an FCC examiner.

Tarshis replied: "The city officials of the city of New
York are honorable and honest, and there is no hanky-
panky."

Then Kraushaar asked: "If there is no public bidding, it certainly opens itself to that charge, though, does
it not?"

Tarshis answered: "I disagree with you completely,
sir."

Kraushaar said: "You have it all the time in the Department of Defense."

Tarshis answered: "You may have it here [in Wash-
ington], but you don't have it in the city of New York." [13]

Today's patronage opportunities were undreamed of
by George Washington Plunkitt, the turn-of-the-century
Tammany ward boss, who defined the difference between
what he called "dishonest graft" (blackmailing and brib-
ery) and "honest graft," availing oneself of inside information for personal enrichment. With a verve that does
honor to the politicians of his day, Mr. Plunkitt noted that
he had made a fortune in politics by purchasing real estate
with the advance knowledge that a new subway line
would soon enhance its value.

[12] Time-Life, a partner of Sterling Information Services (a cable TV
company), seeks to protect its franchise despite FCC rulings that bar
local media ownership of CATV.

[13] *Better TV of Dutchess v. New York Telephone Co.*, Hearing before
the Federal Communications Commission, 1970, pp. 1060–1061.

"I seen my opportunities and I took 'em," [14] boasted Plunkitt, in the best definition to date of honest graft. The subject of dishonest graft, or corruption, is not considered in this book because it has always gained public attention —and outrage—whereas honest graft and its consequences are seldom explored.

Although some reformers tend to regard all patronage as "dishonest graft" because it grants favors on the basis of favoritism, not merit, orthodox politicians consider patronage the pressures and interests on which a democracy rests, well aware that a politician whose patronage is so inflexible that he cannot accommodate rising new interest groups may find himself displaced by them at election time. The successful machine politician relies not only on his ability to satisfy organized local pressure groups, but also on his sensitivity to the political desires of the broad base of constituents who are not organized. Thus, to protect their patronage, machine politicians have often searched out and nominated outstanding candidates to head their tickets: Franklin D. Roosevelt was enthusiastically supported by Ed Flynn's Bronx machine; Harry S. Truman was the protégé of the Thomas Pendergast machine in Kansas City; and Adlai Stevenson was handpicked by the powerful Chicago machine of Jacob Arvey. More recently, W. Averell Harriman and Robert F. Wagner, Jr., were handpicked by Carmine De Sapio, while Adlai Stevenson III was endorsed by Mayor Richard J. Daley as a candidate for the Senate. A distinguished, popular candidate at the top of the ticket often carries into office the judges, sheriffs, and local legislators who are the lifeblood of a machine. Hymie Shorenstein, a Brooklyn district leader a half century ago, was once confronted by

[14] William L. Riordan, *Plunkitt of Tammany Hall* (New York: McClure & Phillips & Co., 1905).

a worried Assembly candidate who had not received the funds he needed to campaign actively. Shorenstein calmed him: "You see the ferryboats come in?" Shorenstein asked. "You see them pull into the slip? You see the water suck in behind? And when the water sucks in behind the ferryboat, all kinds of dirty garbage comes smack into the slip with the ferryboat? Go home. Al Smith is the ferryboat. This year, you're the garbage."

Today, as was the case a half century ago, patronage begins in the clubhouse, or in "neighborhood city halls," where people with problems receive the help of the political organization. Each week in the Williamsburg, Brooklyn, clubhouse of Councilman Leonard Scholnick, about 100 neighborhood residents wait patiently on the rickety folding chairs to consult the Democratic leaders for advice on jobs, apartments, legal matters, and family problems. By helping these constituents, the club hopes to win the loyalty of their family and friends on election day. The Williamsburg clubhouse is one of the few that still sends Christmas turkeys to the poor—a generally defunct practice—but more significantly also intercedes to expedite welfare checks, obtain apartments in public housing, enroll constituents in public health programs, and guide both rich and poor through the maze of federal and state bureaucracy to obtain the far-ranging services to which they are entitled. James V. Mangano, Red Hook district leader since 1934 and general clerk of the Brooklyn Supreme Court, reported that his Democratic club had found jobs in private industry as well as in government for accountants, lawyers, laborers, bricklayers, and carpenters. "Somebody comes to me and says, 'I need a good accountant,'" Mr. Mangano recounted. "I have a list." Jobs in private industry also augment the patronage of Mayor Daley in Chicago—who places as many people in jobs with private industry as he places on the public rolls. Jerome Cavanagh, former Mayor of Detroit, found jobs in the automobile industry and coveted automobile dealerships for his political supporters and, conversely, prevented the awarding of these dealerships to political foes.

Rewards are the basis of political power, and even the lower strata of political leaders are given a wide range of political rewards to cement their power. Mr. Mangano telephoned his congressman last year and set in motion the events that brought Private Joseph C. Caruso halfway around the world, from a line company in Vietnam to his parents' home in Red Hook, indicating that politicians not only support the war but also protect their constituents from its ravages. The same week, Mr. Mangano telephoned his councilman and assemblyman and obtained school-crossing guards for Our Lady of Peace parochial school, arranged for the admission of a retarded child into a specialized school, and arranged for an interdepartmental transfer of an employee of Merrill, Lynch, Pierce, Fenner and Smith, a stock-brokerage house. "I take care of the neighbors' children," the 64-year-old Mr. Mangano said. The neighbors and their children remember. Joseph C. Caruso, Sr., sat on a wooden folding chair and reminisced: "I've known Jimmy [Mr. Mangano] more than 40 years. Everybody here knows Jimmy. He's a generous man. He does people lots of favors."

To do these favors, Mangano must rely on the patronage resources of his friends in the organization placed in other areas of government: Representative John Rooney (who went to the Defense Department in the Caruso case); Council Majority Leader Thomas Cuite and Assemblyman William Giordano (both of whom went to Mayor Lindsay for the school-crossing guards). The profits on wisely invested patronage resources bring large returns in the form of political support. Mr. Mangano fully expects to help those public officials who helped him with his constituents. "If the constituents are satisfied with the service they receive, I assume they'd want the service to continue," he said. Hailed by working politicians in terms of "friendship" and "loyalty," political support takes highly concrete forms when it appears as the quid pro quo for well-placed patronage rewards. The congressman who is lucky enough to favor his district with a new post office may well expect return support in the form of votes at the next election, hefty campaign contributions from contractors constructing the building, or free service at campaign time from party workers grateful for all the new job opportunities offered by a new federal project in their community. Himself the beneficiary of patronage from the executive and legislative leaders who "politically" engineered the passage of the building, the congressman in turn will be obligated to throw his own "support" resources back into the system; perhaps he will make campaign speeches for the President, sponsor fund-raising dinners, or support legislation in which he holds no interest.[15]

Through these favors, nonpolitical members of a community become co-opted in the politician's quest for his own personal advantages, thereby legitimizing the

[15] Rarely does a clear picture of political support appear, because both the public and political analysts are forced to view it in fragments. In "systems theory," a relatively new concept in political science which regards politics as an organic, integrated, and rationally functioning system composed of demands, supports, outputs, and outcomes, the data in the area of political supports emerge as the sparsest category. Perhaps this has occurred because the shadowy nature of patronage and its rewards has made supports so difficult to perceive and to research. The problem of not seeing the entire iceberg is compounded by the inaccuracies in existing data. Reported campaign contributions, for example, which are regulated by law, are notorious for underestimating both contributors and income. For the best exposition of systems analysis, see David Easton, *A Systems Analysis of Political Life* (New York: John Wiley, 1965).

more self-seeking aspects of political behavior. For although men have many motives for entering political life —loneliness, ideological conviction, the desire to escape an unhappy home life, the need to identify with something greater than themselves—the vast underpinning of both major parties is made up of men who seek practical rewards. Tangible advantages constitute the unifying thread of most successful political practitioners; for whatever reason prompts a man to enter politics, if he is to function effectively, he becomes involved in the chase. Political rewards range from nonmaterial ones, like being picked out of a crowd by a governor or receiving an invitation to a White House dinner, or getting appointed to an unsalaried post on an executive commission, to the more tangible rewards: the easy access to government officials; franchises; legal fees; architect's commissions; contractor's fees; judgeships; and of course the nomination for public office.

These furnish the backbone of political machines that thrive despite the popular notion that they were rendered obsolete by television and the revolution in communications, which supposedly enables a candidate to bypass party machinery and approach the voter directly in the comfort of the voter's living room. Anyone who doubts the existence of these machines need only examine the typical ballot, and ponder who selected the judicial and legislative candidates who remain unknown to the average voter. Even the so-called charismatic candidate who may not need a political machine to win must do business with the machine once he is elected, because these machines still control the state legislatures, city councils, and the judiciary. As political realists, three notably "charismatic" politicians—John F. Kennedy, Robert F. Kennedy, and John V. Lindsay—were careful to touch base with their party leadership before undertaking important political projects.

The Kennedys were close to Mayor Daley, Stanley Stein-gut, Charles Buckley, and the other major Democratic leaders, while Lindsay consults with Vincent Albano, the Manhattan Republican leader.

"You can't get the average voter excited about who's going to be an assemblyman or state senator," laments State Senator Seymour R. Thaler, a Queens Democrat who championed hospital reform. "I've got two dozen people who are going to work so much harder, because if I lose, they lose." What they lose, specifically, are their jobs. Mr. Thaler, who also is a district leader, has placed on the public payroll an assistant U.S. attorney, two assistant district attorneys, two marshals, associate counsels to the Assembly Speaker and the Senate minority leader, two appointees to legislative committees, an aide to a congressman, and a staff member of the City Council. At election time, he cashes in these IOU's. "My best captains in the primary," he says, "are the ones who are on the payroll."

Leaders who rely solely on charisma enter politics only at the highest level and with the greatest political risk, because the publicity and exposure they need to win elections are not available to those seeking lower offices. The ideal method to combine the advantages of charisma with solid predictable support was successfully practiced by both Kennedys, who maximized the advantages of modern communications while carefully cultivating support within their party. Joseph F. Crangle, the 37-year-old Erie County (Buffalo, N.Y.) leader and Kennedy supporter, who gained a national reputation as a new breed of political leader who used market research and slide lectures, observed that "If the new politics teaches anything at all, it's that the old politics was pretty good. The McCarthy kids in New Hampshire rang doorbells, made telephone calls and made the personal contact that people associate with the old-style machines."

Patronage crosses party lines and defies reform labels. John Lindsay, who criticized the patronage practices of Mayor Wagner, exceeds him both in the number of patronage jobs and the size of the patronage payroll. While Wagner had $10 million in jobs exempt from the civil service, Lindsay has $32.8 million exempt jobs in antipoverty agencies alone. Under Lindsay, the city's provisional employees—who can be hired without taking the civil service examinations—have increased in total from 1,500 to 12,800. Mayor Lindsay's plan for little city halls, where community residents can have their requests for city services expedited, is similar to the role performed by the Democratic clubhouse. Mr. Lindsay, who pledged during his first mayoral campaign that he would initiate a national talent search for officeholders, found top-ranking jobs for 13 of the campaign's 16 borough coordinators. The mayor's patronage overtures to the state legislature included the appointment of Eli Zaret, brother of Senate Minority Leader Joseph Zaretzki, to a $14,000-a-year post in the city's Department of Real Estate. Both the mayor and the state senator denied that the appointment was politically motivated, but Bernard Ruggieri, Mr. Zaretzki's counsel, noted: "The fact that you do a favor, knowingly or unknowingly, is like casting bread upon the waters. If I were Lindsay and I wanted to build up friends among the Democratic legislators, I'd see that they were serviced. A legislator has to look good with his constituents. The fact that he can bring a delegation into the mayor's office, can make an appointment with a commissioner over a community's request for a traffic light—this is bread and butter."

The experienced politician has little difficulty in casting bread upon the waters, and indeed may view the business of government as one vast bakery. Nearly everyone wants a piece of the action, but some do better than others.

On the national level, these include middle- and upper-class farmers, who receive $4 billion a year in farm subsidies, with each recipient averaging an income of $20,000 a year; oilmen who receive $1.5 billion from oil-depletion allowances; airlines and their users who benefit from $1.2 billion in federal grants; railroads and shipping firms, which receive $1 billion a year in subsidies; trucking firms and motorists who received $5 billion in road subsidies; construction men, who received $2 billion to build private housing; suburbanites who write off interest payments on their mortgages as a tax advantage; and veterans, who receive $7.3 billion annually in federal funds.

Some of these subsidies have come back to the politicians in the form of cake. James Boyd who, as Secretary of Transportation, approved a $25.2 million grant to the Illinois Central Railroad in December 1968, became the railroad's $95,000-a-year president the following month. Charles Preusse who, as New York City's Corporation Counsel, negotiated the sale of the city's power generators to Consolidated Edison at a small fraction of their market value, later resigned his city job to join the law firm that became the utility's general counsel. Joseph A. Califano, a 36-year-old former aide to President Lyndon Johnson, now earns $100,000 a year as member of a Washington law firm that hired him for his ability to help corporate clients maximize their dealings with the federal government. Clark Clifford, President Johnson's Secretary of Defense and a former aide to President Truman, shuttled between government posts and a highly lucrative law practice, where he served corporate giants as a man who knew his way around the federal bureaucracy he had helped create.

Those who would change society—in ways large or small—are advised to pay close attention to the patronage network, which usually tells far more about how government operates than can be learned from congressional debates and political rhetoric; in fact, patronage practices reveal that cooperation plays a greater role in political life than conflict, the often delusive theme emphasized by the communications media. Political ideology and persuasion can be effective in those relatively rare moments when an idea's hour has come, but their importance has generally been overemphasized. Patronage, on the other hand, which often holds the key to national policy as well as state and city planning, is usually well concealed and generally ignored. The highly selective examples in this book are intended merely to illumine the problems and in no way present the definitive portrait. They indicate that patronage can be used for good or for evil, for progress or for regression, to advance social legislation like that of the New Deal era or to try to appoint Supreme Court justices of questionable quality. Patronage exists because of human nature, offering rewards in a democracy in which men have a choice of conduct. It is both an extension of the electoral process, providing public officials with the tools to govern, and a diminution of the electoral process, robbing legislators of the ability to decide issues solely on the basis of conscience and reason. Finally, it is a totally interrelated system, in which franchises granted by municipalities can have profound effects upon the selection of our national leadership and the future of the nation.

2
Clout, Charisma, and Patronage at City Hall

"I don't want patronage. You could build a political machine with patronage, but I don't want a partisan election."
—Mayor Sam Yorty of Los Angeles

"I go over the city jobs, and find a couple of architectural firms haven't had a job over a number of years, and this should be compelling, particularly if some of them were supporters."
—Former Mayor Jerome Cavanagh of Detroit

Chicago, the patronage capital of the world, recently provided an impressive display of the power of Mayor Richard J. Daley's Democratic machine. An organization candidate for alderman, an Italian-American running in a predominantly black ward, died suddenly two weeks before election day. His black opponent, a member of the Congress of Racial Equality (CORE), was heartened by her unexpectedly improved prospects of winning the election when the Daley organization thereupon announced that it was running, as a write-in candidate, a man virtually unknown in the district—one Angelo C. Provenzano. In the semiliterate, economically depressed ward, 90 percent of the voters somehow managed to write in the lengthy, unfamiliar name of Angelo C. Provenzano, who thereupon took his place on the Board of Aldermen, an institution sometimes called the "wax museum" because of its members' unquestioning devotion to Mayor Daley.

Chicago reformers charged that the Provenzano victory bared the brutal power of the Daley organization, which they said had threatened the compliant voters with the loss of their public housing, welfare checks, hospital clinic appointments, and other government services, as well as with the loss of their patronage jobs, especially valued in poor neighborhoods where unemployment is high. The organization, on the other hand, took the benign view that it had won the voters' loyalty in the first place with these services.

To some liberals, the victory was merely additional evidence that Mayor Daley was a political thug, a view that gained national currency as millions watched him on camera during the 1968 Democratic National Convention as he shook his fists at the crowds, mouthed obscenities at Senator Abraham Ribicoff of Connecticut, consulted with an unsavory-looking coterie of advisers seated around him, and invoked the police in a pitched battle against peace demonstrators. The bullnecked, monosyllabic mayor seemed a political anachronism when compared with the new breed of handsome, media-oriented "hero mayors," led by John V. Lindsay of New York, who repeatedly denounce patronage and the "power brokers" who use it. But despite his national notoriety, Daley continues to exercise the unlimited power he has carefully developed (through patronage) in the past, naming governors, senators, and even presidents—contrasting sharply with the litany of impotence recited by the new breed of mayors, who blame their inaction on the locked purses of state and federal governments.

Despite their disclaimers, the evidence indicates that

big-city mayors are among the most powerful public officials in the United States today, and that they wield their
power through the well-practiced art of political patronage
—bestowing the discretionary favors of government in return for political support. Mayor Lindsay, who began his
term of office denouncing the "power brokers"—the powerful union leaders who had always enjoyed access to City
Hall during Democratic administrations—ended his first
term with the support of most of the municipal unions,
after awarding them patronage in the form of the largest
salary increases and best working conditions and pension
rights in their history. More striking examples reappear
again and again to show how New York's mayor, regardless of the antipatronage image he chooses to project, has
learned to use patronage for positive political purposes. A
close examination of the mayor's first postelection capital
budget showed dramatic correlations between the voting
returns of 1969 and the allocation of city funds. The mayor
removed long-promised projects from neighborhoods that
had voted for his opponents, Controller Mario A. Procaccino, the Democratic candidate, and State Senator John J.
Marchi, the Republican, while rewarding neighborhoods
that had supported his re-election bid. Of eleven public
and intermediate schools deleted from the budget, nine
were in neighborhoods that had voted against him, such
as City Island and Clason's Point in the Bronx, Greenpoint and Gravesend in Brooklyn, and Long Island City
in Queens. The Midwood section of Brooklyn, a Jewish, middle-class neighborhood that had supported the
mayor, was awarded one of two new high schools, although the neighborhood was not among those listed by
the Board of Education as among the 15 most in need of a
new high school. The West Side of Manhattan was given
$400,000 to renovate the Broadway mall that slices this
pro-Lindsay district; and Brooklyn Heights, Forest Hills,

Bedford-Stuyvesant, and the Southeast Bronx, which also voted for Lindsay, were similarly rewarded.

Mayor Lindsay and his planning officials steadfastly denied that this shift of city funds was anything more than a coincidence, and sought to give the impression that the ultimate decisions were made by computers buttressed by objective, nonpolitical planners. But sophisticated city officials, including Herman Badillo, former Bronx Borough President, who became the first Puerto Rican member of Congress, concluded that Mr. Lindsay had followed the well-traveled political tradition of rewarding friends at the expense of foes. They did not see these rewards as political pay-offs, but rather as deliberate calculations made during the election campaign. Some areas, such as Clason's Point and Greenpoint, were apparently written off as hopelessly anti-Lindsay, while others were believed to be salvageable by infusions of city services—such as police and sanitation—and by the promise of schools, parks, and playgrounds. Mr. Lindsay himself gave credence to this view by promising these projects to communities during the campaign. He redeemed his promises even when they did not fully succeed, as in the case of a park promised to Bayswater, Queens, which the mayor lost by 80 votes.

The difference between Daley and Lindsay was not that one used patronage and the other did not, but that Daley openly defended the patronage system, while Lindsay publicly deplored it, preferring instead to couch his policies in the delusive vocabulary of good government. Those few big-city mayors who truly renounce the practice of patronage thereby deny their ability to govern. Atlanta's former Mayor Ivan Allen, Jr., a handsome, white-haired, statesmanlike man, boasted near the end of his last term that "No one's asked me for a job since I've become mayor." But a key aide to Mayor Allen conceded that the mayor's hands-off policy was so extensive that the mayor was ignorant of important negotiations that were going on in his own administration, all because "he didn't like to involve himself in the nitty-gritty." Similarly, Mayor Sam Yorty of Los Angeles, who stunned a Senate investigating committee in 1967 with a recital of his lack of powers, failed to see the correlation between patronage and power, and boasted that Los Angeles city government "was purely professional."

Challenging Yorty's concept of mayoral power, Mayor Joseph Alioto of San Francisco argued that although his city charter, like Mr. Yorty's, gives him little power, the charter is meant to be used only as the touchstone, not the final perimeter of political power. "The city charter," remarked Mr. Alioto, "gives the mayor relatively little formal power. Entire commissions can be appointed by someone else, but there is a certain prestige given to the mayor's office which, combined with personality, can get a job done."

Anyone with substantial interests in a city must reckon with its mayor, a factor which mayors throughout the country have used skillfully so as to increase their patronage resources and transcend their nominal charter powers. Those who underestimate the powers of a big-city mayor run the risk of great inconvenience, at the very least, and, possibly, financial ruin—the uglier side of the patronage coin. Some mayors control business permits, for example, by which they can indirectly delay the opening of a new building, or close a factory, office, or store.

The mayors' immense powers derive from soaring budgets ($7.8 billion a year for operating expenses alone in New York City), and the commensurate services required by city government. The purchase by New York City of ketchup and other products made by the H.J. Heinz Co., a small example, exceeded $100,000—for hospitals, jails, schools, and other institutions. Mr. Heinz, incidentally, turned up as one of the major contributors to Mayor Lindsay's re-election campaign. There was no suggestion that this was a campaign pay-off, but merely an indication of how some of those who profit from a city's vast spending power return some of those profits to those in power. Other non-charter powers indirectly controlled by most mayors include the granting of land variances, which enable a builder to enhance the value of property by squeezing more apartments or more office space into an area, partially accounting for the fact that contractors are among the largest group of campaign contributors on the local level to both major political parties. The extent to which the mayor influences the allocation of city funds affords him the opportunity to reward both individuals and groups who have already supported him or who may support him in the future. He may grant: 1) salary increases to city employees (which may also mean rewarding union leaders with city contracts); 2) insurance contracts for insuring city property to cooperative insurance firms; and 3) deposits of city money, often used to reward political supporters, to selected banks, which welcome the opportunity to bank public funds without the necessity of returning large interest payments. The mayor's legislative powers may also mean millions of dollars to an industry concerned with taxi medallions, milk prices, or rent control. All of these powers are negotiable, and as many as possible must be used if a mayor seeks to make major changes in his city—the kinds of revolutionary changes the United States Conference of Mayors and the National League of Cities call essential to make the cities livable.

Despite their efforts to conceal job patronage, most mayors in large cities control a considerable number of jobs, both at City Hall (judgeships, commissionerships, down to temporary office boys) and through private industry. When Mayor Daley uses up the 30,000–35,000 jobs available to him in city and county government, he turns to private industry to help place the party faithful. In return for the many discretionary favors they receive from the mayor, companies quietly offer him jobs to dispense. "With the help of business, Daley has been able to get 30,000 jobs in industry," said Marshall Korshak, a genial, white-haired gentleman, who is Chicago City Treasurer and a top Daley lieutenant. Mr. Korshak uses his own contacts with industry to get jobs for his constituents: "I'm a man who's made a lot of friends . . . at Western Electric, Admiral, Factor, Seaberg, Illinois Bell Telephone. I can get kids summer jobs and people winter jobs. One woman wanted an on-the-job training job, so I called my old friend Sam Kaplan at Zenith—I had worked with him on UJA projects—and got her the kind of job she wanted there."

❛ Old-Fashioned Patronage Clout and Its Modern Application to Chicago Machine Politics

Unlike Mayor Lindsay, Mayor Daley is proud of his patronage powers, does not publicly lament his lack of power, and manages to cull all the rewards he can use for his city from state and federal government. Daley's skillful use of patronage has converted local clout into national power, while at the same time he has won for himself seniority and tenure as mayor which no other mayor in the country has been able to achieve in recent years. By controlling the Democratic organization of Cook County, Daley controls the Illinois delegation to his party's presidential nominating convention, where he can deliver his state's crucial vote to the man of his choosing.[1] Aware of this power, presidential hopefuls compete to ply Daley with promises of future patronage. Daley's powers of endorsement also filter down to the local levels, where he can often deliver the vote for cooperative candidates running for the state legislature, as well as for Congress. Those helped by Daley show their gratitude, and it is no coincidence that Daley was able to get funds for the city's programs, for example, when other needy cities went begging.

These funds reinforced Daley's reputation as an effective mayor, a reputation conceded by his strongest critics, even as they compare him with dictators like Mussolini who, after all, did make the trains run on time! Indeed, the strongest indictments of Daley's administration have centered on the "police state" atmosphere of Chicago: the Chicago police force, accused by the Walker report (an independent investigation of the 1968 Democratic Party Convention riots) of having created a "police riot," was later denounced by a federal grand jury for the unprovoked assassinations of Black Panther leaders Fred Hampton and Mark Clark. Mayor Lindsay, on the other hand, has carefully restrained his police force (the Patrolmen's Benevolent Association of New York has frequently complained of being "handcuffed" by the mayor). Against the present policies of his own party, he has become one of the nation's most articulate spokesmen on a wide range of politically sensitive issues: opposing the war in Vietnam; supporting civil rights; and publicizing the plight of the cities. He has organized mayors both in New York State and nationally to press for a larger share of federal and state moneys. But few mayors have enjoyed more success

---

[1] The large industrial states, Illinois, New York, Texas, and California, because of their sizable voting blocs, are valued most highly at presidential nominating conventions.

in bringing home the patronage than Richard Daley—who has not joined the mobilization of the mayors!

Daley's effectiveness may well give pause to those reformers in other cities who seek to eliminate political parties from municipal elections in order to convert their political systems into closer replicas of the business world. Most smaller cities hire city managers instead of electing a mayor; others elect mayors on a nonpartisan basis. Set off by the sharp example of Mayor Daley, the trend toward nonpartisanship in local government helps to explain just why the cities suffer as badly as they do today, failing to get funds from the state and federal governments with which they have severed their political ties. It is understandable why legislators ignore municipalities that may never be able, because of limitations on their partisan activities, to reciprocate their support. Rather than achieving "good government," political impotence seems to be the fate of misled nonpartisan movements which profess that eliminating political parties erases politics. While state and federal government remains structured on the two-party system, it seems likely that municipalities which have shifted to nonpartisanship will be increasingly unable to deliver services effectively without receiving more substantial help from state and federal governments, help which they may have imperiled by their stance of political neutrality.

Just as "apolitical" governments find it difficult to gain cooperation from other jurisdictions, so do practitioners of personalistic politics, men who perform brilliant political solos before deaf legislative audiences. The question also arises as to where the constituents of personalistic leaders may turn for political accountability once these men leave the political landscape. Thus, the followers of Robert Kennedy and Eugene McCarthy, two such practitioners of "personal politics," who were largely unrelated to their political parties, had no place to redeem their promises—ideological or otherwise—whereas an organization remains in business for decades.

The organization used so artfully today by Mayor Daley was born shortly after the turn of the century, and grew powerful during the Roosevelt years under the leadership of Jacob L. Arvey, a former Democratic national committeeman who is best known for promoting the career of the late Adlai Stevenson, a particularly non-machine type of politician. Arvey called the patronage system "a necessary evil if you want a strong organization, because the patronage system permits of discipline, and without discipline, there's no party organization." He described how a good organization wove a community into an intricate web of personal relationships between the voters, political leaders, and elected officials, with the precinct captain as the focal point. "The precinct captain was the virtual mayor of his precinct," Mr. Arvey recalled. "I tried to make them feel that they were more than political leaders—they were communal leaders. The precinct leaders, then as now, would find out all they could about people moving into the neighborhood—what kind of man he was, Democrat or Republican, right or left, and what his interests were. On moving day, he would send people to take care of the children, and put a dozen eggs in the kitchen . . . he tried to become your friend, and it's very hard to vote against your friend." Stressing the value of the precinct captain as the hub of the organization, Mr. Arvey advised that "if you have a well-organized group of precinct captains, loyal to you and conversant with the issues, they can deliver the votes, unless there's a great issue involved: Vietnam, civil rights, or busing."

Ward leaders would rather deal with rewards than with issues, for when the community becomes embroiled in a "great issue," the political organization is threatened by both indigenous and outside pressure groups which divide the loyalty of the voters and often weaken the influence of the machine. Issues threaten Chicago's political organization only sporadically, and in Chicago today, the precinct captain is as important as he was at the height of Jake Arvey's power. Even Republicans in Chicago attest to their value within their own organization. State Representative Arthur Telcser professed that he "would rather have a good precinct captain working for me than $4,000 in campaign contributions." [2]

Mayor Daley's army of precinct captains stands out as a model of well-organized, loyal mercenaries, whose loyalty is reinforced by the increasing number of rewards available to them. By decentralizing his patronage down to the district leaders, Daley has forever bound up party workers who owe him not only their personal jobs but their entire power base as well.

Vito Marzullo, an old-time ward politician and staunch defender of Daley's patronage system, listed his own extensive powers derived from and nourished by the Daley organization. As alderman from Chicago's 25th ward (which houses a population of 75,000 to 80,000 people), Marzullo has personal patronage that extends to 125 jobs in state, county, and city government. The beneficiaries of these jobs serve as his inner corps of political work-

[2] This stands out in sharp contrast to cities like Detroit where the precinct captains have a minimal role. In 1961, a research team found that only 8% of the citizens could recall having been contacted by party workers, while a mere 16% were aware that party workers functioned at all in their precinct. Only one-fifth of the precinct leaders used tools that Chicago workers would consider necessities (like a card file of their party's supporters); while less than a third of the precinct leaders had reported activities like door-to-door canvassing or party meetings. Detroit elects its officials on a nonpartisan basis. See Daniel Katz and Samuel J. Eldersveld, "The Impact of Local Party Activity on the Electorate," *Public Opinion Quarterly*, Vol. 25 (Spring 1961), pp. 16–17.

ers, who must be constantly available to Marzullo for a wide range of political functions performed on a year-round basis. To his constituents, Marzullo offers the gamut of government services, for which he is always on call. Entitled to these services regardless of party affiliation, Chicago citizens are made to feel obligated to the alderman who expedited their problem through the bureaucracy. Chicago's municipal government reinforces this illusion by empowering the aldermen to channel applications through city departments for speedier and more efficient service. "Poor people don't have corporation lawyers; we get them lawyers. They don't even know where the hospital is; we show them," explained Alderman Marzullo. "Someone may introduce a petition to raze buildings in my district. They have to introduce it to the Buildings Department, to the Law Department, and then take it into court. This takes several months. I know people in the Buildings Department, which speeds things up." Another citizen may ask for a reduction in his water rates, which he claims are excessive because of a leaky pipe in the city's water system. In order to get action on the pipe, he must get a council order, which again brings him right back to his alderman. The same procedures extend to zoning variances and many other city services. Marzullo said he spent two evenings a week in his district office just to act on these personal matters.

The art of obligation as practiced by the most expert political organization in the country shows on an exaggerated scale how government can co-opt the citizen even in the most picayune decisions, such as fixing leaky water pipes. After a while, the citizen forgets that as a taxpayer he has a right to expect speedy and efficient service from government, and begins to feel grateful to the alderman or ward leader whose talents had converted government services into government favors. The voter might be satisfied enough to translate his gratitude into tangible forms of political support: campaign contributions, doorbell ringing at election time or, at best, a permanent reluctance to attack the party.

Proudly, Mr. Marzullo theorized on how his organization had achieved the ultimate in democracy and humanism by bringing the politician closer to the people than any other political alternative. Defensive about his party, Marzullo found it hard to understand why Chicago's patronage traditions had achieved such notoriety across the country. "We provide these services," he said. "If this is a crime, then I'm a criminal."

Generous in parceling out its favors, the Daley organization demands a substantial return from its participants in terms of money, work, and verbal support. The organization's tithe system was described by Lois Wille, of the *Chicago Daily News*, who quoted a typist making $80 a week, forced to buy a ticket priced at $50 for a party function at the Playboy Club. "You can't tell the organization 'no,'" said the typist. "If they say pay, you pay." The $50 ticket came as an additional assessment on top of her regular monthly dues of 2% of her salary to the 4th ward, and five subscriptions to the ward newspaper. "Sure, there's a lot I don't like," she said. "But the organization got me the job when I couldn't find work anywhere else. I'm not exactly a great typist." She added that when her precinct captain needed help, she would go out and make pre-election house calls for him.

Consistent verbal support is also an important quid pro quo extracted with great success by the Daley machine. Many of Daley's top aides and appointees exhibit Pollyanna-like loyalty to the mayor, a quality rare among mayoral aides in other cities, many of whom aspire to top office themselves. Even deputies long transplanted to other cities continue their adoration and admiration for the mayor, which often beclouds their own judgment of the facts. John Duba, who formerly served Mayor Daley as Deputy Mayor and Public Works Administrator, seriously argued that "Mayor Daley has no patronage power at all . . . his patronage favors are geared for the city as a whole, not to individuals."

To all observers, the Daley machine is gaining sufficient strength to encompass almost every conceivable part of city life. "I don't know of any powers Daley doesn't have," said Mike Royko, political columnist for the *Chicago Daily News*. The fingerprints of the Daley organization appear even in the unlikeliest places. When the Chicago convention hall burned down, for example, it was learned that the insurance was written by George Dunn, president of the County Board. Similarly, much of the airport insurance was written by Joseph Gill, a member of the Park Board. Frequently, ward committeemen in Chicago open insurance businesses just to take advantage of all the government business available to them.

On paper, Daley's patronage power seems small, and despite painstaking research, government documents would not reveal the extent of the rewards available to him. The *Christian Science Monitor* reliably reported that 97 percent of Chicago's city-government jobs fell under civil service, at least in name. And Daley, who formerly held the patronage-dispensing job of Cook County clerk, is ironically credited with having strengthened the civil service system by providing more money for recruitment and in-service training. Yet the mayor has at the same time circumvented civil service through the use of "temporary employees," leaving no stone unturned in his search for more patronage. According to recent estimates, nearly 40 percent of Chicago's public employees were classified as "temporaries," which means that they may hold jobs for 180 days. Some politically active employees have held these 180-day temporary jobs for twenty years, after getting appointed and reappointed. Should a Republican suddenly become mayor of Chicago, these jobholders would be thrown out of work, as they were on the state level when Richard Ogilvie became governor. Other estimates have placed the temporary jobs at 5,500, over and above the civil service payroll of 39,000. It is not unusual for someone whose civil service classification calls for a salary of $6,000 to draw $14,000, through the skillful use of "temporary" jobs. No one was surprised at the failure of state legislation to eliminate these temporary jobs at the 1969 session of the legislature. The mayor's clout extends down to Springfield, a result of selectively parceling out jobs to Republicans, who now control Illinois state government.

Temporary jobs are small rewards, however, when displayed against the massive array of non-civil-service jobs that Daley controls in Chicago's independent agencies which are responsible for running such service areas as parks, sanitation, sewers, recreation, and health. The mayor appoints all the members of the board of the Chicago Park District, and picks ten out of the fifteen representatives of the Cook County Board, which is tantamount to complete control over the county. In comparison with other cities, Chicago's budget seems small simply because so many of her services are run by these so-called "independent" agencies, firmly under the dominance of the mayor and his party.

Mayor Daley uses these high-status positions on boards and agencies to institutionalize the city's elites, a successful technique for preventing potential sources of opposition from materializing. In fact, Daley owes his success in the field of labor relations primarily to this technique, again proving the close correlation between the use of patronage and administrative skill. Using patronage to neutralize potential as well as actual opposition, Daley has co-opted labor leaders into his organization by giving them high-status—as well as paying—jobs in government. Now part of the family, union leaders become like Daley's precinct captains, faithfully delivering votes, cooperation, and support.[3]

By keeping the union leaders domesticated through the use of patronage, Daley has kept Chicago relatively free from the crippling strikes which have plagued other cities, and has been able to influence the unions to adopt more flexible attitudes toward construction. Ada Louise Huxtable, architecture critic for *The New York Times*, points out that Daley, alone among big-city mayors, has "persuaded" the building-trades unions to use prefabricated materials, thus promoting new construction in Chicago at a much faster pace than other cities have been able to achieve.

On the negative side, the close relationship between Mayor Daley and the union leaders leads unwanted construction companies to find themselves beset with labor troubles that may cause financial losses, and ultimately

[3] To name but a few of the labor leaders benefiting from mayoral patronage: William McFetridge, chief of the city's janitors, is on the Police Board, which helps run the Police Department, the Chicago Park District, the antipoverty board, the Buildings Commission, and the Railroad Terminal Authority. Steve Bailey, chief of the city's plumbers, was appointed to the Board of Health, and equally important, runs the annual St. Patrick's Day parade. Thomas Murray, head of the electricians' union, was named to the Board of Education, and his son was vice-chairman of the Daley-run City Council. Joe Germano, head of the steelworkers, was named to the Library Board, as was Murray H. Finlay, an official of the clothing union. John Massee, boss of the Building Services and Municipal Employees Union, was named to the Chicago Housing Authority. William Lee, head of the Chicago Federation of Labor, helps run the antipoverty program, as does Thomas J. Nayder, secretary-treasurer of the Chicago Building Trades Council.

persuade the unwanted bidder to abandon the contract. Columnist Royko argued that despite competitive bidding on construction contracts, "if you're not wanted, you stay out, because they [the organization] can make it difficult for you."

In county government, Daley controls jobs in the courts, jails, sheriffs' offices, and even in the hospitals. In these areas, where life and liberty are so often at stake, patronage abuses stand out more clearly than they do elsewhere, to the general detriment of the institutions involved. Traditionally shielded from public scrutiny, institutions governed by patronage in the health and criminal-justice fields continue to worsen, as employees with backgrounds of political service take precedence over those with technical training. Bill Davidson attributed the conditions at the Cook County Jail partly to patronage politics: "The jail . . . has always been a source of patronage jobs. . . . Jack Johnson was a cop before he was made superintendent of the jail; his predecessor, Irvin Balzek, was a tailor. . . . The guards appointed by the sheriff are chosen from a list of names compiled by the Chicago ward bosses of the party in power in the county. Those names are generally precinct workers and their relatives. . . . On election day, the jail is virtually unmanned as the guards report for duty at the polls." [4]

The director of Cook County Hospital complained that he was forced to employ political workers with neither the knowledge, experience, or motivation to do the job. This ended in 1969, when the legislature placed the hospital under a special board, created by Governor Ogilvie, who now uses the hospital for *his* patronage placements. The governor has said that he does not favor uni-

[4] Bill Davidson, "The Worst Jail I've Ever Seen," *Saturday Evening Post*, July 13, 1968, p. 19.

lateral disarmament in the patronage wars. Frequently, politicians under pressure create special boards which give the appearance of good government—at least for a while—but in reality just transfer the patronage to someone else, like the governor. What the public forgets, as they forget in the issue involving appointed versus elected judges, is that someone still has to do the appointing, and chances are very strong that the appointing official will use his power to take care of his own patronage obligations.

The envy of all serious practical politicians, Mayor Daley's organization functions with virtually no effective opposition, thanks to the carefully nurtured patronage traditions of Chicago. George E. Mahin of the Better Government Association estimates that Daley controls jobs worth fifty million dollars a year, but this figure is believed low by students of the Chicago organization, including Alderman Leon Despres, one of the Mayor's few opponents on the Board of Aldermen. Despres, who represents the Hyde Park section of Chicago (home of the University of Chicago), argues that Daley controls between 30,000 and 35,000 jobs, including county and city jobs, not to mention the jobs available to him through industry.[5]

Elected for his fourth term, Daley withstands political change in the way that Chicago weathers the icy winds which blow off Lake Michigan each winter. Other mayors with far more attractive and liberal images, such as Jerome Cavanagh of Detroit, say that they turn to Mayor Daley—who is always accessible to them—for political advice when they are in trouble. Aided by an army of dual-

[5] The office of mayor in Chicago owes its tremendous power in no small part to the mayor's hegemony over Cook County. Chicago occupies two-thirds of the land area of Cook County.

functioning municipal-political employees, Daley has succeeded in obligating everyone, citizens and party workers alike, to his organization.

Banfield and Wilson call Chicago a city "in which an extreme decentralization of authority has been overcome by an extreme centralization of power, the power being based on specific inducements," over which the mayor exercises the role of broker.[6] Every government decision, by being treated as a favor, extracts a price; and with citizens (even those outside the party) so effectively bound up into the net of government, the body politic in Chicago stands firm as a monolithic, one-party state. Voters often dissent, but they rarely rebel, which led one dissenter, State Representative Arthur Telcser, to call this exercise of patronage "the root evil of politics because it keeps people in human bondage." Chicago city government gets things done; but by ensnaring its participants into a political monopoly, it has moved the city further and further away from the American ideal of an open society. Daley, as many mayors agree, presides over the most efficiently run city in America, but a city that still functions as a one-party city, its opposition effectively institutionalized or otherwise kept at a minimal level.

"Mayor Daley's power is inherent in the system, not the man," explained Illinois Lieutenant Governor Paul Simon. As a product of the system, he is an interchangeable part and could just as easily be replaced without any resulting changes in patronage practices. "The liberals get too excited over Daley," said Simon, a liberal himself. "He has inherited the system. If he doesn't use the power, it will be used by someone else."

[6] Edward C. Banfield and James Q. Wilson, *City Politics* (Cambridge: Harvard University Press, 1965), p. 104.

❬ *Can Charisma Produce Clout? The Experience
of New York's Mayor John V. Lindsay*

Contradicting Paul Simon, Mayor John Lindsay considers the Daley style of politics passé, long overdue for a
change, which Lindsay believes will occur when Daley
leaves office. "Times are different," according to Mayor
Lindsay. "After Dick Daley leaves politics, Chicago will
come down like a house of cards . . . times are different." The Daley patronage system just does not jibe with
modern needs, new styles, and the importance of image
required by the constant exposure demanded of the mayor
by the mass media. The mayor concluded: "There's the
new politics coming along . . . it takes a different view
of patronage . . . instead it emphasizes the involvement
of the community."

Unlike Mayor Daley, who advanced slowly through
the ranks of his regular Democratic organization until he
reached the seat of power, Mayor John Lindsay won his
first election as mayor basically without the help of the
city's Republican organization, which contributed little
except its endorsement to his victory. As a result, Lindsay
did not feel obliged to delegate much patronage to his fellow Republicans, and was defeated four years later in his
bid for the party's nomination,[7] a defeat also partly attributed to the fact that Lindsay stood too far to the left
of his party.

Lindsay said he won the mayoralty through mass

[7] Republicans have always found that they have enjoyed more patronage in New York City under Democratic rule than under "fusion government," according to Theodore Lowi in his excellent study of mayoral patronage: *At The Pleasure of the Mayor—Patronage and Power
in New York City 1898–1958* (New York: The Free Press of Glencoe,
1964), p. 13.

appeal—what he called "charisma" [8]—which he believed would give him the latitude to run the city without lowering himself to the tawdry patronage practices of his predecessors. Lindsay's victory was hailed, naturally enough, as a victory for good government, a view encouraged throughout by the mayor himself, who always preferred to be cast in the role of "reformer"—a label adopted by most candidates not running as incumbents. Looking clear-eyed into the cameras, Lindsay talked good government while he planted the image he had created for himself firmly in the public mind. With his youthful, all-American good looks, tall, raw-boned and sandy-haired, Lindsay was loved by the media: throughout his term he enjoyed strong editorial support while becoming the idol of the TV networks, news magazines, and newspapers. To the viewing public, whatever political styles Lindsay brought with him could be trusted; not so Mayor Daley, whose tough appearance frightened millions who saw him so prominently displayed during the Democratic convention of 1968.

[8] With apologies to Max Weber and to the other nineteenth-century philosophers, whose original conceptualization of "charisma" has been recently cannibalized by politicians and the media to mean little more than personal charm and the ability to speak well before a group. In its original meaning, "charisma" meant the ascription of certain extraordinary, almost godlike powers to an individual, like Joan of Arc, for example, whose ascension to power is explained by historians in terms of charismatic phenomena. For an excellent analysis of this subject, see Matthew Lipman and Salvatore Pizzurro, "Charismatic Participation as a Sociopathic Process," in *Psychiatry : Journal for the Study of Interpersonal Processes*, Vol. 19, No. 1, February 1956, pp. 11–30. The authors argue that the attribution of charisma to a leader "exists quite independently of the leader's actual abilities . . . defined not by what the leader can do, but by what people believe he can do." In fact, Messrs. Lipman and Pizzurro conclude that charisma is incompatible with democratic social institutions due to the condition of "servility which genuine moral leadership has . . . sought to correct."

Political images convey visual reality; and campaign rhetoric projects what the political leader wishes the public to believe. But here the accuracy ends, for the evidence somehow gets lost in the shuffle as the voter finds he is forced to decide psychedelically amid a passing array of images, insecure about what constitutes reality. Under closer scrutiny, two realities emerged from Lindsay's tenure as mayor, both contradicting the image he projected about the role of patronage in his administration. The most obvious discrepancy revealed that he *couldn't* govern effectively without using patronage resources, and he admitted this himself privately at the end of his first term. And secondly, perhaps more important, was that he *didn't* govern without patronage, though his patronage was more hidden than Daley's, his rewards were directed toward different groups, and his organization was more personal than the Chicago mayor's.

On the surface, Lindsay attacked patronage, which he denounced as political horse-trading, an unnecessary hindrance to effective government. Dramatically, he attacked the patronage practices of his predecessors; and as evidence of his good faith, he promised to eliminate patronage in his administration by leading the fight to abolish the job of city marshal, a notorious mayoral patronage outlet.[9] Said Lindsay: "It will be a fight, for patronage seldom has been legislated away with the willing consent of those who have benefited from this patronage. . . . Yes, let's abolish this embarrassment to our court structure. . . . Let's expel this sordid compound of privilege

[9] All 83 of the city's marshals are appointed by the mayor for six-year terms, which enables them to outlive the mayor politically. Used primarily by the Civil Courts to enforce the collection of money judgments, marshals can parlay their offices into profitable business ventures by being permitted to extract percentages (5% on the first $10,000 and 3% on amounts in excess of $10,000) on the funds they collect.

and patronage. Let's bring this dark aspect of our judicial system into the light of a free and open society. . . . The reform deserves our finest efforts, for what we can do is to reaffirm that there cannot be one law for the affluent and another for the impoverished." [10]

An impressive array of the city's good-government groups who had long fought for the abolition of marshals —the Citizens Union, the Municipal League, and the Association of the Bar of the City of New York—applauded Lindsay's antipatronage stand. But Lindsay found that investing heavily in an image of reform succeeded only in winning power initially, not in maintaining power or solving the problems of city government. The people he chose to exclude from patronage he called "power brokers," a convenient term used to whittle down the number of groups competing for the city's available rewards. Since the mayor's approach was so personal—based on his own obligations rather than on political realities, Lindsay alienated some powerful groups, and the results were disastrous for New York City.

On his first day in office, Lindsay denounced as power brokers the city's major union leaders whom he accused of entering City Hall through the back door during Democratic administrations. Offending some of New York's most powerful labor leaders, this immediately triggered a transit strike which paralyzed the city for close to two weeks. In quick succession, the city was struck by its teachers, sanitation workers, social-service case workers, and incinerator workers. The city's nurses resigned *en masse* (and were reinstated after the city met their demands), and the city's policemen and firemen began job actions—refusing to perform nonessential services, such as

[10] Text of an address by Mayor John V. Lindsay, prepared for delivery before the Association of the Bar of the City of New York, January 29, 1968.

towing away illegally parked cars—to exert pressure for salary increases.

Unlike Daley, and his own predecessor Robert F. Wagner, Lindsay did not conceive of his role as a behind-the-scenes mediator and conciliator, but rather at stage-center, providing moral leadership. Unfortunately, every time the mayor took a moral position on a wage increase, his union opponents also made their position a moral issue, and each side became rigid. If a sanitation strike was a moral issue to John Lindsay, it could be no less to John DeLury, president of the sanitation men's union.

After entering office on the offensive against those who engaged in back-room deals, Lindsay ended his first term being photographed with Harry Van Arsdale (head of New York's Central Labor Council, probably the most powerful of the labor movement's "power brokers"), learning the hard way that he had to dispense the city's favors to all those with power bases strong enough to challenge him. Instead of using his patronage powers to appoint New York's labor chiefs to prestigious positions, a much cheaper technique honed to a fine point by Mayor Daley, Lindsay rewarded the unions with their biggest salary increases in history. In contrast to Daley who institutionalized the opposition before it attacked him, Lindsay offered his patronage after the opposing sides had hardened into postures of dramatic confrontation and stretched the city's emotional energies well beyond their breaking point. When Lindsay finally sought reconciliation with the labor leaders, whom he invited to social gatherings at Gracie Mansion, he was rewarded by re-election support by the sanitation men, transit workers, and the largest municipal employees union, District Council 37, which won an agency shop from the Lindsay administration. Lindsay himself did not feel that large wage packages brought with them a proportionate degree of support and appreciation. "The kind of thing we do, people expect anyway," he said.

In retrospect, Mayor Lindsay defended his initially rigid posture on the grounds that at the beginning of his first term the city's labor leaders refused to take him seriously. In an atmosphere like this, negotiation was impossible, even though, the mayor alleged, he had offered them all kinds of favors to lure them into cooperating with him. Said Lindsay: "I was a patsy, a freak . . . they told me I was a sitting duck until they could get in someone who dealt in traditional methods. I tried everything. They were always stand-offish. Quill [Michael Quill, the late president of the Transit Workers Union] told me that there had to be a transit strike. He could do nothing about it; he was being challenged from within his union. . . . I was the patsy." The same problem, Lindsay complained, existed with the rest of the city's power elites: "There were always icebergs between us," said Lindsay, referring to Van Arsdale again, as well as to Theodore Kheel (a well-known labor mediator) and to the late Francis Cardinal Spellman. "With Cardinal Cooke, there is a whole new world; he will allow me to do favors for him."

Whether he learned it on the battlefield, or knew it all along, Lindsay found that the politician as messiah could not survive for long in a pluralistic society: that he could not govern without an organization, or maintain an organization without tangible rewards. While Mayor Daley was fortunate enough to work with a ready-made organization, Lindsay was forced to build one out of his available supporters. He tried formally to create an organization by forming "little city halls" which he said would bring government closer to the people and prevent the breakdown in communications, common in urban settings, between the public and government. Boston's Mayor Kevin White and Mayor Ivan Allen of Atlanta also in-

stituted little city halls, with White frankly admitting
their political function: to deliver government's rewards
to the people with the mayor's label securely attached.
"We're trying to institute political clubhouses through little city halls," said Mayor White. Mayor Allen, on the
other hand, regarded his little city halls as strictly administrative units designed to facilitate the dispersal of
services. Whether they dispense services, dole out patronage, or act as ombudsmen, little city halls really exist as
patronage-dispensing units, in the same way that Chicago's wards and Brooklyn's clubhouses provide employment for the poor and franchises for the rich. For this
reason, New York's Democratic City Council refused to
finance Lindsay's venture into building a political organization, sensing it would compete with local Democratic
clubhouses.

Failing to get his little city halls funded, the mayor
built his organization around programs and favors over
which he had more exclusive control: land variances, high-
level jobs, judgeships, and the antipoverty program. His
major patronage power fell in the area of zoning variances
—which made it easy or difficult for people to use and
profit from land—a source of patronage which is no
stranger to other mayors, although they prefer keeping
this power unpublicized. Publicly, mayors complain they
are powerless to prevent urban sprawl, which is ironic in
view of their vast patronage power over land use. This
gives them power over zoning ordinances, which often
enable selected builders to enhance the value of their
property by squeezing more apartments or more office
space into a given area. "The whole real estate industry
wants rezoning to R-10 [the highest density allowed],"
said Commissioner Beverly Moss Spatt, a maverick member of the New York City Planning Commission, and
daughter of the late Maximilian Moss, whose patronage

power as surrogate of Kings County made him one of the most powerful politicians in the country.

Although each city's system differs, the key to the mayor's power over land use turns on the extent to which he controls the zoning board of his particular city. In New York, whose example is common to many American cities, land variances are granted by the City Planning Commission, and also by the Board of Standards and Appeals, both of which the mayor controls with nearly absolute authority. He can use his power over zoning ordinances either to accrue political support for himself, promote the interests of the city, or both. Sam Minskoff, a New York builder, obtained a zoning variance in exchange for building two theaters at Astor Plaza in Times Square, because the Lindsay administration wanted to preserve the theater district. Mr. Minskoff turned up as a major contributor to Lindsay's re-election campaign.

Many of Lindsay's zoning patronage activities have been fought and exposed by Commissioner Spatt, whose own loyalty is bound by the Democrats who appointed her. Objecting to a tax abatement and zoning change sought by the city on behalf of the builder of high-income apartments at Chelsea Walk, Mrs. Spatt pointed out the patronage involved in this kind of favor: "Suffice to say," she wrote in her dissenting report, "cutting a developer's taxes in half is a subsidy to him, and at the same time means the city gets less in the total revenue pot." In addition, she revealed that if the zoning change went through to permit apartment dwellings to replace the printing industry located in the area, 600 employees would have lost their jobs. "This is but another step in Lindsay's attempt to subsidize the rich," charged Mrs. Spatt.[11]

[11] In another rather humorous instance of subsidizing the rich through city favors, the mayor allowed George Plimpton, well-known author, socialite, and editor of the *Paris Review* to rent Welfare Island for the

Another example of the mayor's use of zoning patronage, the zoning change which accompanied the sale of St. Joseph's convent in Flushing, Queens, triggered the most emotionally charged zoning battle in the city's history. Lindsay himself admitted the quid pro quo for effecting the zoning change in terms of his newly developed relationship with Cardinal Cooke. "We wanted to do something for the Catholic Church," he remarked. The convent, located in a residential section of Queens, was sold to two private developers, Leonard Litwin and Martin Swarzman, who sought to build a $15 million shopping center in the area previously occupied by the convent. Their intention more than doubled the selling price to $2.2 million, paid by developers—who were somehow sure of getting the zoning change to the higher density needed to build the shopping center (from R7-1 to C4-2) when they made the purchase from the church.

Had it not been for the violent response from a community fearful of becoming a vast shopping mall, the sale and zoning changes at St. Joseph's would have taken place hidden from public scrutiny, the familiar pattern of land-use politics. Residents in the Flushing area agreed with Commissioner Spatt, who predicted the change would ruin the neighborhood by upsetting its residential character and introducing a commercial quality to the area. Directly across the street from the proposed shopping center stand the Flushing Public Library, the Free Synagogue of Flushing, the Rabbi Max Meyer Religious School, the First Baptist Church of Flushing, Public School 20, and the St. Michael's Roman Catholic church and school.

---

nominal sum of $50 in order to hold a private party for the benefit of the magazine. The party's 800 guests, many in formal attire, danced to a rock 'n' roll combo out of earshot of the 2,800 chronically ill patients in the city's Bird S. Coler and Goldwater Memorial hospitals on the island.

"Quite a place to build a shopping center, wouldn't you say?" Mrs. Spatt asked. "With children darting in and out of the traffic that would be created there?" In her dissent, Mrs. Spatt charged that the proposed rezoning "violates desirable land use, circulation, and economic principles, and inevitably will have detrimental consequences for the Flushing community and for the city." Community groups opposed to the shopping center sent out a flyer that asked: "Would you build a shopping center in the middle of Central Park?" Despite the violent opposition from the community, the zoning change was effected, a direct result of pressure applied from the mayor's office through Donald H. Elliott, chairman of the City Planning Commission. It is now in litigation in the courts.

Chelsea Walk and St. Joseph's dramatically showed how zoning patronage, improperly exercised, violates sound principles of city planning, openly sacrificing the quality of life for the residents and workers to private considerations. In both cases the sacrifices were costly in human terms, and probably unwise politically in the long run.

"Planning is designed to get political support," explained planner Edwin Friedman, formerly with the City Planning Commission, and now employed by the New York State Division of Planning Coordination. In fact, he added, the vigorous opposition from politicians to the Master Plan for New York can be attributed to the fact that once such a plan existed, there would no longer be room for zoning contracts.[12] The whole method of effecting zoning changes, he said, proved the political nature of the

[12] "Contracts" is a term commonly used among professional politicians to mean a private agreement over a political question, such as a zoning change. Similar to a legal contract, although not legal or binding in court, this kind of contract conveys the same solidity, and carries the same meaning, as one that is binding: the promise of delivery of services or goods in exchange for a prespecified quid pro quo.

changes: "It depends on who wants the change. General Motors goes through the mayor's office; an individual goes through his assemblyman." The borough presidents, assemblymen, district leaders, congressmen, and city councilmen all influence zoning changes. An official involved in negotiating and setting the zoning line for the new Hunts Point Meat Market remarked that the "residential line would not have been drawn where it was had Dave Ross [former majority leader of the City Council, now a judge] not lived there."

In New York City, the process of zoning changes runs in a well-systematized fashion. Certain law firms are known to specialize in zoning cases, and their lawyers cultivate their political contacts as carefully as they study zoning law. One well-known lawyer, Abraham (Bunny) Lindenbaum, owes his well-developed zoning practice to the political connections he developed as a city planning commissioner during the Wagner administration. As commissioner, he openly solicited campaign contributions for his boss, former Mayor Robert F. Wagner, at a luncheon given for that purpose, and was forced to resign his seat after the luncheon became public knowledge.

While politicians agree that most zoning changes involve patronage, few divulge the quid pro quo, which is financial as often as it is political. Explained one city planner, who lamented the lack of reform in the zoning area: "There is no way of knowing what is behind the façade of zoning changes. Pay-offs occur two, three years later . . . sometimes in the form of stock tips. . . .We can't trace any wrongdoing in paying off political debts . . . there is no tin box any more." What does emerge clearly is a picture of zoning as big business, and zoning as a particularly valuable form of mayoral patronage, the political value of which is only slightly dented when it encounters the tragic and often futile opposition of the community. Functioning as patronage, zoning politics has caused unhealthy land speculation, where property is bought and sold like stock in anticipation of something that may not materialize. With urban land-use policies forced to conform to the exigencies of political profit and loss, cities have become overly congested and poorly planned, as political men seek new sources of support through the politically lucrative system of zoning patronage.

The politics of zoning is national, despite the distorted impression given by the literature on the subject of urban planning.[13] Irregularities in zoning patronage were the subject of grand jury investigations in Los Angeles and in Fairfax County, Virginia. In Los Angeles, the grand jury recommended charter changes to eliminate favoritism, and in Fairfax County the grand jury indicted members of the county board and several real estate developers.[14] Unfortunately, only when zoning patronage

[13] The vast literature on urban planning almost never mentions, much less describes, zoning ordinances as an item of political patronage and as an important factor in land use. In fact, except for Martin Meyerson and Edward Banfield's *Politics, Planning, and the Public Interest* (Glencoe, Ill.: The Free Press, 1955), planning literature rarely includes political variables as significant parts of the planning process. A new book specifically entitled *The Politics of Zoning*, by Stanislaw Makielski (New York: Columbia University Press, 1966), fails to recognize the existence of politically ordained zoning variances and their impact on the local planning process.

[14] See *A Program to Improve Planning and Zoning in Los Angeles*, Citizens Committee on Zoning Practices and Procedures—First Report to the Mayor and City Council, Los Angeles, California, July 1968; and *Planning and Zoning for Fairfax County, Virginia*, Zoning Procedures Study Committee, September 1967. Both reports, written by an impressive array of citizens and planners from each area, neglect also to analyze (or even mention) political factors which had definitely functioned in each case.

61.523

reaches scandalous proportions does the public become aware of its existence.

In Chicago, John Daley, a cousin of the mayor's, is a lawyer with an extensive zoning practice; and the law firm of Alderman Thomas Keane, a Daley lieutenant, also has a large zoning practice. Before a zoning change is effected in the city of Chicago, the zoning department sends the alderman of the district in which the change is to occur a notice, giving the alderman virtual veto power over the proposed variance. Alderman Vito Marzullo called this practice real grass-roots participation. "It's the neighborhood," he said, "which has to approve the zoning change." In the last analysis, however, the alderman has the final say over the variance, another bone of patronage handed out by the Daley organization to its faithful adherents.

Alderman Leon Despres told of zoning favors on a higher level in Chicago, presumably from the mayor's office, in the sale of land formerly occupied by the Edgewater Golf Club. According to Despres, soon after the club sold the land, a zoning ordinance was passed allowing the land to be used for intensive use—a shopping center and town houses—thereby tripling its value. The purchase of the links was therefore not entirely speculative, charged Despres, since the men knew beforehand that they would get the ordinance. Despres also charged the city with selling two streets worth $200,000 to Republic Steel for $40,000, on the rationale that they wanted to keep Republic Steel in the city.

Recognizing the political fertility of zoning patronage, the mayor also uses this power to burnish his image as a public servant, putting the power of land use behind what the public would consider worthy social policies. Freed from excessive charter restrictions, zoning offers the mayor a handy outlet by which he can bypass the usual

checks and balances and bargain with a free hand. Mayor
Joseph Alioto, for example, granted Warner Brothers the
right to film the motion picture *Bullitt* in San Francisco,
including extensive filming at the airport, in exchange for
a $50,000 swimming pool in the Hunter's Point ghetto.
He also "influenced" the builders of Rockefeller Center
West, a five-block area in downtown San Francisco, to
construct theaters by telling them: "We'll close a street
in the area if you build the theaters." Unless induced by
specific compensations, builders shirk the construction
of legitimate theaters, which too often amount to economic
liabilities.

Mayor Lindsay also claims his zoning policies have
been hand-crafted for the good of the city. Everyone given
a variance in the development of lower Manhattan, he
said, was "required to give something back to the city."
United States Steel Corporation and Uris Brothers have
given parks to the city and have continued to be responsible for their maintenance and upkeep. At Lincoln
Center, pedestrian malls were built as the quid pro quo
for being allowed to build in the area. Permission to close
the streets to be used by the World Trade Center was not
given until the Port of New York Authority agreed to increase the taxes it paid to the city. Tax abatements were
given, and land made available at low cost under urban
renewal programs for Beekman Downtown Hospital, on
the general understanding that the hospital would reciprocate by cooperating in the future with the mayor. (Although unmeasurable, tax abatements appear to constitute
another hidden but very important form of mayoral patronage. In Boston, according to Mayor Kevin White,
contractors sometimes build on the basis of tax agreements
which guarantee that they will not be taxed on their assess-
ments, but rather on a percentage of their gross profits.)
Design represents a major theme in the Lindsay ad-

ministration's use of zoning favors. In return for design esthetics, such as putting up a small park or adding attractive street furniture, a builder will be granted the most coveted of all zoning rewards: an increase in density which more than compensates him for the cost of the vest-pocket park, or the added furniture. In contrast to zoning changes which help only specific individuals or groups, the mayor conducts land patronage of this kind quite openly, seeking as much publicity as he can get. Considered "political" in the broadest sense of the term, "what the Mayor is getting back in the form of a quid pro quo is public approval and cooperation from builders, in accordance with his plans for the city," said Deputy Mayor City Administrator Timothy Costello, describing the mayor's planning powers. "He will get re-elected if the community is behind him."

Although the most important, zoning stands out as only one of the many areas of discretionary power used by Mayor Lindsay to garner political support. Practically invisible to public view, the general area of purchasing can also be used, despite rigid city regulations, for patronage purposes. To illustrate: scarcely one year after the city purchased $800,000 worth of drugs from the Bristol-Myers Corporation, the same company came through to aid the mayor in his re-election campaign by lending him the use of its private plane to attend a conference in Charleston, South Carolina, sponsored by the Southern Christian Leadership Conference. The city later settled a $700,000 antitrust action against Bristol-Myers and other drug companies, exercising its discretionary powers. Some city residents felt that acceptance of the plane ride placed the mayor in the position of dealing with a friend in his negotiations with the drug company, instead of dealing solely on behalf of his constituents.

Lindsay has also used awards of architectural and

engineering contracts as fruitful nonpublic patronage.
Aided by the fact that both national architectural societies
refuse to allow their members to participate in competitive
bidding—for strictly professional reasons—these contracts
continue to be awarded on a discretionary basis in every
city, state, and county in the nation. "When you give contracts to people who haven't had them before, you build
up your support and possibly your campaign funds," said
Mr. Costello. "There is an increased number of people
who have contributed for the first time."

Lindsay's favorite architect, Philip Johnson, has won
contracts from the city for the development of Battery
Park City and Welfare Island. According to Roger Starr,
director of the Citizens' Housing and Planning Council,
"an architect has a better chance of getting a contract
from the city if he calls in Johnson as a consultant." Mr.
Johnson returns Lindsay's favors by hosting dinners for
New York's "beautiful people" at which he enthuses about
the mayor. "These people will support Lindsay in the fall
because of Johnson . . . a great boulevardier," said Mr.
Starr. Actually, Philip Johnson and his circle made up
the natural Lindsay constituency, and one could not imagine their supporting a Mario Procaccino for mayor.

Lindsay's patronage also included awarding major
research grants to "think tanks" like the Rand Corporation. "This was really a gift," said Deputy Mayor Costello,
whose office is responsible for conducting in-government
studies. Other departments also find their research function duplicated by Rand and other private research companies benefiting from city research contracts.

The Lindsay administration vastly expanded its use
of these private consulting contracts, which were awarded
without competitive bidding and were usually unknown to
the public, from $8 million in the last year of the Wagner
administration to $75 million in 1969. "The point is that

old-fashioned municipal governments must reach out for management talent and modern technology," Mr. Lindsay told a City Hall news conference after a newspaper report revealed the unpublicized expansion of the city's use of consultants. In a style reminiscent of Mayor Daley, Mr. Lindsay issued a brief statement on the subject, but refused to hold a question-and-answer session with the testy remark: "I've made the only comment I wish to make."

Mayor Lindsay's expanded use of consultants raised some interesting questions in view of continuing evidence connecting these contracts with the Lindsay administration's patronage obligations. Peter Abeles, president of Abeles and Schwartz, which conducted a $12,000 study of Washington Heights for the City Planning Commission, explained: "We got this contract because I knew Don Elliott through reform politics. He offered me a job working for the planning commission, which I didn't want to do. He asked me, 'What can you do?' I said, 'Washington Heights.' It's all done on the basis of who you know and how much time you're willing to spend on self-promotion."

An employee of McKinsey and Company, a concern with $1.5 million in management consultant contracts with the city in 1969, also explained the predominance of the political role of a consulting contract. "There is a problem," he admitted, "when the consultant is assumed to be more objective than a civil servant or academic, or more knowledgeable than a political hack. We are not more objective, we have our own biases. We become eligible for contracts because we are the right social people, we have the right values, and we're trustworthy, just as other kinds of people, who wear different clothes and have different values, receive their contracts from the clubhouse."

He described the consultant's role as "helping the executive maintain and consolidate his position, and not help solve the problem," which explains why the studies are not only unavailable to the public but even to public officials other than the mayor. Ten New York City councilmen brought a lawsuit to compel the Lindsay administration to show them a Rand study on housing which formed the basis of Lindsay-administration housing legislation on which the Council was asked to vote. Because of their secrecy, prior studies are sometimes unknown to present commissioners, who then freely dole out grants unaware of the existence or findings of previous studies on the same problem. A $50,000 study of Queensboro Bridge traffic in 1970 was the fifth such study since 1968, the eighth since 1963, and the tenth since 1948. City officials said that they knew of no recommendations of any study that had been implemented. Transportation Administrator Constantine Sidamon-Eristoff conceded, moreover, that he was unaware of the existence of six of the ten studies, and remarked, "Come over to my office sometime and I'll show you all the studies we have lined up all over the place."

Lindsay-administration officials said that management studies had saved the city $200 million a year by accelerating construction of capital projects. Asked to substantiate the claim that these projects actually had been accelerated, the officials cited an increase in construction starts, or ground-breakings, rather than construction completions, or ribbon-cuttings. Moreover, the public was asked to take the administration's word that management studies had aided in the acceleration of construction starts, because the studies were unavailable to the public.

On the other hand, Milton Musicus, the city's new Municipal Services Administrator, found "relatively worthless" several studies on Con Edison and added: "The old studies, frankly, don't mean very much." An $80,000 study of the Lower Manhattan Expressway was so unsophisticated that "I wouldn't have accepted that from a college freshman," said Albert H. Woehrle, former manager of the highway-planning unit of the Tri-State Transportation Commission, an intergovernmental body. A $150,000 transportation study of the Bronx by Frederick H. Harris was 75 pages long and contained detailed descriptions of the history of the Bronx, the topography of the Bronx, and the traffic patterns of the Bronx—the thrust of which was that whether one was in Riverdale or Mosholu Parkway, traffic tended to move toward Manhattan in the mornings and away from Manhattan in the evenings. Similarly, a $70,000 study of the Staten Island ferry conducted by the former college roommate of the Borough President of Staten Island concluded, among other findings, that ferry traffic was heaviest at 8 A.M. and 5 P.M.

While deriding patronage in the offices of city marshals and pothole inspectors, Lindsay managed to find government jobs for his two unsuccessful running mates —appointing Milton Mollen, candidate for controller, to the Criminal Court, and Timothy W. Costello, candidate for city council president, deputy mayor city administrator. Of his sixteen borough coordinators, all but three received jobs in his administration. Although Lindsay has complained publicly about civil service, he has excelled— like Mayor Daley—in circumventing this law. He increased the number of temporary jobs—exempt from civil service—from 1,500 to 15,000 (90 percent of these jobs are in the antipoverty program). The city has an additional 55,000 noncompetitive jobs, of which 18,000 are in education (school-lunchroom helpers and other aides), 29,000 in hospitals, and 1,700 in health. The mayor has also used the office of corporation counsel as a fruitful patronage area, particularly suited to all the young lawyers who helped him in his campaign. Patronage in the corporation counsel's office has led many of Lindsay's critics to accuse him of running a city-financed on-the-job training program—thus enlisting troops to call upon for his political campaigns. The critics claim that due to its inexperienced legal staff, the city has lost many cases in court.

Simultaneously, the Lindsay administration vastly expanded the city's use of private law firms, from four cases in the 12 years of the Wagner administration to 15 cases in the first five years of the Lindsay administration. Most were antitrust cases, and the private firms were given 12½ percent of the funds they recovered. Two cases were handled by Sheffield, Webster, Mr. Lindsay's old law firm. Paul O'Dwyer, unsuccessful Democratic candidate for senator, was named counsel on a transit case by the Board of Estimate, but the corporation counsel reduced his fee from what he had requested to $35 a day, in marked contrast to the $700 a day paid by the city to some private management consultants.

To circumvent even further what he considers an outdated civil service system, Lindsay has begun (and many other mayors have joined him) the extensive contracting out of services formerly performed by city employees. In addition to contracting out city research to private firms, the mayor has also contracted out the entire $750 million hospital budget for New York City, with the approval of the state legislature. The private, voluntary hospitals vied to operate the medical programs of the city hospitals, at a substantial profit, through a newly formed public corporation.

What Lindsay showed in his use of patronage favors was that although he professed fusion, nonpolitical government, he could not survive for long in the political arena if he took this posture seriously. To Lindsay, community involvement and participation represented desirable features of government, while political machines on the Daley style did not—confusing the important fact that the two forms of political organization bore remarkable similarities; only their styles and surface presentations were different. Unsavory as it appears, the Daley organization also involves the community, extracting from its workers an exceedingly high level of participation. Where it differs from the Lindsay organization lies in its selection of sectors of the community that are to be included in the organization. Since few political organizations have ever succeeded in including everyone, it is almost inevitable that certain sectors are bound to be ignored. While Lindsay, for example, at first denied certain union leaders the access and recognition they had enjoyed under Democratic leadership for so long (and which their counterparts received from Mayor Daley), he was busy extending his patronage and building up support in other areas: real estate developers, high-income apartment dwellers, architects, research corporations, and, to some extent, lower-income blacks and Puerto Ricans who benefited from jobs in the antipoverty program.[15] From these groups, despite his image as a man who fought the machines, Lindsay actually pieced together one of the most formidable political organizations New York had ever seen, lubricated by $3 million in campaign contributions (an all-time high for a municipal election), which came

[15] This policy paid off at the polls on November 4, 1969, when Lindsay, according to *The New York Times*, "won re-election with an unusual combination of support from higher-income New Yorkers and low-income Negroes and Puerto Ricans," with large segments of the middle class voting "against his continuing in power." In fact, the mayor's highest percentages came from heavily Negro areas: upper, central, and south Harlem; Crotona Park; and Bedford-Stuyvesant. *The New York Times*, November 6, 1969, p. 37.

mostly from the financial district,[16] the Wall Street law firms, and from industrialists. In the end, Mayor Lindsay admitted the necessity, fortunate or otherwise, of effectively using patronage to run New York City. "You've got to have people in government who are politically smart," said the mayor. "This means they have to understand that part of politics is the art of obligation."

❡ *Patronage Opportunities and Political Realities: How Different Mayors Grant Favors*

While mayors complain of political impotence, which they attribute to their continuing financial dependence on state and federal government, and to the albatross of civil service, the office of mayor emerges as one with vast power. Often equipped with an acute instinct for survival, mayors have developed this power by refining the known techniques of political patronage, seeking new routes and rejecting others that seem too limited to be viable. Mayors plead poverty, but city budgets under their jurisdiction have soared to all-time highs which, in some cases, mayors can develop into new sources of political support and new areas of obligation.

Some mayors use patronage to prevent the organization that helped them get elected from dissolving. Mayor Ivan Allen of Atlanta was elected by an unstable coalition of blacks and businessmen, which he glued together primarily through his ability to get and give federal patronage in the form of grants for the benefit of both groups. Beginning with the Kennedy administration, Atlanta has, under Democratic rule, benefited well above the average

[16] Gustave Levy, chairman of the New York Stock Exchange, was chairman of the campaign finance committee.

city from OEO (Office of Economic Opportunity) and Model Cities grants. In return, Allen was willing to go to Washington to testify in favor of President Kennedy's Civil Rights bill when Kennedy asked him to come. Unlike most other cities, Atlanta has been lucky enough to have developed a strong city-federal relationship without having to cope with senators and congressmen in between, who seize on issues and government grants that will put them in a favorable light with the voters. "I have never gone through a senator since I've been here," said Dan Sweat, Allen's chief aide in charge of federal grants. Sweat added that senators do appear to take credit for programs they had nothing to do with getting: "The only time [Senator] Russell's been off the hill to OEO was when the first OEO grant was announced in 1965 . . . even though he voted against it . . . he just doesn't like poor people and black people."

Some mayors have successfully increased their patronage power through the clever use of the private sector for public purposes. Industry has always received favors from government; now the quid pro quo requires that industry supply tangible evidence of public-spiritedness along with the more traditional private forms of support. In Pittsburgh, the entire theme throughout the administration of former Mayor Joseph Barr expressed the relationship of business to government. "The key to Pittsburgh," explained Mayor Barr, "is how the city works with industry. The companies know they must put something back into the cities. You can't go back into the suburbs anymore and put your feet up and have a martini. Those days are gone forever." Mayor Barr eased zoning codes so that the steel companies could expand their plants and build housing for their employees. In exchange, industry has put some of its resources back into the city. U.S. Steel and Jones & Laughlin conducted tests costing them $100,000 to determine whether an area of the city was mined too much for the city to build housing on the site. As gravy, Mayor Barr added, several companies located in Pittsburgh donated $30,000 to the city to entertain the mayors at their annual conference in June 1969. Industry also frequently lends Pittsburgh some of its top consultants without charge.

In Detroit, Jerome Cavanagh cultivated a strong relationship with the automobile industry in order to expand his extraconstitutional powers over city government. In fact, Cavanagh criticized his predecessors who did not use this fertile field of power. "I object," he said, "to some former mayors whose relationship with the automobile industry was purely social." In contrast to them, Cavanagh worked hard to "get the automobile industry more actively involved in the problems of the city, and to participate in government." Like Mayor Barr, Cavanagh persuaded the automobile industry to lend the city some of its talented administrators as consultants. He also convinced the industry to initiate training programs for the hard-core unemployed, and these were among the first and most successful in the country. What Cavanagh did for the automobile industry in return was not spelled out with the same detail, but the mayor admitted that he had the power to veto automobile dealerships proposed for political opponents, and to obtain franchises for political friends and others who would cooperate with him. He also justified doing favors for the automobile industry in terms of the general health of the city. "What was good for General Motors was good for Detroit," when Cavanagh, using his powers over land use, rezoned lands adjacent to the Ternstadt Plant of General Motors from residential to commercial purposes in order to keep the company from moving out of the city. If the company had left, the city would have lost 4,000 jobs, according to Mayor Cavanagh. In Detroit, land variances are granted by the Board of Zoning Appeals, appointed by members of the Common Council, who are advised by the mayor's Industrial and Development Department. "So the Board of Zoning Appeals knows what the administration wants," Mr. Cavanagh explained.

Atlanta's Ivan Allen enlisted the support and help of the city's business interests by threatening that everything would go up in smoke if they refused to cooperate with government. In an age in which the threat of race riots means continual anxiety to urban dwellers, the promise of racial peace signifies a great deal—assuming the mayor can deliver. Indeed, Mayor Lindsay capitalized with substantial success on the absence of riots during his first term—and this was a large factor in his re-election. "Last summer I made eight calls and got seven emergency swimming pools," said Allen, who claimed there was no quid pro quo involved. "The business community has responded on hundreds of occasions by matching funds, paving streets . . . etc." In effect, Allen offered industry peace from race riots if it coughed up substantial contributions of facilities and money for the city. A businessman himself, Allen ran a successful furniture business before becoming mayor. "Allen" furniture stores are seen throughout Atlanta, although Allen stressed that the city made no purchases from his company.

Mayor Kevin White of Boston also described how he had bestowed city favors on industry for what he considered the public good. "I will occasionally give a developer a break in his assessment, in hopes that he will provide jobs and do a good job," said the handsome young mayor. Mayor White noted that in Boston, as in other major cities, contractors are major campaign contributors, but also noted: "Political contributions are not a quid pro quo necessarily, but insurance against retribution or abuses." He added that he felt the "biggest single patronage item in the cities rested with the selection of developers for urban renewal projects."

The main danger in exercising and developing mayoral patronage lies in the question of where to draw the line between the legitimate and illegitimate use of this kind of power. Former Mayor Cavanagh, who thoroughly understands and enjoys the application of the patronage system, is leery of "left-handed," or dishonest, contracts. He cited one national contractor who had built housing developments in three major Eastern cities. When the contractor arrived in Detroit, he greeted the city's top housing official by asking "Who do we see?" meaning, "Whom do they pay off to get the contract?" Warned Cavanagh: "If the word gets around that you could do this in the mayor's office, in the long run it's like opening Pandora's box." [17] Mayor Joseph Alioto also differentiated between the legitimate and unfair uses of patronage, citing the state of California's milk-price-fixing law as an example of what he called "legalized patronage." "This means millions of dollars to that industry," Mr. Alioto explained.

Job patronage available to mayors varies widely, with few statistics to pinpoint with exactness what is already known. A study conducted by Jean J. Couturier, executive director of the National Civil Service League, showed

[17] In spite of his justification of patronage, Cavanagh was embarrassed when some of his own patronage practices were publicly revealed. It was disclosed that Cavanagh lobbied for the city sponsorship of $30 million in tax-free development bonds to finance expansion and relocation for Detroit's Peerless Cement Co. The president of the company, John Sweetland, is a long-time friend of the mayor's, and raised more than $5,000 for the mayor in his primary campaign against G. Mennen Williams for the U.S. Senate. Mayor Cavanagh denied that his friendship with Sweetland had anything to do with selecting Peerless for bond sponsorship.

that city employees usually excluded from merit-system coverage were those who worked on highways, health, hospitals, sewage, sanitation, parks, and recreation. "These categories represent 663,000 of the 1,434,000 full-time municipal employees in 1962," testified Couturier before the U.S. Senate Subcommittee on Intergovernmental Relations in March 1969. "This 46% of the municipal work force is the traditional source of patronage in American government because unlike in Europe, the merit system here was developed from the top down," he continued. His survey also indicated that civil service coverage decreased proportionately with the decrease in city size.

In the same league politically with senators and congressmen, powerful mayors with national clout have been able to amplify their job patronage through Washington. When the Democrats were in the White House, admitted Mayor Cavanagh, his patronage included federal jobs: "The chief talent scouts for the Johnson administration would always call me to get my view," said the Mayor. Kevin White also described federal patronage in Boston which went through the mayor's office: "Boston did especially well during the Kennedy era," and he added: "Having the Speaker of the House [John McCormack] from Boston also helps." White said that he frequently asked the Speaker for emergency 30-day jobs for "someone who is desperately in need of funds."

Regardless of the job patronage they already control, mayors complain about civil service. Mayor White called for curtailing or circumventing civil service, which he labeled "a detriment to effecting change quickly in an urban society." Civil servants, he explained, are unaccountable to political organizations, enabling them to remain free from the checks and balances which elected officials must cope with. Protected by law and by increasingly powerful municipal unions, they can resist changes in policy without suffering either the loss of their jobs or a cut in their salary. No corporation president could run his company, the mayors argue, with this empty shell of command over his employees: authority without power or control. Adding to their difficulties as mayor is the public belief that they do command, causing the shower of blame which inevitably rains on them when services fail to run optimally.

❰ *Minority Group and Antipoverty Patronage*

The turmoil of the black revolution centers in the cities, forcing mayors to accommodate their patronage policies to the demands of minority groups. Dramatically, the leaders of the revolution have shown that they, along with the country's other nonwhite racial minorities, have entered the competition for government's discretionary awards, allocated disproportionately for so long to the white community. In an attempt to mitigate the already exacerbated tensions between the races, many mayors have begun to delegate more and more patronage to Negroes, as well as to other ethnic groups, primarily through such channels as prestigious appointments; the use of black contractors, banks, and insurance agencies; the antipoverty program; direct access routes to the mayor; and the allotment of increased mayoral time to the ceremonial activities of minority groups.

Appointing blacks to highly visible positions in city government was first used by the mayors to recognize ethnic groups, and later to cool the ghettos by showing their inhabitants how they too were sharing in the rewards of government. Warm weather, it was found, invariably brought with it beefed-up efforts by mayors, fearful of summer riots, to offer recognition and patronage to the black community. In fact, the only minority-group patronage former Mayor Joseph Barr of Pittsburgh could recollect in his entire administration was a program run by businessmen to hire ghetto youths for the summer. Mayor Kevin White admitted that he engaged in "black patronage," which, he explained, amounted to appointing Negroes to prestigious boards. If the city's civil service system did not inhibit him from "bringing Negroes into the base of the political system," he alleged, he would probably be able to do more for the black community. "Boston's a city that never saw a black come in the front door," said White, who won the mayoralty in a close vote against Louise Day Hicks, a conservative candidate supported by a strong white backlash vote. As concrete examples of this kind of token patronage, White told of appointing a black to chair the Board of Trustees of Boston City Hospital, and of his attempt to get Wayne Emory of the Boston Celtics basketball team to head the city's recreation department.

Mayor Joseph Alioto reaped political popularity among San Francisco's Chinese and Japanese populations from his continuous efforts to recognize these groups through his power over land use. To obtain a Chinese bridge over a street, and a Chinese-American cultural center, Alioto gave a developer a variance he needed to build a hotel. The mayor was also instrumental in closing two streets for a builder who agreed to construct a Japanese-American cultural center—including a specialized theater for Kabuki dancers—as part of the hotel-office shopping-center complex. "We must use the opportunities for buying valuable properties into promoting extra things," said Alioto, referring to his efforts to continue the Japanese and Chinese traditions of his city.

Mayor Allen, helped to the mayoralty by the support of the black voters, granted his city's black community access and recognition it had never experienced before under previous mayors. With a copy of Martin Luther King's book *Where Do We Go from Here?* prominently displayed on his desk, Mayor Allen described one of his first acts as mayor specifically intended to grant recognition to the black community. Right after Allen was elected in 1962, a group which included five black students came to the mayor to complain about having been denied service in the City Hall cafeteria. Marching down to the lunchroom with them, Allen told the cafeteria staff he would serve the students himself if they refused to do so, causing the entire room of people to walk out rather than witness blacks being served. The cafeteria was integrated from that day on, encouraging Allen to attempt to desegregate other areas of city life. "The business community backed me," said Allen, "and also the press." Allen also reciprocated the black community's support by spreading among them the more tangible rewards of government, such as depositing some of the city's funds in black banks. "We opened the same privileges to Negroes that whites have always had," said Allen. The city of New York also attempted to give black-owned businesses preferential treatment, and announced that two Negro-owned demolition concerns, the Winston A. Burnett Construction Co. and the Trans Urban Demolition Co., would be awarded two emergency contracts totaling $1,620,000 without public bidding. Both contracts included the provision that the companies hire and train workers from slum areas.

Other mayors, such as George Siebels of Birmingham, Alabama, take a more limited view of black patronage than Mayors Allen and White. Mayor Siebels considers that his most important favor to the black community is the policy he initiated of taking predawn (5 A.M.) tours of the ghetto, followed up by letters to all citizens he sees dumping garbage on the street, serving them notice that "As mayor of this city, I am putting you on notice and give you 10 days to clean up." According to Mayor Siebels, a gracious, white-haired Southern gentleman whose great-grandfather was a U.S. senator and chief justice of the Alabama Supreme Court, "two-thirds of the Negro population understand and appreciate this." He said he had also proposed the establishment of Matt Leonard Day, to honor a brave Negro soldier from Birmingham who had posthumously received the Congressional Medal of Honor. Siebels' limited tokenism typifies the attitude of some Southern mayors whose cities have not substantially been affected by the nationwide attempts of racial minorities to share in the rewards of patronage. Mayors like Siebels truly want to improve the condition of the Negro population in their cities and change the poor image their cities have projected over the last few years. Siebels was particularly concerned over the bad image Birmingham impressed on the nation during the Bull Connor (the city's former police chief) era, and would much rather, he said, link Birmingham with progress in the mind of the country. But underlying his sincere intentions, Siebels' idea of promoting self-help as the only form of mayoral patronage (getting the Negroes to clean up their own slums before they can, if ever, share rewards with everyone else) amounts to old-line plantation paternalism in modern dress.

Many argue that token black patronage, such as appointing blacks to highly visible, prestigious positions, often creates more psychological harm and general frustration than good, in holding out to the community hope for advancement that is unrealistic. With the passage of the antipoverty bill, mayors in cities lucky enough to get funded found they now could enlarge on their tokenism if they wished, and offer rewards to all occupational groups in the black community, not only to celebrities and highly skilled employees.

Although the program's jobs and contracts were not given exclusively to blacks or other racial minorities,[18] the program at its current levels of funding has given mayors and other local politicians the opportunity to extend their patronage beyond traditional sources. Kenneth Sparks, Acting Assistant Director of Public Affairs at the Office of Economic Opportunity (headquarters of the antipoverty program), offered the following figures to show the scope of the jobs made available by the program: "In Fiscal Year 1968, some 144,500 nonprofessional positions were filled out of 170,000 available by Community Action Agency grantees and their delegates. In that same year, some 92,300 professional positions were held. Of course, there is a breakdown within these figures for year-round employees and those designated to summer programs only."

What the antipoverty program offered minority groups was the opportunity to participate in government in the same way that the traditional machines enlisted citizen involvement: giving away a piece of the action. And while the antipoverty program did not break up the city machines (as some of its advocates argued), it did threaten them; for what it accomplished was the broadening of the patronage base to undercut those political leaders who traditionally dispensed patronage. For this reason, many Republican leaders, such as George Romney of Michigan, tried to save the program while many Democrats, particularly Democratic mayors, worked behind the

---

[18] James Ridgeway, who covered antipoverty programs for the *New Republic*, argued that the patronage in the program existed only for the white middle class, what he termed "diddling social scientists" who flocked to Washington to fill the numerous positions open at the newly created OEO. Most of these employees, he alleged, went on to lucrative positions in industries that considered them valuable for the contacts they had made during their service in government.

scenes to weaken it. Mayor Daley, for example, never re-
laxed his tight control over the antipoverty program in his
city, often vetoing grants to the city which threatened to
circumvent his organization. The Green amendment,[19]
passed in 1968, aided mayors like Cavanagh and Daley,
who keenly felt the threat of newly developed competing
groups, by returning to these mayors some of their original control over patronage in the poverty program. Before
the Green amendment was passed, 50 percent of local com-
munity-action agencies were required to represent the
poor, with the remaining 50 percent to come from citywide
civic organizations. The Green amendment changed the
requirements to provide that up to one-third of the members of the local community action agency be elected or
appointed city officials. Board members on local community agencies held control over the patronage (mostly jobs
and contracts) which issued from the antipoverty program. Even with the addition of the Green amendment,
mayors like Kevin White were not interested in the jobs
offered by the antipoverty program. "Whatever job patronage was involved in the program," said White, "was
not worth the headache. I didn't want the jobs. Besides,
I knew that once Nixon won, I would be asked to pick up
whatever programs he succeeded in tossing out. Blame is a
big factor with mayors."

In New York, as in other cities, there were clear-cut
cases of "poverty politicians" successfully competing with
the entrenched organization, fully justifying the fears of
mayors like White, Cavanagh, and Daley. Shirley Chisholm, the first black congresswoman elected to the House
of Representatives, built her power base out of the antipoverty program in the Bedford-Stuyvesant area of Brooklyn. Shunned at first by the Brooklyn Democratic county

[19] Sponsored by Representative Edith Green, of Oregon.

leader, then Stanley Steingut, Mrs. Chisholm found she could act independently owing to the patronage at her disposal courtesy of OEO. "These people were able to get ten times the job placements in Youth-in-Action that Stanley [Steingut] could ever give them," said a poverty official working in Brooklyn. Other black politicians in New York were able to hold up successful examples like that of Mrs. Chisholm to force the Democratic machine to be more responsive to the patronage demands of the black community. Sensitive to the effects of this pressure, John Burns, New York State Democratic Chairman, formally asked the party's national committee to enlarge his own state committee to include more Negroes and Puerto Ricans before the presidential nominating convention of 1968.

Atlanta politicians, who nurtured the antipoverty program with almost the same care with which they catered to industry, found that using the program effectively brought them racial peace in situations that might otherwise have erupted into racial warfare. Jealously guarding its own turf, the newly created antipoverty organization in Atlanta warded off outside groups coming into Atlanta to organize the black community against the existing government. When Stokely Carmichael arrived in Atlanta to lead some demonstrations, he was run out of town by an eccentric Negro known as Malt Liquor (his real name is John Patrick), who headed both EOA (Economic Opportunities of Atlanta) and the job-recruitment section of the city's Model Cities program. "He was extremely influential in the black community, a real man of the streets," said mayoral assistant Dan Sweat, describing how effective Malt Liquor was. Malt Liquor appointed his cronies to antipoverty jobs, even though many of them had police records. "Yet even with his gang of hoodlums, we needed him," said Mr. Sweat.

Mayor Lindsay also found the antipoverty program

extremely useful, particularly in augmenting his job patronage, and in making inroads into the powerful Democratic machine in New York. "The community corporations," said the mayor, "cracked up traditional systems . . . the traditional Democrats were more fearful than my crowd. I supported the Poverty Program . . . they [the black community] knew I would support it . . . now I don't have to call them for pay-offs. They'll support me in the fall [mayoral election of 1969]." Lindsay's use of the antipoverty program involved very substantial rewards for the ghetto community. His aides were given sets of jobs—and many allege cash as well—and told to go out on the streets and sign people up. One of the mayor's antipoverty aides, Arnold Seguerra, told how he had parceled out the jobs within his control: "Many of the jobs I gave out went to my friends . . . many of them were men with criminal records . . . they wouldn't have been able to get any other city jobs." In June, at the start of Lindsay's second mayoral campaign, Seguerra left his job temporarily to work for the mayor's re-election. Although those who received jobs with the antipoverty program would probably vote for Lindsay—if they were registered—constructive critics of Lindsay's antipoverty patronage policies charged that the mayor erred in not leading his new patronage beneficiaries to register as Republicans, as traditional machine politicians would certainly have done; he then, they allege, would have had enough support to win the June 1969 primary which he lost to State Senator John Marchi.

Regardless of how it is used, most politicians fear "poverty patronage" and the problems it has brought with it as an unknown variable. They know the political dynamite inherent in the system of giving out jobs and contracts (and hence, power) to groups and individuals without the unifying discipline and guidance offered by a central organization. Often, after making the initial appointments, the mayor loses his interest and his control, and the idealistic purposes of the antipoverty program are eclipsed by the grab for power. When it becomes clear that along with its substantial benefits, the programs have politicized people toward violence and unpredictable, anomic political attitudes, angry congressmen become less and less willing to fund programs that they feel might result in their own political destruction. The funds decrease as the competition increases; and in cities like New York, competition among groups for poverty-patronage power has caused almost as much hostility among groups within the black community as the more public conflict between blacks and whites.

Dr. Canute Bernard, of New York's South Jamaica Community Corporation, has publicly accused his board of operating exclusively on patronage principles, to the general detriment of the program. The patronage Dr. Bernard described existed on every level, from the regional antipoverty board to the local board, on up to the mayor's office, with the fights between these three units leading to the ultimate failure of the program, as evidenced by the poor ratings the group received from OEO.

Initially, said Dr. Bernard, the top levels of city and national governments left the poverty board substantially alone, reminding him of the colonial attitude under which he had grown up in Jamaica, West Indies: "Don't bother me; just keep your boys quiet." As in Atlanta, the mayor's office was happy to allow the board and the local politicians fairly autonomous power in exchange for racial peace in South Jamaica. After a while, as everyone began to take racial peace for granted, many hungry eyes looked toward the jobs offered by the program. And jobs, said Dr. Bernard, constituted the major patronage offered by the program. Of the $970,100 allocated to the South Jamaica Community Corporation, 90% went to pay salaries, with the other 10% going to the board's delegate agencies. Over one-third of the staff members were paid over $6,000 each in annual salaries, with the executive director drawing a salary of $19,000. The board and its staff members added up to 140 people. According to Dr. Bernard, no separation existed, even prior to the Green amendment, between the local political machine and the poverty board: the assemblyman and the Republican district leader controlled all appointments to the board, while the executive director of the board, along with a majority of the board's members, were members of the district leader's club. Lacking the "one-third poor" as stipulated by OEO guidelines, the board represented instead members of the community belonging to the status quo: real estate men, insurance brokers, etc. "The emphasis of the poverty program is jobs," said Dr. Bernard, "while the end product does not reach the people who need it most: the welfare people."

To correct what he considered a bad situation, Dr. Bernard and his friend Dr. Gerald Simpkins (a dentist who had been active in antipoverty work in the South), ran against the local politicians and won control over the board. With his new power, Dr. Bernard tried to divert some of the funds to filter down to the poor. He quickly found that the patronage policies of his predecessors impeded his progress all along the way. At first, he discovered that he had inherited all 140 staff and board workers, and could neither fire them, nor hire anyone new. "If you appoint a man, you can't knock him; that's the political game," explained Dr. Bernard. "As a result, all my money went to pay the salaries of these men, who were not doing the job of formulating programs for the real people for whom poverty money is intended . . . we were supposed to be developing programs and we weren't. A corporation according to its charter has the right to remove someone who's not producing, and we didn't have that power." It was no surprise that they were rated "F" by OEO, charged Bernard, after their program showed an "outreach" (how far the program extends into the community) of twenty youths, after $200,000 had been allotted to them.

Dr. Bernard argued that he didn't want the antipoverty program devoid of spoils; he just wanted the community to get the available patronage. "There has to be a spoils system in a given context," he explained. "Just leave a piece of the pie so these people can eat, too!" After trying to run the program with this philosophy in mind, Bernard was soon deposed from power, through what he called a coup d'état, initiated by the local Republican and Democratic machines, and implemented by the mayor's office. "Lindsay couldn't fight his own organization," said Dr. Bernard. Ostensibly through the auspices of the Community Development Agency (which oversees local community corporations), the police came and took over the corporation, giving the CDA the right to run the organization until new elections could be held.

Mayoral patronage based on OEO was further illustrated by Dr. Bernard who described the differences in access before and after his fall from power. While he ran the board, he said, he had direct access to the mayor: he could call him and get an immediate response. The access was mutual; Bernard provided the mayor with access to the black community of Jamaica, bringing together his friends and community leaders who would sit down with the mayor and with Donald Elliott, chairman of the City Planning Commission, and discuss community problems. Now, claims Bernard, he can't even reach Lindsay on the phone, and was never able to tell his side of the power struggle to the mayor.

Power struggles like this within the antipoverty

program occur often. Clearly political entities, they will produce the same kinds of conflicts for available rewards, over which political units in a democratic society continually grapple. In many cases, they have reached the criminal stage, which unfortunately has led many critics to discredit the entire program. In Boston, for example, the leaders of a training program to teach hard-core convicts to become mechanics were murdered. According to a National Broadcasting Company White Paper on the murder, both the murderers and the dead men were members of the program, known as the Consortium, and had been locked in a power struggle over the government funds brought in by the program. Less extreme cases of malfeasance more frequently involve misappropriation of funds. In New York, the antipoverty program has suffered from problems of this kind stemming primarily from bad hiring policies: hiring men with criminal records to fill middle management positions with extensive financial power, and then hiring poor administrators to supervise them. *The New York Times* publicized the mismanagement of poverty funds (brought to light by a report issued by the U.S. Department of Labor) in New York's Community Development Agency, which is supervised by the city's Human Resources Administration.[20] Citing millions of dollars in loss, the *Times* revealed that almost "40% of the 43,000 names on the weekly payroll of the Neighborhood Youth Corps in 1967 cannot be proved to belong to actual persons, according to the latest available tax records." [21] In addition to giving out "no-show" jobs, fake HRA checks worth $1,017,615.01 were uncovered as part of a complex plot involving poverty workers. Involved in these payroll irregularities were a group of antipoverty program em-

[20] Which administers the city's welfare budget.

[21] *The New York Times*, Sept. 14, 1968, p. 1.

ployees who described themselves as the "Durham Mob," after the North Carolina city where they originally banded together. Sidney Hall, a 28-year-old member of the Mob, worked as an assistant payroll officer, in which capacity he was suspected of rigging HRA computers so that they clicked out thousands of payroll checks to "phantom" Youth Corps enrollees.[22]

As in the case of Dr. Bernard's experience with the SJCC, patronage did not cause New York's failure to administer its antipoverty program, but rather the application of sloppy, ill-used patronage practices, where rewards went virtually unchallenged to the wrong people, who then contributed to the destruction of the program's credibility. The *Times*, for example, quoted a frustrated member of the mayor's staff who believed that patronage obligations honored by the mayor to out-of-state Republicans caused the agencies' major problems and precluded future flexibility. "There have been many times when HRA wanted to appoint someone they thought they needed," he said. "But the names come from a list in the Mayor's office, some of the names come from big Republicans all around the country."[23]

As a new form of mayoral patronage, antipoverty teeters insecurely on a partly unhinged perch. At one time, a successful mayor was considered someone who was able to read the two-inch-thick OEO catalogue and knew how to apply for the grants it described. This took, of course, more than a mayor with exceptional analytical abilities; it required a mayor with "clout" on the national level. Ivan Allen, who benefited originally from antipoverty grants, cooperated extensively with President Kennedy who, lacking a working relationship with Southern senators, con-

[22] *Ibid.*

[23] *Ibid.*

tented himself instead with a Southern mayor. In other cities, the program ran away with itself, precisely because of the way in which it dispensed rewards. Edmund Weber, staff director of the Senate Subcommittee on Intergovernmental Operations of the Senate Committee on Government Operations, called OEO a "shattering experience, because of the way grants were dumped on localities without the proper bureaucratic systems and technical expertise and guidance to deal with these grants." "The great mistake of OEO," explained Weber, "was that they took only people with zeal . . . who were superimposed on an outdated personnel network on the local level." Weber traced a large element of the nation's conflict and dissent to the problems created by the situation he described. Sound planning principles were sacrificed to the contingencies of political obligation; and due to the delicate nature of the program, many who wished to help held back, afraid to become embroiled in the struggles for power. Congressman Thomas Rees of California admitted that it was too difficult for him to criticize the operation of the Poverty Program, fearing he would be criticized by some of his constituents for being "anti-Negro or anti-Mexican."

To its credit, the antipoverty program caused great fragmentation within the black community, an important first stage in its politicization. Starved for so long of a proportionate share of government's rewards, ghetto communities were now given a small amount of money, contracts, and jobs, and told that they now exerted "community control." The competition for funds contributed to the development, proliferation, and struggle among these groups, over the rewards being offered to them. After the money and jobs began to dry up, so did some of the hope the program created within these communities. (The Nixon administration, cognizant of the fact that the Democrats held power in the cities, began to direct antipoverty money in block grants to the states, which were not inclined to turn the money over directly to the cities.) Many attribute the frustration of the ghetto populations to the mercurial nature of poverty money: people who had grown to expect expanded opportunities for jobs and contracts watched government officials, local political leaders, and their own community leaders jockey for the spoils while the federal government, confronted (as with foreign aid) by increasing public criticism of the program, slowly withdrew much of the money it had originally allotted.

The antipoverty program's biggest accomplishment was that it involved citizens traditionally ignored by the machines in the only genuine way that people can be brought permanently into politics: giving them a share in the rewards and decisions of government. It is doubtful that once they have tasted involvement of this kind, and received some of the discretionary favors of government, they will easily let go and retreat into obscurity. Like all other forms of political patronage, poverty patronage has acted both positively and negatively, most often pendulum-like, at the same time. It has given mayors who chose to use it an effective vehicle by which to offer substantial recognition and rewards to neglected groups within the city's body politic, and thereby enabled them to exert control over yet another sector of the city's economy.

3

Patronage
in the State House

"Everybody's got a reason for doing something in politics."
—Jack Morris, patronage aide to Governor Buford
Ellington

*"If you want to put politics first, then patronage is necessary.
If you want to put government and efficiency first, it isn't."*
—Governor Lester G. Maddox

Governor Lester G. Maddox summoned his commissioners to his elegant office of polished woods and crimson draperies, and sought their help in persuading a rebellious Georgia legislature to enact his revenue program.

"I said to the governor, 'Let's wheel and deal and do some trading,'" recalled George E. Bagby, former Speaker whom Maddox appointed fish and game commissioner. "Tell them you're going to put that roll call behind your desk, and when they come looking for jobs and roads and contracts, you'll be looking at that roll call," advised Mr. Bagby, who wore gold eagles above the shoulder patch of his gray uniform, and a Sam Browne belt around an ample middle. "I said, 'Governor, this is nut-cuttin' time. They're going to try to cut your nuts off, and you've got to try to cut theirs.'"

Governor Maddox would have none of it. The governor, a perky, Rotarian-type enthusiast who greets visi-

88

tors with an energetic handshake and an automatic "hello, friend," regards patronage as "discrimination at its worst." Political observers agree that Mr. Maddox has substantially reduced the discretionary favors provided by the Georgia state government. "People believe that waste and looking after friends is proper," Mr. Maddox said, referring to patronage. "It is, if you want to put politics first. Then patronage is necessary. If you want to put government and efficiency first, it isn't [necessary]."

When Marvin Griffin took office as governor, he fired 2,000 jobholders in one day, but Governor Maddox says with pride that "nobody's gone because of their opposition to Lester Maddox, or been put to work because of their support." Under Governor Maddox, the state's gasoline, formerly purchased from friends of previous governors and supporters of influential legislators, was purchased through competitive bidding—at a saving of $500,000 a year, according to the statehouse press corps. The state's computers, formerly rented from politically influential companies for $8 million a year, are now purchased through competitive bidding, although this area remains politically sensitive.[1] Mr. Maddox also initiated reforms of the state's parole system. "The most influential, meanest crooks could get attention," the governor said of previous administrations. "Now all people, not just influential people, are given the same consideration."

In the area of race relations, Mr. Maddox, an unabashed racist, stunned his critics as well as his White

---

[1] One apparent lapse, reported by *The Atlanta Constitution*, was the case of Dr. William R. Dyer, a chiropractor who was a friend of Mr. Maddox'. Dr. Dyer was a consultant to Honeywell, Inc., while that company was making a $500,000 sale to the state. Dr. Dyer resigned from the Pardon and Paroles Board after newspaper criticism that he had been the successful bidder of sales to the state of canoe paddles and life-preserver cushions, from a business run from his home.

Citizens Council supporters by action far more liberal than his "liberal" predecessors—Governors Ellis Arnall or Carl Sanders—by opening up state patronage jobs to blacks. Governor Maddox has appointed 15 Negroes to the Georgia draft boards, 58 Negroes to the Revenue Department, and even placed Negroes on the Georgia Bureau of Investigation. "I told all departments to hire whoever they could get, as long as they were qualified," said the man who entered politics after closing his restaurant rather than obey a federal order to serve Negroes.

The man who greeted blacks at the door of his restaurant with ax handles is frequently photographed serving them his famous fried chicken at receptions at the Governor's Mansion, where he receives 100,000 constituents a year. Before Maddox, a visit to the Governor's Mansion was a form of favoritism enjoyed by a relatively small number of influential constituents. "We've had more people in the Mansion in the last 30 months than in the last 30 years," the governor boasts.

Governor Maddox' disdain for patronage has undermined his leverage with the legislature, to which he owed his election because no candidate received a clear-cut majority. The governor argued in vain that the proposed one percent increase in the sales tax was a necessary program, and should be enacted solely on its merits. After the proposed legislation was defeated, Mr. Maddox called a special session of the legislature, which contemptuously adjourned without even reconsidering the tax bill.

Curiously, Mr. Maddox has received little credit for his fight against patronage, or for his efforts to bring blacks into every level of state government. Regarded as a racist by good government forces and civil liberties groups because of his pronouncements against integration, he finds that his rhetoric is given more attention than his deeds. Almost poignantly, Mr. Maddox shows visitors a sheaf of cartoons, which he carries in his breast pocket, which depict him as a country bumpkin with long floppy ears that rest on his shoulders and huge, black-framed eyeglasses. "You think these cartoons are funny until they happen to you," he says. "Well, maybe I need big specs, there's so much needs looking into around here, and big ears to hear what's going on."

Governor Maddox is a prime illustration of a very basic political principle that public officials who do not know how to use patronage are invariably poor administrators. Without patronage for leverage, public officials find it difficult, if not impossible, to persuade legislatures to enact their programs. Without patronage, these officials find it difficult to control even their own commissioners, who have their own constituencies. The public official who expects legislators and commissioners to bestir themselves on his behalf usually needs something material to offer them, for few people have sufficient time and money to work for nothing.

Paradoxically, some of the literature on administrative science takes the opposite view: that a strong executive reduces patronage and the interference of private interests in government while strengthening the public interest instead. Ideally depicted in the two Hoover Commission Reports and in the 26 Little Hoover Commission Reports (on the states), the strong executive presides over a complex of agencies coordinated efficiently by staff aides and his executive budget, without the aid of patronage techniques.[2]

Governor Maddox, a political maverick without an organization to reward, had little use for the state's patronage traditions. "Maddox never was an organization

[2] See Robert Highsaw, "The Southern Governor—Challenge to the Strong Executive Theme," in Frank Munger, ed., *American State Politics* (New York: Thomas Y. Crowell Co., 1966), pp. 74–80.

man," analyzed Reg Murphy, editor of the *Atlanta Constitution*. Barred by the state's constitution from re-election, Mr. Maddox lacked the urgent need to build an organization or to conduct a no-holds-barred fight for his legislation. Designed to prevent the governor from becoming too powerful, Georgia's succession law at the same time inhibits the state's legislative progress by encouraging the governor to indulge his personal whims instead of forcing him to become an effective legislative leader.

Mr. Maddox is frequently referred to by Georgia's political observers as the last of America's true Populists. Like the Populists who achieved such great momentum in the late-nineteenth century, Maddox keeps emphasizing his adherence to the values and aspirations of the little man, the poor, the hard-working lower-middle class, who he feels have no voice in government. Like the Populists who took up the platform of free silver to counter the influence and wealth of the Eastern banking establishment, Maddox has wedded his policies to the welfare of everyone —which he believes to be the essence of democratic government. What Maddox has shown by combining anti-patronage rhetoric with the new Populism is how antithetical patronage and pure democracy really are. For patronage is a selective way of governing, with special groups and persons chosen arbitrarily to receive the rewards of government. Maddox and Populism, theoretically at least, stand for the opposite view—dispensing government's rewards on an equitable basis, for the good and benefit of all.

Governor Maddox' aide, George Bagby, recalled former Governor S. Marvin Griffin as a man who knew how to apply the political pressure points of patronage. Mr. Bagby, then a legislator, had announced his intention to vote against a bond issue sought by Governor Griffin, whose lieutenants sent back word that Mr. Bagby's brother would lose his job in the state highway department unless the legislator complied. Mr. Bagby strode to the well of the House, and told the legislature that he had a public message for his brother John. "Dear John," Mr. Bagby began. "You always told me to do what was right, and that's what I'm going to do. So if they fire you, John, you come on home. There's ham in the smokehouse and flour in the bin, and we'll part the hoe-cakes just like we always have." Governor Griffin obliged. "Yes, John, you go on home," he said in a public response. Not surprisingly, Mr. Griffin and Mr. Bagby remained on excellent terms. "It was the last year of his administration," Mr. Bagby recalled. "He knew I was just trying to get on top of the next administration, and I did." The angry rhetoric and political spectacle may have fooled the press and the public, but not the "pols."

Southern politicians, although unusually canny, hold no monopoly on political finesse. New York's Governor Nelson A. Rockefeller, the antithesis of Mr. Maddox, unashamedly relishes the levers of patronage power, and is considered an exceptionally strong executive. Mr. Rockefeller gave a virtuoso performance of converting patronage power into political clout during the 1968 session of the New York State Legislature. By threatening to withhold "personal favors" from legislators unless they switched their votes, the governor persuaded the legislature to reverse itself on a $6 billion slum-clearance bill. The legislation, which was defeated early one afternoon, was passed at 11:30 that evening by a vote of 86–45, after 34 legislators changed their votes. The bill was originally defeated 63–69. "These guys have never seen this side of me before," said the governor, who is, if nothing else, a man who knows how to get things done. Mr. Rockefeller slyly explained that he had merely told the legislators: "I would be unable to do their personal favors . . . such as signing bills and appointments." John T. Gallagher, a Queens Republican who twice voted against the program, urged his colleagues not to succumb to "a phone call, a threat, a whispered promise in the back of the chamber."

The following year, Governor Rockefeller was accused of buying the votes, through patronage, of two Democrats who bolted their party to support a Republican-sponsored tax increase. Charles F. Stockmeister of Rochester was later appointed by the governor to a $29,300-a-year post on the Civil Service Commission, and Albert J. Hausbeck was rumored to be in line for a $23,500-a-year post on the State Harness Racing Commission. Eugene Nickerson, Nassau County executive and a Democrat, brought a lawsuit to invalidate the governor's appointment of Stockmeister. Mr. Nickerson charged that under the Public Officers Law, it was a felony to accept or promise a reward in return for a vote. Governor Rockefeller denied having made any patronage "deal," a heinous word in good-government circles, but admitted: "Let me say that what they did on the budget doesn't make me feel punitive toward these individuals."

If the Public Officers Law were enforced,[3] and those who accepted or promised a reward in return for a vote were actually incarcerated, few of the state's legislators would remain outside prison bars. Although "deals" are denounced with regularity, they are an essential tool of the democratic process. The alternatives to "deals" are legislation by fiat, in which a chief executive employs almost dicatorial powers; or anarchy; or political stasis—a vacuum in which nothing gets done.

Governors also use their discretionary favors to bail out legislators from otherwise hopeless situations in their home districts. In this way, patronage helps governors to

[3] Mr. Nickerson brought a civil suit, focusing on technicalities involving Mr. Stockmeister's eligibilty for the post.

build up future power with legislators, who, they hope, will remember gubernatorial largesse the next time their vote is needed on a crucial issue. This helps explain why a governor who knows how to use patronage can administrate more effectively than one who doesn't—for a governor who holds IOU's in his pocket has a sound basis for action on his legislative program, and does not waste time on programs he cannot get through or budgets he cannot pass.

A few governors have used their discretionary powers over government contracts for their personal as well as political enrichment. Even when contracts come under competitive bidding, loopholes exist which circumvent bidding laws, enabling one firm to receive preferential treatment over another. "Honest graft" of this kind is accomplished by wording the specifications of a contract to fit only one firm, and leaking advance notice on a bid to one firm to give it time to meet the specifications.

Walter Hickel, Secretary of the Interior, was able to get a subcontract totaling $1 million for his plumbing-and-heating firm for Anchorage Airport while governor of Alaska, although his firm was not originally low bidder. Drew Pearson, who broke the story, quoted C. R. Lewis, who headed a rival firm which was reportedly low bidder. "I'm a Republican State Senator," Lewis said, "and Hickel is the Republican Governor. It's a bit sticky for me. . . . There were four general contractors bidding and with three of them, my company was low. With the fourth, they said we were not low, that the Governor's firm was low." "For weeks, we couldn't get the figures out of them," Lewis continued. "We couldn't find out who was low bidder. With the other companies, we had no trouble. We got the figures right away. But with the fourth, we just ran up against a blank wall, and in the end, the Governor's firm got the subcontract."

The governor's job patronage powers vary greatly from state to state. The governor of Pennsylvania reportedly controls over 50,000 jobs, while Oregon's governor must content himself with less than a dozen. In Wisconsin, the governor dispenses less than 26 jobs, while the governors of New York and Illinois each directly control thousands.[4]

These governors sometimes share their appointment powers with their party organizations—depending on the relative strength of the party; the degree to which the governor owes his election to the party; the number of obligations already built up between them; the degree of competitiveness between the state's two parties; and the party's need to build and maintain an organization.

Any politician who would seek to wrest control of the New York Republican Party from Governor Rockefeller, or deny him the nomination for a fourth term as governor, would have to allow for the fact that Mr. Rockefeller has placed most of the Republican county leaders on the state payroll. His patronage powers include control of 1,050 exempt jobs, 24,500 noncompetitive jobs, and 14,000 provisional jobs. All are excluded from civil service. Exempt jobs, such as those of commissioners and their top aides, have no fixed job requirements. Noncompetitive jobs, such as those of inspectors and examiners, are considered too difficult to test, and provisional jobs, such as those of antipoverty aides, also are exempt from civil service because they are temporary positions—although they may last an appointee's lifetime.

In Illinois, no one knows the true figures for job patronage because, in the words of Ralph T. Smith, former Speaker of the Illinois House of Representatives who was

---

[4] No survey-type data exist comparing gubernatorial job patronage on a state-by-state basis. The information on this subject contained in this chapter comes from interview sources and published material.

recently appointed to succeed Everett Dirksen in the U.S. Senate, "there are obviously ways you can gimmick up the civil service system." Illinois governors use their job patronage cruelly, an inevitable consequence in a state with so much patronage to dispense and such a strongly competitive two-party system. The new Republican governor, Richard B. Ogilvie, a persistent critic of the patronage practices of Chicago's Mayor Richard Daley, dismissed 10,000 state employees who were appointed by previous Democratic administrations, and Democrats fear that the transfer of power is not yet complete. "We [the Democrats] would have done the same thing," conceded Lieutenant Governor Paul Simon, the state's highest-ranking elected Democrat. Mr. Simon notes that, because of the emphasis on patronage in Illinois, "a legislator can go to his chairman and say, 'I stole, I voted wrong,' and he'll pat you on the back." Governor Ogilvie's dismissals, according to Simon, extended to civil service employees, many of whom were harassed out of their jobs. One conservationist, who had just purchased a new home in Springfield, the state capital, was transferred to Chicago and had to quit rather than take a loss on his new home. "If he had accepted his new assignment, he knew he would probably have been transferred again," Mr. Simon said. "Ogilvie has even abolished civil service jobs as a way of firing civil servants."

Other, far more tragic cases cited by Mr. Simon included two janitors in the state armory, both patronage employees, who were fired when the new administration came in. Since one had epilepsy, and the other was lame, neither was able to get a job in private industry. Both had less than six months to work before receiving their state pension.

Both parties support Illinois patronage practices, and despite their frequent public attacks on each other's use of patronage, would be uncomfortable living under any other political system. Arthur Telcser, a young Chicago Republican member of the state legislature, found to his dismay that he could not persuade his fellow Republicans to enact a bill he had sponsored—at the behest of the governor—to limit the patronage system. His bill would have abolished the use of temporaries—a classification by which civil service employees can still be patronage employees—since they are appointed and reappointed every 180 days. Without the job security of civil service they can also fail to be appointed at the end of the 180-day period (the practice for firing state employees when a new administration takes over), in order to free the job to make room for the new governor's political obligations.

Ross Barnett of Mississippi was a governor who entered his statehouse with more obligations than most. He personified the personalized approach to politics reminiscent of Andrew Jackson. During his 1959 campaign for governor, Barnett promised a state job to anyone who wanted one. When he was sworn in, office seekers trooped into Jackson from all over the state, and the waiting line wound around the capitol rotunda and down the street. Governor Barnett found hundreds of jobs, but not enough for everyone. Campaigning for re-election in Brandon, Mississippi, the governor met someone who had voted for him, had influenced all his relatives to vote for him, and still couldn't understand why he didn't get a job. The governor answered that that was precisely, yes precisely, why he was a running a second time—to find jobs for everyone he couldn't take care of the first time. Mr. Barnett lost his bid for re-election.

Governors sometimes enter the statehouse with their own organizations that are superimposed on the party. Clarke Reed, Mississippi State Republican chairman, describes the system: "The bulk of meaningful job patronage in Mississippi is found in the state government, over which the Republican party has no influence or control. However, for that matter, neither does the Democrat party in the state. The Democrat political pattern in Mississippi has been one of personal factionalism and with most state job patronage in Mississippi accruing to the Governor, state appointments are generally made upon the recommendations of his key men or 'colonels' in each county. While there is some overlapping between this organization and the regular Democrat party structure it is by no means controlling."

Aware of increased black registration in the South, some Southern governors have appointed men just to handle the appointments of Negroes to state jobs. Governor Buford Ellington of Tennessee appointed H. T. Lockard, who was vice chairman of his campaign, his patronage chief for black appointments. "While he didn't carry the Negro vote," said Vernon Jordan, director of the Voter Education Project of the Southern Regional Council, "he got enough to make Lockard his administrative assistant. Whatever patronage Negroes are going to get, they're going to get through Lockard."

In Tennessee, as in most other states, the governor parcels out his patronage power to a patronage lieutenant in each county, who becomes his vassal there, building great power of his own in the county but being ultimately answerable to the governor. Memphis, home of one of history's most powerful political machines—that of Boss Ed Crump—continues the traditions of bossism despite the demise of Mr. Crump. Following the death of Crump, everyone heralded the end of a powerful and cruel local dictator, whose methods offended almost everyone, but whose tenure was unshakable because of the machine he had developed. No one lamented his death, but all complained about the political anarchy which he left, for no

leader could fill the gap. Slowly, within fifteen years after
the decline of the Crump machine, new patronage kings
have arisen to put the pieces of Memphis politics back together again.

Jack Morris III, one of the new and much more genial breed of patronage kings, dispenses patronage for
Governor Ellington in Shelby County, home of the city of
Memphis and the domain of the late boss Crump. Unlike
Lockard, Morris holds no formal position in state government (he runs an auto glass business), but like Lockard,
was given his patronage power because he helped deliver
votes to Ellington in his last race for governor.

"The old Crump machine couldn't deliver any more,"
said Morris, "and the Governor couldn't depend on remnants. With the old crew he got 17 percent of the vote.
This time he lost the county by $\frac{1}{10}$th of 1 percent, but he
couldn't have won the election without this high a percentage from Shelby county (49.9 percent)." Yet there are
still members of the Crump machine active in the party,
contributing money and votes, and they must be reckoned
with. For this reason, Jack Morris shares the title, if not
the power, of patronage dispenser with an old Crump lieutenant, Bert Bates, an old-timer who recalls the terror of
the Crump machine. "Today," said Bates, "a man can
speak and breathe freely." Other remnants of the Crump
machine are seen throughout the city of Memphis: E.H.
Crump Stadium, E.H. Crump Boulevard, and the E.H.
Crump Company.

Jack Morris regards himself as a help both to the
governor and to the state departments that need qualified
people. "I act as a clearing house for state employees,"
Mr. Morris said. "State jobs are so lousy—a hotel and restaurant inspector makes $395 a month—that all you can
get for that is a drunken boozehead. I was able to get a
retired bank president a state job. He wanted to do some-

thing." "I'm in touch with all departments," Mr. Morris continued. "In Shelby county there are 1800 employees, more than one-half civil service. A job opens up, I'll have to tell 9 people 'no' and one 'yes.' You take credit for the guy you hire, and you tell the others: 'Well, I did my best for you—it must have been somebody up the line.' "

Unless he is lucky, the lack of patronage powers can mean certain defeat for a governor in his re-election bid. Representative Thomas M. Rees of California explained former Governor Pat Brown's defeat to Ronald Reagan in terms of job patronage. "Patronage helped cause Brown's defeat," Mr. Rees noted. "His biggest fund raisers were attorneys. After eight years in office, most were appointed to the bench, after which they wouldn't touch politics with a ten-foot pole." Many politicians complain of the ingratitude of patronage recipients whom they have appointed to government jobs, especially jobs which may be covered by civil-service-type guarantees of job protection and tenure. Using their jobs as an excuse, these "ingrates" say that they have been "hatched," after the Hatch Act [5] which prohibits political activity on the part of government employees. Surprised by the sudden purity of their appointees, their patrons believe that this is invoked as a ruse to get out of working for the politician who was good enough to appoint them in the first place.

---

[5] The first Hatch Act was passed in 1939 (53 U.S. Statutes 1147 [1939]). It applied restrictions on classified and unclassified public employees other than those in top policy posts, prohibiting political activities, which were clearly defined in the statute. Violations could mean fines and/or imprisonment for the offender. The second Hatch Act, passed in 1940, clarified and extended the original act's prohibitions to state and local employees paid in full or in part by public funds. Many states and municipalities have passed "little Hatch Acts" modeled after the federal statute. For further background, see Paul Van Riper, *History of the United States Civil Service* (Evanston, Ill.: Row, Peterson, 1958), pp. 339–343.

Mr. Rees, who spent eleven years in the state legislature (eight in the Assembly and three in the Senate), explained that California's civil service law left very little room for the governor to operate in, except in the area of judgeships. In California, the governor appoints all municipal and superior court judges, plus supreme court judges. "California is civil service to the hilt," Mr. Rees said. "The state went through a reform period that was Hiram Johnson with a vengeance, leaving the Governor with very little patronage except for four or five appointments in each department, and some per diem appointments on state commissions."

He added that civil service had inhibited California government from operating at optimum efficiency, a viewpoint shared by many politicians who believe that civil service thwarts government progress. Civil servants, considered by some to be "human paperweights," can sabotage an administration through laziness, inefficiency, or by being just plain ornery. Unaccountable to anyone, they can easily thwart those who are accountable to the electorate. Civil service advocates believe that the failures of the system can be resolved within the system, and that civil servants can be given incentives and rewards to enhance their effectiveness, just as patronage offers incentives and rewards to enhance the political effectiveness of the party faithful.

❡ *State Officials with Patronage Clout*

The extensive patronage powers enjoyed by the governor often conceal the influence of other, less visible state officeholders, particularly those with discretionary fiscal power. Mistakenly regarded by the public as glorified bookkeepers, many state financial officers (controllers, for example) have built power bases independent of the governor's, with patronage opportunities that often equal and sometimes exceed the governor's. This gives them an advantage over the governor, who is less insulated from public pressure and less free to operate without the constant fear of criticism and newspaper headlines, which the governor and other visible elected officials must accept as a way of life.

Jim Gillis, a veteran Georgia politician with an alligator smile, wields the power of the purse with a quiet skill. Mr. Gillis, Georgia's highway director, is probably one of the most powerful men in the state, having enjoyed longevity in politics and a post in almost every administration since 1937, when President Franklin D. Roosevelt named him his federal patronage chief for Georgia. Like others awarded patronage on the state level, Gillis won his power after proving his vote-getting abilities. When Roosevelt tried to purge Senator Walter George, Gillis' county was the only one carried by the Roosevelt nominee —Lawrence Kemp. The vote was 1,640 for Kemp, 51 for George, and 89 for Governor Talmadge. Gillis' federal patronage helped him to build his political capital on the state level, so that now his power is virtually unchallenged.

As state highway director, Gillis keeps millions of dollars in banks throughout the state, deposited entirely on a discretionary basis. And Gillis similarly awards all highway contracts on a discretionary basis. Everyone agrees that "If you're a highway commissioner, you have to come up to 'Mr. Jim,' " as he is called. Asked if people appreciated all the roads he had engineered through for them, he replied, "If you give them one road, they ask for three more"—proving again the hardships of wielding power.

Cutting across state, federal, county, and city political boundaries, the role of highway director stands out as one of the most crucial patronage positions in the country. For a man who holds unpaid patronage debts on all levels of government cannot be fought on any one level without seismic reverberations throughout. Recognizing the threat posed by Gillis' power, former Governor Griffin tried to remove Gillis almost as soon as he was inaugurated, but soon found that Gillis' power was so great that even he couldn't take it away. "Ol' Marv was nailing hides to the smokehouse wall, as he had promised in every speech he made from Deepstep to Brasstown Bald," recalled Reg Murphy, editor of the *Atlanta Constitution*. "The man he went after hardest was Jim L. Gillis, the major domo of the State Highway Department. Griffin was threatening to reorganize the state highway department to get rid of Gillis. Gillis was fighting back as best he knew how," Mr. Murphy continued. "And he was at his best reminding legislators of the roads he had paved, as well as those he proposed to pave in the future." [6]

Like Gillis, New York State Controller Arthur Levitt, a modest, phlegmatic man, has displayed a remarkable longevity. A Democrat, he has been bracketed for four terms between a Republican governor, lieutenant governor, and attorney general, the sole Democrat elected on a statewide ticket in fifteen years, with the exception of Robert F. Kennedy's election to the Senate in 1964. As in the case of Gillis, Mr. Levitt's success has been attributed neither to his personality nor his political ideology (both conservative, but within the mainstream of Democratic politics), but rather to his control over state funds.

As controller, Mr. Levitt controls the investment and deposit of $4 billion in state funds, more than the entire federal budget of the 1920s. Mr. Levitt has deposited state

[6] *Atlanta Constitution*, October 23, 1968.

funds in 75 percent of the state's commercial banks, with large deposits in banks controlled by influential politicians. He also buys stocks, including investments in companies controlled by influential Democrats, and uses state funds to purchase municipal and school bonds—all on a discretionary basis—and his investments can be gilt-edged securities to local mayors seeking re-election.

The controller's favorite banks include the Kings County Lafayette Trust Company, a small institution which has $900,000 in long-term state deposits, and $2 million in no-interest, short-term deposits, out of $200 million total assets. The bank's chairman is John J. Lynch, the long-time chairman of the Brooklyn Democratic Party, many of whose leaders are stockholders in the bank. The Central State Bank of Brooklyn, whose president is James A. Farley, Jr., son of President Roosevelt's campaign manager and Postmaster General, has $150,000 in long-term state deposits, out of $47 million in assets. The bank's directors include Democratic Assemblyman Alfred A. Lama, chairman of the State Assembly's Banking Committee. The American Bank and Trust Company, of which New York City Controller Abraham D. Beame was a director, has long-term state deposits of $100,000.

Controller Levitt also deposits funds in banks controlled by influential Republicans, a key factor in ensuring his longevity and additional evidence that the two-party system is more cooperative than competitive. The Century National Bank, whose chairman is Vincent F. Albano, New York County Republican Chairman, has $100,000 in state funds on long-term deposits.

Few politicians regard the interlocking directorates of the banking world and government as a conflict of interest. In fact, politicians expect this kind of legal profiteering as a legitimate reward for the years they devote to public service at pay which is lower than what they feel they might earn in the business world. Banking language is common among politicians—"Now you've got money in my bank" is a common phrase to express political indebtedness.

The close relationship between banks, private industry, and politicians has become an accepted part of our political culture. "I don't know of any bank, insurance company or corporation that isn't politically connected," said Thomas M. Whalen, the director of investments and cash management in the New York State Controller's office. "You look at any bank and you'll find that they have a damn good Republican on their board and a damn good Democrat. This is part of our American way of life."

Controller Levitt's counterpart in Illinois, Adlai Stevenson III, the State Treasurer, recently elected U.S. senator, has tried to eliminate the patronage inherent in the office by depositing state funds on a competitive basis, eliminating the old system of the favored bid. Concerned with his image as a liberal Democrat, he nevertheless left himself some discretionary power, which he turned to social uses by depositing state funds in banks owned or operated by Negroes and banks trying to help their communities. His attitude toward patronage, different from that of his father—who allowed the party to fill most patronage posts when he was governor—has not endeared young Mr. Stevenson to the political hierarchy led by Mayor Daley, who nonetheless endorsed Mr. Stevenson's candidacy for the Senate.

In Illinois, the secretary of state has "more patronage power than anyone else," according to Representative John B. Anderson of Rockford, Illinois. Without having to "gimmick" the civil service as the governor does, Illinois Secretary of State Paul Powell runs the largest Secretary of State office in the nation, reportedly controlling over 2,800 patronage jobs in the offices under his jurisdiction: motor vehicle registration, corporation charters, index division (which administers election laws), the registration of securities, and the state libraries. Reminders of Powell's power appear everywhere. Gardeners working on the shrubbery on the capitol grounds wear shirts with orange and blue emblems on their backs, which read "Paul Powell—Secretary of State." "Powell doesn't have a single employee under the civil service," said former Speaker Ralph Smith, with some envy. "Powell can also let contracts and issue drivers' licenses and vanity plates."

❪ *Patronage and the State Legislators*

Mr. Smith need not have envied Mr. Powell. As Speaker, Mr. Smith controlled more patronage than any other legislator, including the power to make committee assignments, contract out voting machines, and hire 100 employees. In fact, Mr. Smith grew so powerful in this post that he was appointed by Governor Ogilvie to take the Senate seat made vacant by the death of Senator Dirksen.

Since state legislatures, like Congress, operate on a committee system in which the committees do the real work and hold the real power, the Speaker's power to make committee appointments was substantial patronage indeed. Unlike Congress, where key committee chairmen make the appointments, in Illinois the Speaker exclusively controls committee appointments, which Mr. Smith naturally enough considered his prime patronage. "We scratch around to find people knowledgeable in appropriations, municipalities, education, etc. . . . then we orient them politically," he explained.

Once appointed to an influential committee, the legislator may also augment his available job patronage with the departments whose funding is controlled by his committee. Describing how committee members enhance their patronage, Lieutenant Governor Paul Simon noted that "A member of the Appropriations Committee goes to the Revenue Department. Do you think he'll be refused on a job request?"

The patronage accorded to each legislator as an individual depends both on his influence and the extent to which he chooses to develop his patronage opportunities. Each legislator in Illinois is allowed two or three personal patronage employees. Representative C. L. McCormick, who controls only two or three jobs as a state legislator, augments his patronage with 20 to 25 jobs he controls as county chairman. If he is lucky, he may be able to boost the number to 35, placing his appointees mainly in highways, parks, and hospitals. "The civil service code covers way too many people to suit me," complained Representative McCormick.

Representative Arthur Telcser, who says he abhors patronage, nonetheless has 30 jobs in the county treasurer's office, the county sheriff's office, and the state house. "I use my patronage to the fullest extent," Mr. Telcser conceded. "After all, the Democratic state legislators in my wards each have 200 jobs." "I can't fight an elephant with a pea shooter," he added.

Although Mr. Telcser objects to the word "patronage" to describe favors he can do for his constituents, he frequently uses his influence with state government to help individual constituents. Like a congressman, he functions primarily to cut red tape, and to expedite his district's relationship with the government bureaucracy. The success legislators have with state departments shows how the system reinforces the continual attempts of elected politicians to obligate people. One constituent, for example, was able to transfer her relative from a state mental health facility recently affected by scandal to another, more prestigious institution only after Mr. Telcser made a call to the Department of Mental Health.

The legislator can also favor constituents by obtaining vanity license plates for them, automobile license plates with personalized initials and low numbers. To get such a license in Illinois, as well as many other states, a citizen goes to his state representative, who then gets the plate from the secretary of state. It still costs the citizen $10, but he afterwards feels obligated to the man who was able to expedite this favor for him. Ideally, he also believes that he has an inside track in the event of future problems, and a vested interest in the legislator's re-election.

Patronage thus often brings the citizen closer to his government, but there is a subtle difference between integrating the voter into the political process and tying him to an individual politician. In this way, government reinforces patronage by making and approving opportunities for legislators to obligate their constituents.

Bright young legislators who are especially ambitious try to make patronage opportunities out of everything that isn't nailed down, and they find ample opportunities in the continuing programs enacted by government. In New York, Assemblyman Leonard Simon, who represents the Brighton Beach neighborhood in Coney Island, capitalized on the state's Medicaid program and claimed credit for the program among his constituents. The legislator personally signed up scores of patients in the new apartment houses that tower above the Atlantic Ocean. "It wasn't Rockefeller's Medicaid, or President Johnson's Medicaid," Mr. Simon recalled. "It was Simon's Medicaid." His constituents referred to "Simon's crutches," "Simon's [false] teeth," and "Simon's eyeglasses." Unfortunately, when the state cut back its Medicaid program, his constituents did not blame Rockefeller

or Johnson, but Simon. "Simon, why are you taking away
my dental work?" they asked.

Patronage-oriented Simon, a Democrat, kept his district in mind when he endorsed Mayor Lindsay's bid for
re-election. Publicly, Simon professed that he was moved
to endorse the mayor because the "survival of the city was
at stake." Mayor Lindsay hailed the assemblyman's support, at a Gracie Mansion press conference, as "an act of
great political courage." Away from the glare of the klieg
lights, Mr. Simon conceded that he had first offered his
support to Mario A. Procaccino, his party's standard-
bearer, but Mr. Procaccino had declined Simon's request
for direct access to City Hall, and had told him instead
that he would have to work through the Brooklyn Democratic organization of Meade H. Esposito. "I then got the
call from the mayor," Mr. Simon recalled. "He promised
me direct access to community services. We're going to
get direct action on tax abatements for the co-ops," Mr.
Simon said, referring to the many Mitchell-Lama mort-
gages guaranteed by the state in his district. "We're getting a new subway route, a more direct route to Coney
Island," he continued, "and we're also getting more traffic
lights, and more police protection in the parks." Best of
all, Mr. Simon was promised direct access to City Hall by
Mayor Lindsay.

The clear-cut patronage agreement between the
mayor and Assemblyman Simon—services and access in
exchange for campaign support—is the kind of agreement
that is usually kept hidden from the public. Especially on
top of all the campaign rhetoric, which talked in terms of
"great political courage" and the "survival of the city,"
the agreement between the two men seems almost cynical
in its contempt for the public intelligence. Why, then, did
Mr. Simon admit that his support could be "bought" even
though the price was so high? As an assemblyman, Mr.

Simon is not free enough to throw his support away from his party's choice unless he can convince his voters that it is well worth the price of party disloyalty. By extracting promises for beefed-up community services, Simon showed that he understood that his district's commitment to party took second place to its desire for civic improvements. Flanked by his community leaders when he announced his endorsement, Mr. Simon showed that ideology meant little to the voters to whom he was accountable.

Under further scrutiny, Mr. Simon's action also illuminates one of the causes of what is so often called "the crisis of the cities." The promise of traffic lights and police protection to communities in a desperate attempt to grasp political power ignores the importance of rational city planning, as services are then allocated on the basis of the political complexion of communities rather than according to real needs. Does Brighton Beach need more police protection than Bedford-Stuyvesant or East Harlem? (The first fourth platoon of additional manpower during high-crime evening hours in Queens was installed, not in Jamaica, despite its high crime rate, but in Fresh Meadows, because of its superior political clout.) What communities would sacrifice traffic lights already on the drawing boards to brighten up Mr. Simon's more politically astute district?

Mr. Simon happened to be a particularly aggressive state legislator who created his own opportunities. Others rely on the ample opportunities built into the system in the form of jobs and financial patronage to reward their friends and supporters. In Albany, for example, the state legislators control a legislative payroll of over $6 million, which consists mostly of salaries for legislative aides. These aides earn from $750 to $1,500 for a 3½-month session (sometimes extended), and are not always expected to appear in Albany. More bluntly, many of these jobs are called "no-show jobs," amounting to cash patronage for the legislators who are lucky enough to have them under their control.

The $2-million Assembly payroll reflects the Brooklyn power base of former Speaker Anthony J. Travia, now a federal judge. Of a total of 750 Assembly employees, 106 are from Brooklyn, 34 are from the Bronx, and 29 are from Queens.

In many states, including Maryland, the legislators are given outright control of some of the governor's patronage. This helps to speed the governor's personal appointments through the legislature, since the Senate must approve all the appointments. If they have some patronage of their own, they are more obligated to the governor, and will tend to cooperate with him more readily. As described by Don R. Kendall, chairman of Maryland's Republican State Committee, "Many state boards and commissions are filled by the appointment of the Governor, but with the consent of the Senate. In reality, State Senators have available at least some of the patronage jobs. The State Senator may, or may not, listen to the advice of the Party committee."

❅ *Patronage Swapping in the State Legislature*

Although conflict and combat dominate the mass media's accounts of the legislative process, cooperation emerges as the most pervasive force. The conflicts are reported because they are visible; the cooperation often remains buried in committee rooms, or in telephone conversations between county leaders and state legislators.

In Tennessee, a cordial relationship between the banks and the legislature was worked out by Jack Morris III, Governor Ellington's patronage-dispenser for Memphis, showing how legislation used as patronage creates

yet another web of mutual obligation between legislators
and their beneficiaries. "The banks were interested in a
new interest rate, from 6½ to 8 percent," Morris recalled.
"The governor said, 'You help those legislators,' and we
sat down with the presidents of the banks. For a bank to
go to a legislator, it would look bad," Mr. Morris observed. "For a legislator to go to a bank, it would look
bad." With Morris' help, the state's major banks divided up the entire legislature. "So I would call the legislator, and ask: 'How you coming in the campaign?' "
"Well, I can use some money," was the invariable response. " 'Well, this bank wants to make a campaign contribution,' " I would say. "Then, when the time came to
pass legislation, I would call the legislator and say, 'That
bank president who made that campaign contribution
wants to have a talk with you.' " The interest-rate increase
was speedily enacted.

The exchange of favors flows continuously between
legislators and their "constituents." Legislators publicize
the small favors they can get for their constituents as a
way of promising future favors for potential political supporters. Less public, but much more substantial, are their
favors to their corporate constituents: an interest-rate hike
of 2 percent, for example, can mean millions to the banking industry. Because the favors to corporate constituents
are much more substantial than obtaining vanity license
plates, for example, the legislators expect more in return
from the beneficiaries of their major largesse. Large campaign contributions stand out as the most obvious quid pro
quo (despite restrictions on corporate gifts, contributions
are made by officers of the corporations). But there are
other gifts: legal work and insurance contracts, finder's
fees, bank stock, and stock tips.

"I've been offered bank stock many times, even the
money to buy the stock," said Lieutenant Governor Paul

Simon of Illinois, who always rejected the offers. In Illinois, banks and insurance companies are especially close to state government. Former Speaker Smith admitted that "their influence can make a difference in a close vote." After all, the former Speaker said, "Who knows better what should be the law on insurance than the insurance business? Who knows better what should be the law on banking than the banking industry?" "Naturally," conceded Mr. Smith, who is himself the chairman of a small bank, "their interests are not always compatible with the interests of the people. They're blowing their own horn, which they have every right to do."

The unions also dispense favors to legislators. Campaign literature for 80 New York state legislators is printed, without charge, by three unions: the Seafarers Union, the Teamsters, and District Council 37 of the American Federation of State, County and Municipal Employees. These unions also supply sound trucks and personnel during election campaigns. "I won't take from the banks and insurance companies," said one Democratic state senator, "but I take from the unions. I'm going to vote their way anyway."

Unions offer finder's fees as a way of rewarding cooperative legislators. The Municipal Employees Union and the Teamsters lend money from pension funds to business clients or legislators unable to obtain bank loans. For this service, the legislators obtain finder's fees, or commissions, of 5 percent or more. This is how it works: "I'm a restaurant and I need $1 million," explained Nicholas Kisburg, the Teamsters' legislative representative in Albany. "I go to the legislator, he goes to Hoffa and gets me into the pension fund. I get my money and he gets a finder's fee." Mr. Kisburg later explained that he was speaking theoretically about other unions, and not the Teamsters.

Well aware that many legislators are lawyers, grateful corporations and pressure groups channel legal business to reciprocate for past and future favors. State Senator Anthony B. Gioffre, a Westchester Republican, said that his law firm, Gioffre and Gioffre, in Port Chester, New York, represented the National Bank of Westchester as local mortgage-closing attorneys. He said that he had received the law work beginning in 1966, when he was elected to the State Senate and assigned a seat on the Committee on Banking. Although he claims that there was no connection between his election and the law work, the coincidence must be noted.

Politics means lifetime security, as well as immediate profits, for those who build their clientele through contacts made as state legislators. A former New York state legislator recently elected to the bench described the law work as "an opening of the door to a guy who will work for his money, but would not otherwise have the opportunity to get the client." Another state legislator said that "one of the virtues of being a legislator is you pick up banks and insurance companies as clients."

Politicians feel that they deserve these fringe benefits of public service. The nitty-gritty involved in reaching the seat of power is usually hard, dreary work: hours of telephone calls to voters; continual ceremonies to attend; getting out "bodies" to register, vote, and attend functions. Coupled with the insecurity inherent in any elective job, the politician regards business opportunities as a way of ensuring his security in the event that his political fortunes fail.

Next to law work, insurance means extra income to more legislators than any other source. Government insures itself at all levels—county, city—as well as insuring government employees and people using public facilities. Insurance means extra income to about 20 percent of the

207 New York state legislators, who are affiliated with insurance companies—either as brokers or stockholders. Assembly Minority Leader Stanley Steingut and Brooklyn Democratic leader Meade H. Esposito are partners in the Grand Agency. Mr. Steingut also is president of I. Steingut and Co. The liberal assemblyman maintained that he had never accepted government business, but asked whether political connections had helped obtain private clients, Mr. Steingut replied: "It's all friendship—and service." Erastus Corning, mayor of Albany, is also an insurance broker. His company receives $100,000 in annual premiums for insuring the property of Albany County. The business was obtained without competitive bidding, because the uniform insurance rates are fixed by law by the State Department of Insurance, and no insurance company can undersell another. The mayor is president of Albany Associates, an insurance company that also has written insurance on plumbing and heating contracts for the South Mall project, a $610 million office-building complex being built by the state.

The late George Swetnick, New York City councilman and district leader of the Seneca Democratic Club in the Williamsburg section, explained why insurance on government properties makes ideal patronage. "The prices are the same. If the state is going to get insurance there are no bids. It's who you want to give it to. If you have your choice between a friend of yours and someone who isn't a friend of yours, you pick your friend."

❡ *Patronage and the Party Treasury*

It is almost axiomatic that states run by powerful parties are usually states with a great deal of patronage at their disposal, and through no political accident these parties have well-filled treasure chests. Parties from big patronage states like Illinois, New York, Indiana, Oklahoma, and Pennsylvania impose a tithe on jobholders in order to build a war chest to use at campaign time. In Indiana, for example, where everyone with a patronage job pays 2 percent of his salary to the party, the party in power can "reasonably expect to start a campaign with a war chest of $500,000." [7]

Approval of the tithe system comes not merely from reformers and regulars alike. Representative Andrew Jacobs, an Indiana Democrat, claims he is grateful for the solidarity created by the 2 percent system. A courageous, young liberal Democrat from Indianapolis, Mr. Jacobs has frequently taken on his own establishment in Congress to protest the war in Vietnam and what he considers the overemphasis on defense spending. "I pay 2 percent of my *net* salary to the county committee," Mr. Jacobs says. "Everybody in my office pays. This creates a campaign organization. There are 1,000 precinct committeemen in my district. They go out and knock on doors for me. I'm very grateful. Therefore, I don't mind paying the 2 percent. . . ." "At the State House," Mr. Jacobs adds, "there is much grumbling about the 2 percent because there it is not as personal as it is in a congressional office. Like the unions in the 1930s, there is a source of pride in giving, in paying dues. . . ." [8]

Mr. Jacobs concluded that "for an apathetic society like ours, 2 percent is still the best system." Otherwise, he

[7] Robert J. McNeill, *Democratic Campaign Financing in Indiana* (Institute of Public Administration, Indiana University, and Citizens Research Foundation, Princeton, N.J., 1966).

[8] In Missouri, according to Dr. Alexander Heard, state employees must contribute to a pool called the "flower fund." Ostensibly to cover the costs of flowers and other non-business expenses, the cash is readily convertible to campaign funds. See Alexander Heard, *The Costs of Democracy* (Chapel Hill: University of North Carolina Press, 1960), p. 152n.

explained, the temptation is too great for the party to rely solely on "fat cats" (large contributors), further estranging the citizen from the political process. Former President Johnson was aware of this problem when he attempted unsuccessfully to garnishee everyone's income tax with a small contribution to both political parties.

Many disagree with the 2 percent system. Robert J. McNeill termed the "two percent club" an ancient, if not honorable, institution in Indiana. Wrote McNeill: "Its advocates justify the 'two percent club' on the theory that everyone knew that it took a lot of money to run a political campaign, and that money had to come either from the utilities or special interest groups or from party workers." Mr. McNeill reported further that "nearly 8,000 of the state's 22,000 employees are patronage appointees." More recently, Richard Martin, Indiana Governor Welsh's press secretary, defended the system on the grounds that it is "cheaper than an employment agency fee." [9]

States with plentiful patronage opportunities extract a quid pro quo at even the lowest level of patronage benefits. Professor Frank Sorauf, formerly at Pennsylvania State University, interviewed highway patronage workers in Centre County, a rural county located in the center of Pennsylvania. He found that party contributions were expected and given, although they were not systematically collected, as in Indiana. "In one respect—financial contributions—" wrote Professor Sorauf, "the highway workers came in overwhelming numbers to the aid of their party. Of the 123 [whom he interviewed], fully 97 (79%) declared themselves party contributors while on the job, even if only once or twice." [10]

[9] *Ibid.*, footnote 7.

[10] Frank Sorauf, "State Patronage in a Rural County," *American Political Science Review*, Vol L (December 1956), pp. 1046–1056.

Other states without job patronage find funding the party extremely difficult. Lacking concrete opportunities to obligate people to the party, many party leaders wish they had more patronage, although in many states, publicly to lead a movement for more patronage would be tantamount to political suicide.

A thinly veiled lament comes through the statement of John Allen, Oregon's state Democratic chairman. "Keep in mind that some states are more affluent than others. . . . In Oregon, with less heavy industry and a very independent voter, largely divorced from strict party lines, we will be fortunate to raise $20,000 although we should raise $25,000 with assistance from the Democratic National Committee in the form of speakers."

Beneficiaries of big government patronage—business, contractors, and the like—are "taxed" by the party which has acted in their interest. Naturally, nothing so crude as the 2 percent system is applied here, but often individuals within a firm doing business with government appear as large contributors, with the basic understanding that they represent the company. The South Mall project at the state capital in Albany yields a total of $200,000 in annual insurance premiums to Peter D. Kiernan, president of Rose and Kiernan of Albany, a contributor of long standing to the Albany Democratic machine run by Daniel P. O'Connell. This insurance of South Mall contractors was awarded without competitive bidding, subject to state approval. Mr. Kiernan said that the contractors involved were long-time clients of his firm.

In Tennessee, architects who design state buildings are selected without competitive bidding, as is the custom everywhere else. "There's enough of them so we don't have to go to ones that are not on the team," explained Jack Morris. "The selection can be vetoed, however, by the state architect on the grounds of incompetency." "At campaign time, we systematically call each architect," Mr. Morris added.

In Connecticut, a high official of the Republican State Committee, who declined to be quoted, said that "awards of architectural and engineering contracts, where no competitive bidding is practicable, are handed out on a patronage basis." Here, too, one can assume that the firms who get state business don't have to be reminded to contribute to the party. No one has ever questioned or studied the relationships of architectural esthetics to political factors, in spite of the fact that political influence on architectural contracts is such an established fact of life. The results may prove too explosive.

❡ *The Machines: Party Leaders*
and Their Influence on Patronage

At a caucus called by the Democrats for Good Government of Montclair, New Jersey, to select a new town chairman, John Feeney stood up and advised his fellow committeemen: "Let's get someone who'll go down to Newark and bring back the patronage." Mr. Feeney was promptly elected party secretary-treasurer.

Whatever they profess publicly, bringing home the patronage dominates the private activities of party leaders, even reform leaders and good-government groups. In fact, their success depends on their resourcefulness in developing new patronage opportunities while keeping a firm grasp on the old.

In selecting candidates to run for higher office, party leaders usually give reliability more weight than other considerations, such as creativity and talent (which may frighten them), and explains why so many public figures, including President Nixon, Mayor Daley, and former

Mayor Wagner, seem so bland. What they lack in imagination, they make up for in dependability, and they can be relied on to accede to the dictates of the party's hierarchy on most matters, including patronage. In her description of Massachusetts state politics, State Republican Vice-Chairman Mrs. Ruth Vance pointed out what is crucial in party-patronage dynamics: that candidates must have local backing, what she termed "united support from their own area" before obtaining a position at any level of government. She told how her system worked. It was fairly typical:

> "The applicant approaches the Town Chairman who approaches the State Committee Member who forwards the necessary information to this office and we take it up with the Governor's office. If they are well qualified and have united support from their own area, their chances for appointment are good.
>
> "The kinds of jobs are varied—from a Governor's appointment, to the local Housing Authority, to Honorary Boards and commissions, to paying state positions. Other kinds of favors which we can provide are State flags for service men, vanity license plates, etc."

Party officials at even the lowest levels of the party hierarchy are given substantial patronage powers—even if they are only able to ratify or veto a candidate for government office. In this way, the party binds its members to the organization by giving each local party functionary the opportunity to make others obligated to him.

Each Democratic committeeman in Cook County, Illinois, for example, influences the hiring and firing of at least 60 workers, according to Lynn Williams, a committeeman from Winnetka. Representing the dissident wing of the Democratic county organization, Mr. Williams argues that patronage binds committeemen through fear to the party, resulting in an unimaginative, intellectually bankrupt, static party organization, unresponsive to intra-party reform. "Committeemen themselves are under patronage pressure," Mr. Williams explained, "some because they hold appointed jobs and hope for advancement or want to be judges . . . others because they fear reprisals against their patronage workers if the committeemen don't stay in line. Within the last 60 days, one committeeman told me he agreed with my proposals for strengthening the party, but feared to say so, lest his 20 or 30 patronage jobholders be fired."

Pennsylvania also uses patronage extensively to cement the party structure from the lowest ranks to the highest. "Pennsylvania is substantially a patronage state," said a high party official. "There are certain areas completely covered by civil service as well as departments in which it is totally absent." In his study analyzing county road patronage in Pennsylvania, Professor Sorauf described how the party decentralized its patronage. "The county organizations are . . . able to place some patronage appointments in Harrisburg and within the county in positions with the Forest and Waters Service, various state institutions within the county, and the state fish hatchery." As in Indiana, highway jobs dominate the job patronage scene. "Although the patronage resources available in Centre County are not limited to the 140-odd highway jobs, these are the most important part of the local spoils."

While Cook County and Centre County represent counties which cooperate with powerful party machines on the state level, weaker local parties offer their representatives far fewer jobs and favors. In Montclair, New Jersey, whose five wards are dominated by a reform wing of the regular Democratic county organization, town chairman Dr. Winona Lipman laments the scarce patronage allotted both to her and to the committeemen in her organization. Each pair of committeemen representing an election district share but two patronage jobs between them, and meager per-diem jobs at that: manning the polls on election and primary days for a stipend of $30. In some of the more affluent districts, committeemen find it difficult to find someone to work the 12-hour day at the polls for $30. With so little patronage cement, party discipline is relatively low; the rate of participation and amount of service the party can extract from county committeemen are minuscule compared with Cook County. The party considers itself lucky if 50 percent of its committeemen show up at meetings—even those labeled "urgent"—while even lower percentages turn out at functions intended to produce crowds for visiting candidates. Nevertheless, the rate of issue participation is much higher among Montclair Democrats who are not bound by the fear displayed by the Cook County committeemen. Even without the party's official sanction, or protection, many Montclair committeemen stand out in town politics for their active participation in issues affecting the community, such as school integration policy, traffic planning, and civil service for the firemen and policemen.

In the same way that state party leaders decentralize their patronage to the county, national party leaders channel their patronage to the states. Starved of federal patronage for eight years, Republican party leaders, especially in the Senate, expressed unconcealed glee at the patronage prospects provided by the election of Richard Nixon. The South won the election for Mr. Nixon, amid general expectations that it would share many of the fruits of victory.

Some Southern Republican leaders believe that federal patronage from Mr. Nixon will revitalize the two-party system—a hope encouraged by Strom Thurmond's closeness to the White House. In South Carolina, Republican State Chairman Donald L. Fowler notes that local Republican party leaders "have a certain influence over

who is appointed to federal jobs in South Carolina because of the current Republican administration. They
[the leaders] have a patronage committee which systematically surveys job applications for federal positions."

In Georgia, another state where the Democrats have
exercised complete control on the state level, Republican
leaders "are requested to provide recommendations for
U.S. Attorneys and United States Marshals in each of the
three judicial districts of Georgia," according to G. Paul
Jones, Republican state chairman. "In addition," Mr.
Jones continued, "we are asked to give political recommendations for any other position that will be filled by
the President at the national level in which a Georgian is
being considered. Whenever we are called upon to give a
recommendation, we always contact the county chairman
of the county of residence of the individual recommended."
He proudly counted off the names of Georgia's recent federal patronage appointments—Under Secretary of Agriculture, Commissioner of Internal Revenue, Assistant Secretary of Labor, and Assistant Secretary of the Interior.

Applauding the opportunities presented by federal
patronage for improving party morale, A. Conover Spen-
cer, executive director of New Jersey's Republican State
Committee, said: "We also are most pleased when we receive federal appointments which in many instances help
build the morale of the organization and *give the workers
a goal upon which they may set their sights*" (italics
added).

Republican party leaders also have received word
from Washington that in 1970 the census-taking will present patronage opportunities for low-level party workers.
Said G. Paul Jones: "We understand the U.S. Census,
which will be conducted in 1970, will utilize the Republican political organizations in the various states and counties for hiring the necessary enumerators and other census

personnel." Although some party leaders publicly shun the whole concept of patronage, most state chairmen would agree with Mr. Jones, who said: "We expect them to look first to the Republican organization in seeking this advice, and in attempting to measure public opinion."

A survey of party leaders throughout the nation revealed a wide disparity in the patronage available to them. Several state chairmen and party officials reported that they had absolutely no job patronage at all: Minnesota, Washington, Oregon, Ohio, Colorado, Nevada, California, Missouri, and Oklahoma. Of these, some leaders attributed their lack of patronage as the primary reason their party remained the "out" party in their respective states.[11] Speaking of the Democrats in Missouri, Republican State Chairman Elmer Smith estimates "the opposing party has several thousand State, County, and Municipal jobs filled by their party workers." Since Missouri has a "divisive two-party system of battling political parties, there are few crumbs available to the outs," Mr. Smith complained. "Since the Republican party in Missouri is the minority party and controls only one statewide office, and approximately one-third of the State legislative seats, there are no patronage jobs where the State party leaders can influence the selection of the employees. . . . The two major cities in Missouri are controlled by the Democratic Party and few jobs are available for Republican workers."

In contrast to Missouri, less fratricidal two-party states have resolved their differences sufficiently to share the spoils. In Maine, both parties give each other partial insurance against ever being completely left out in the cold, and work together in doling out patronage. State

[11] From a national survey taken by the authors on party patronage. Unfortunately, the return rate on the questionnaires came to a meager 26 percent, indicating the difficulties presented by attempts to quantify and systematize patronage data.

Republican Party Chairman Cyril M. Joly, Jr., explained that "We have a Democrat governor and a Republican Council, so the two work together swapping jobs and I occasionally confer with the Republican Council in this regard."

Party control over patronage often stands as the most reliable index of party discipline and party strength. Comparing his own party unfavorably with the Republicans in his state, Arizona's State Democratic Chairman Richard Duffield called the Republicans "better disciplined than the Democrats." Elaborating on this point, he continued, "there is a closer liaison between its elected officials and the party organization. I presume that the party organization has substantially more influence in the selection and appointment of persons to both paying and non-paying jobs."

On the other hand, party leaders with a great deal of patronage power (as well as many who seek the rewards of patronage) often hide their patronage power by telling job and contract seekers that only elected officials, not themselves, wield patronage power. In this way, they will not be blamed by unsuccessful office seekers who have approached them for patronage. Taking this view, Oklahoma's party leaders claimed to have little influence in the selection of patronage appointees, a paradox in view of the fact that Oklahoma is one of the best-known patronage states in the nation. Contradicting the more prevalent view in which party leaders say that they are at least consulted in patronage situations, J. C. Kennedy, Democratic State Chairman in Oklahoma, said, "Very few jobs, if any, remain open for party leaders to fill. They sometimes are asked to recommend or approve names, but it is left to the elected officials at all levels to make the selection."

Most party officials without much job patronage admitted that they were in trouble. Representative Thomas Rees, a California Democrat, argued that the lack of job patronage created an erratic political situation in his state. Without jobs, he said, the party organization lacked stability, and was forced to function between extremes of political opinion in an atmosphere of "whipsaw politics." [12]

Many states with little job patronage obtain jobs in private industry for the party faithful—a technique used by some mayors to create an organization. In Oregon, where the governor himself controls only a handful of patronage jobs, Democratic Chairman John Allen explained: "Party leaders and elected officials have opportunities to provide jobs for party faithful within local, state and private business by either appointment [patronage] or introduction to employers."

Other state chairmen without formal job patronage claim that they don't need jobs to keep the party together, because they cater to a sophisticated public which accepts their issue orientation toward politics. "We don't care much about favors of patronage in the usual sense," said Bruce Terris, chairman of the Washington, D.C., Democratic Central Committee. "We were elected because of our commitment to Robert Kennedy, and we care much more about the issues—ABM, Vietnam, welfare, police, schools, transportation. . . . So even if we had more in-

---

[12] In his study of reform politics, James Q. Wilson pointed out that the governor of California controlled no more than 600 political appointments, but channeled a great deal of "honorific patronage" (unsalaried appointments to advisory boards and commissions) instead. Although honorific patronage, according to Wilson, carries little value in mobilizing lower-class voters, it has "considerable value in attracting contributions of time and money from middle-class Democrats for whom prestige may be as valuable as additional income. Thus, 'clean,' honorific patronage in California predisposes politics toward middle-class activity." See James Q. Wilson, *The Amateur Democrat* (Chicago: University of Chicago Press, 1962), p. 203.

fluence than we do, we would have been interested in issues and people to carry out reform, not patronage and favors." Complaining that "the detail involved is so terribly time-consuming," the Republican State Chairman of Ohio, another well-known patronage state, said that he was glad they had no patronage, adding that "the importance of patronage to the state organization is highly overrated in any event."

The states' differing views of patronage are understandable in the light of testimony by Jean J. Couturier, executive director of the National Civil Service League, before the Subcommittee on Intergovernmental Relations in March 1969. He reported that although some 36 of the 50 states had some sort of merit system, there were no hard figures on how many of their employees are actually employed under merit principles. "Excepted appointments, provisional employees, noncompetitive positions, temporary and part-time employees are not accounted for," Mr. Couturier noted. "Nor is it certain that the two key tenets of a merit system—objective recruitments and selection and some meaningful form of tenure—are fully provided for in those states which do have civil service law." [13]

In his incisive study of party politics in America, John Fenton classifies states without patronage as "issue-oriented" in contrast to the more traditional patronage states which are "job-oriented." Fenton's examples of job-oriented states include Ohio as well as Indiana and Illinois. In issue-oriented states, Fenton argues, people who enter politics are not primarily oriented toward jobs or

[13] Nowhere are there concrete figures available, analyzed in quantitative terms, comparing patronage jobs with those under civil service. Departments one would expect to compile these figures, such as the Bureau of the Census and the Office of State Merit Systems (in HEW), have failed to do so.

privileges. "Following World War II, programmatic or issue-oriented parties emerged in California, Michigan, Wisconsin and Minnesota . . . out of the increased issue-orientation occasioned by the New Deal and the war." [14] Those who enter issue politics, Mr. Fenton concludes, do so out of their desire to translate certain policy preferences into public policy." [15]

Like living on love, few politicians can survive for long on issues alone. Issues are more often used as shortcuts by the "out" party to get in; patronage is used to stay in. In many cases, issues are like patronage, in that the "out" party promises the public certain broad favors, which invariably narrow down to favoring certain groups. No one would question whether school bussing or oil depletion allowances constituted an issue or not, yet under closer scrutiny we find that the resolution of these issues inevitably favors one group at the expense of another. Political systems analysts call this "the authoritative allocation of values," the power of government to order its priorities to reflect the values of society, which in the last analysis hinges on government's tremendous discretionary power, inherent in the American system of politics.

Issues, and issue-oriented politics, have sporadic mass appeal, rather than the day-in, day-out appeal that a job or insurance contract or legal referral has for the political professionals. Consequently, issue-oriented politicians often have a hard time keeping their adherents active in the political arena on a consistent basis. The supporters of Eugene McCarthy, for example, who supported his political career in strictly issue terms—his opposition to the Vietnam war—either had nowhere to turn or

[14] John Fenton, *People and Parties in Politics* (New York: Scott Foresman & Co., 1966), p. 51.

[15] *Ibid.*, p. 50.

dropped out after McCarthy lost interest in his own move-ment. Without the rewards promised by power, the issue by which he hoped to attain power could be easily forgot-ten, and McCarthy even relinquished his seat on the For-eign Relations Committee, bringing ultimate disenchant-ment to his supporters.

Consequently, those who attach themselves to issues outside the arena of partisan politics frequently express feelings of political impotence and disenchantment with the democratic process. For without political leverage gained from practicing "the art of obligation," issue-oriented activists usually find that they are powerless to change the course of history.

4

From the Clubhouse to the Bench and Back Again: Judicial Patronage

> *"Above all else they [the judges] belong to the political club, and are cheerful in performing the interesting assignments their leader has for them. They are exemplary in their loyalty to their political party. They look on judicial appointment as the reward for their loyalty and devotion to the party, and they look forward to judicial service as socially and financially rewarding."*
> —Former Attorney General Herbert Brownell

> *"I have no patience with living-room liberals who rant about corrupt politics, but recoil from rolling up their sleeves and trying to improve conditions. . . . The political parties, from among their active memberships, can staff all the courts with outstanding, distinguished judges."*
> —Judge Bernard Botein

❡ *The Judgemakers and the Botein Committee*

In August 1968, Frank Rossetti, the beefy, taciturn leader of Tammany Hall, and Henry McDonough, the late Democratic chieftain of the Bronx, visited the offices of Francis T. P. Plimpton, president of the Association

131

of the Bar of the City of New York. Classic stereotypes of themselves, the chunky "pols" faced socialite Plimpton, who represented New York's legal reform establishment, to discuss meting out the 125 new judgeships in Manhattan and the Bronx recently created by the New York State Legislature. "The biggest judicial pie in almost half a century is about to be cut," announced *The New York Times*, although the formal selection would not occur for another month, when delegates from the entire Democratic party would convene at the judicial nominating convention.[1] Plimpton's group, a coalition representing the Citizens Union, the VERA Foundation, the Association of the Bar of the City of New York, and the Reform Democrats, hoped to wean away from the party leaders some of the power over the selection of judges. (In New York, Democratic nomination is considered tantamount to election.)

Confronted with intense pressures and bad publicity regarding their judicial patronage practices—not to mention the threat of a primary battle—the county leaders agreed that the time had come to demonstrate their honorable intentions toward judicial selection. Their meeting with Plimpton ended with an informal agreement that Judge Bernard Botein, then Presiding Justice of the Appellate Division of the First Department (which encompasses Manhattan and the Bronx), would head a screening committee in charge of seeking well-qualified candidates for elective judicial offices. Botein, a judge of impeccable reputation, said he had represented a compromise between the politicians and the bar associations.

Speaking for the other party leaders, Rossetti told

[1] The new judgeships included 50 Supreme Court judges (34 for the city), 25 Civil Court judges, 20 Criminal Court judges (6 for the city). The party would select Supreme and Civil Court judges, while the mayor would select Criminal and Family Court judges.

Plimpton that he didn't trust the bar associations but would trust Botein: "He's tough, but fair."

In its original form, the agreement worked out between the county leaders and Plimpton provided that the leaders would submit to the party judicial convention only those candidates approved by the Botein committee. To the chagrin and outrage of the reformers, the party leaders broke the agreement and nominated three Supreme Court justices who were rejected by the committee. The Association of the Board also rejected the three nominees, in addition to Paul Fino: Manuel A. Gomez, a Criminal Court judge known to shout at defendants whom he often called "idiots," rejected "by reason of lack of judicial temperament"; State Senator Ivan Warner, who had admitted under oath that he was present and had failed to report an incident in which a fellow legislator had proposed to "fix" a narcotics case for $100,000; Isidore Dollinger, district attorney from the Bronx, rejected "by reason of his age (64) and lack of recent professional and litigation experience"; and Representative Paul Fino, rejected "because he had not affirmatively demonstrated that he possesses the requisite qualifications for the court for which he is a candidate and because he had failed to cooperate with the committee in its endeavor to evaluate his qualifications." [2]

The four men were duly nominated at the Democratic Party's judicial conference, and despite the abortive cries of "doublecross" from the reform coalition, handily won election that November as the Democratic candidates. Former Bronx Borough President Herman Badillo charged that the leaders' reneging on the agreement was "an outrage to everyone who believes in good government and respect for the judiciary." The party leaders, for their part, said that they had agreed to submit the names

[2] *The New York Times*, November 3, 1968.

of the candidates to the Botein panel, but had not agreed to be bound by its findings.

"There was very heavy political pressure on McDonough and Rossetti," Mr. Plimpton said a year after the episode. "McDonough just folded under the pressure. It was a flat breach of faith," he continued. "They made a specific promise to Botein. They wouldn't make one to me. They stalled and stalled." The episode showed that the party leaders respected the contracts that they had made with each other, and with those to whom they had promised judgeships, far more than they respected their agreement with the "good government" forces. What the reformers could not understand was that their agreement never held the same weight as formal political contracts made between politicians, which were based on long-standing relationships and cemented by previous favors rendered among the participants. In effect, all the political leaders had ever received from the reform groups were challenges, criticism and, to the extent to which they could get their complaints into the media, adverse publicity. According to the laws of patronage politics by which New York's political leaders lived, there seemed to be no logical reason why these groups deserved instant power without coming up the hard way, the way the leaders had, in order to build up the patronage IOU's necessary for negotiating solid political contracts.

A spokesman for the reform groups explained his view of the controversy, salvaging some positive effects from the incident. "Dollinger, Warner and Gomez were political debts the leaders had to pay off . . . they were not bad enough for the leaders to have been frightened off by them; they had to make these appointments. The Botein incident pointed out that you can't rely on party leaders . . . they had all given their word that they would rely on the committee's judgments. Some good was done: at least five men were not named as a result of committee pressures."

Safe from a primary threat, the party leaders did not seem overly concerned with the barrage of criticism leveled at them for their cavalier behavior. Instead, they privately congratulated themselves for having managed to institutionalize their opponents, hoodwinking them into believing that they were all working together, while at the same time keeping the patronage exclusively to themselves. By keeping the Botein committee busy until September when the deadline passed for circulating nominating petitions, the party regulars held off the reformers (and the Reform Democrats) from initiating embarrassing primary fights. More cynical members of the reform coalition blamed Judge Botein for being so easily duped: "Judge Botein is always being taken to the cleaners by the politicians," one said.

Although reform groups in other parts of the country have been more successful in changing the system of local and statewide judicial selection, in New York the district and county leaders have managed to retain the use of judgeships as a patronage tool of the party, and make no secret of how the system works. Before formal nominations are submitted, district leaders who represent a particular judicial area will get together and select the Civil Court judges who will come from their respective areas. Before agreeing on a slate of nominees, the district leaders engage in an intricate process of bargaining among themselves,[3] and if they can't reach a decision, the county chairman resolves the dispute—usually by selecting his own candidates. It rarely comes to this, however,

[3] Since districts are not equal (depending on the size of their assembly districts), some clubs wield more influence than others, and these are given voting power proportionate to their strength. Often, the stronger clubs find they can swing judicial nominations toward their candidates.

since the district leaders are reluctant to relinquish their patronage power to the county leader. Some Reform Democratic leaders, stressing intraparty democracy, require their clubs to decide in open session who is to be nominated; and should anyone wish to promote a candidate, he can come to an open meeting at the clubhouse and make a presentation on his candidate's behalf.

On the Supreme Court level, the party hierarchy in a show of democracy runs judicial conventions to nominate the justices. At the convention, the county leaders bargain with each other before they alone decide where the judgeships will go, according to former Municipal Court Judge Dorothy Kenyon, who represents Reform Democrats at these conventions. "The district leaders wait for instructions from the county leaders," she explained, rendering the selection of Supreme Court justices "an even greater farce than the selection of lower court judges." At least when the district leaders get together to select lower court judges, "there is no pretense of democracy; the other is a charade, a high comedy." Judge Botein called the judicial convention an "obscenity . . . a device to retain control over the district leaders."

The real problem with the party-dominated judicial patronage system—and it is the prevailing system nationally—is that the judiciary is compromised by its closeness to the political process. How independent can the judiciary be when the judicial decision-makers can hardly be expected to turn against the political system that produced them? Politicians and judges retain close ties with each other, reinforced by the ample quantities of courthouse patronage grateful judges mete out to the party faithful. Young lawyers still flock to the clubhouses, eager to serve the party in a wide range of menial tasks, accepting as rewards the driblets of refereeships, trusteeships, and guardianships while they wait in hopes of capturing the ultimate prize for political service: the judgeship. By the very nature of the route they took to get to the bench, judges are obligated to party leaders who chose them and party workers who campaigned for them. "Each one nourishes the other; it is a very healthy plant because it is viable," observed Judge Kenyon.

Each month, the Brooklyn Democratic organization sends a list of recommended appointees to the Surrogate, and to the State Supreme Court justice sitting in Special Term Part II—where special appointments are made by carefully selected judges who serve one month at a time and are known to have especially strong ties to the party apparatus. "Ignoring the list is like ignoring their [the county leader's] recommendation of a law secretary," remarked a newly elected judge on the Brooklyn Supreme Court bench. "You can't get anything done—the elevators get stuck, your cases are misfiled, nothing gets typed. . . ."

Other county leaders in New York City also send around lists: how closely judges follow their patronage dicta reflects the power of the individual county leader. Manhattan's Surrogate Sam Di Falco, for example, parcels out guardianships [4] freely to his friends and former law partners, a luxury he would not be permitted were he part of the more tightly disciplined Brooklyn organization.

Still other judges say they don't need lists, having remained active enough in the local organization to recognize the party faithful without the guidance of the county

[4] *Guardian ad litem:* "a guardian appointed by a court of justice to prosecute or defend for an infant in any suit to which he may be a party"—Black's *Law Dictionary*. The attorney appointed guardian by the court usually receives a steady fee drawn from the estate, based on the *size* of the estate rather than on the amount of legal work involved.

leader, even though they are required by law and by the American Bar Association's *Canons of Ethics* to sever all their political connections upon becoming judges. Many judges find this organically impossible, however, and former Supreme Court Justice Abe Fortas, who was later forced to resign his seat, drew heavy criticism from the Senate for continuing to advise his old friend and mentor President Lyndon Johnson. One New York State Supreme Court justice, when asked whether his current interest in the clubhouse conflicted with his judicial functions, protested that he "only sat in the back of the room at club meetings where [he] could give advice when it was requested."

Added to their bounty of courthouse-directed legal business, politicians often extract other courthouse favors as well. The kind of courtesies that politicians receive from the courts was described by a New York City councilman from Queens: "You get all the courtesies of the house," he said. "When you enter the courtroom, wherever you are on the calendar, you go right to the top. When the judge calls you into his chambers to make a settlement, he says, 'Now, councilman, I don't want you to take advantage of your position as councilman in dealing with learned counsel for the insurance company,' and then gives you twice as much as you would have gotten otherwise."

Along with the legal work controlled in tandem by party leaders and judges, there are also numerous categories of court jobs available as party patronage: county clerks, judges' clerks, bailiffs, Public Administrators, secretaries, and recorders. William J. Pierce, Professor of Law at the University of Michigan Law School, complained of all the "paraphernalia around the court used as party patronage." In some states, he said, court reporters are allowed to charge $1 a page for transcripts, which augments the salaries they already draw from the state. Rela-

tively unknown to the general public, this kind of patronage contributes to the high cost of appealing decisions, and
in many cases may preclude the poor from appealing an
unfavorable decision.

Good-government groups periodically express their
dissatisfaction with the continuing relationship between
the political party and the bench through ancillary personnel in the courts. In a confidential study, the Citizens Union reported that more than one-third of the Supreme
Court judges in New York City hired clerks who were
district leaders or county chairmen. The report charged
that the cozy relationship perpetuated was basically un-
ethical: "The district leader as a co-tenant of the judge in
the judicial chamber does not fit into the picture which
the public should have of the court as an agency removed
from politics." Representative Ed Koch also emphasized
the conflict of interest inherent in this system.
"Can you imagine," he said, "a political adversary coming before a judge whose secretary was a district leader?"

The judicial system has remained the mainstay of
New York's Democratic county leaders, who reward their
district leaders and party officers with jobs in the courthouse. Bronx County leader Pat Cunningham says that
he does not personally attend to judicial patronage. "If a
judge wants guidance on an appointment," said Mr. Cunningham, "he calls my secretary, Joe Cohen." Despite Mr.
Cunningham's disclaimer, many of his officers on the
Bronx County committee enjoy his well-placed judicial appointments.[5] Patronage jobs, many of which are in the

[5] Those on the county committee who occupy judicial patronage posts
are: 1st vice chairman John J. Sullivan, county clerk in the Surrogate's Court; 2nd vice-chairman Howard F. Tyson, director of administration of the Civil Court; 3rd vice-chairman Mildred O. Klett,
secretary to a judge; 6th vice-chairman Margaret Persuda, secretary to
a judge; and 7th vice-chairman Agnes Jones, former secretary to a
judge.

courts, are held by all but four of the forty-six district leaders in Meade Esposito's Brooklyn organization.[6]

The judges themselves have little to do with appointing court personnel, in contrast to their control over courthouse legal business. The patronage, like the judgeships, flows from the party. In Illinois, according to State Representative Arthur Telcser, all court personnel must go through their ward committeemen to get their jobs. The judge is only allowed to appoint his own bailiff, and even his choice of bailiff may be influenced by the party. The Clerk of the County Court in Chicago, one of the party's chief patronage-dispensing offices, controls about 1,400 court jobs. Mayor Richard Daley once held this job.

❪ The Judgeship

Of all the jobs now left to the discretion of party leaders, judgeships stand out as the most desirable. "Every lawyer wants to be a judge," many politicians admit; witness the high ratio of lawyers involved in the political process. Judgeships are desirable for a variety of reasons. The security afforded by the generous tenure of judgeships offers politicians, scarred from continuous struggles to maintain their power, relatively peaceful retirement professions. A federal judge is appointed for life, while a

[6] The district leaders, by assembly district, who hold court jobs are: 36th A.D.—Gasper S. Fasullo, law assistant in the Surrogate's Court; 43rd A.D.—Bernard Bloom, deputy public administrator; 44th A.D.— Alexander G. Hesterberg, counsel to the public administrator; 47th A.D.—Sebastian Leone, law secretary; 49th A.D.—Joseph N. Sciarra, law secretary; 50th A.D.—Harry Mortimer, former law secretary;— 51st A.D.—Joseph Levine, law secretary; 52nd A.D.—Frank Cunningham, law clerk; 53rd A.D.—James V. Mangano, general clerk of the Brooklyn Supreme Court.

State Supreme Court judge in New York is elected for a period of 14 years, regarded by many as a virtual lifetime appointment. Removed from the fray of political wars, judgeships also offer party veterans the dignity of being part of a high-status profession, a dignity they sorely missed during the long years they wore the label of "politician."

As a group, judges draw higher salaries than any other professional corps of public officials, exceeding the pay of bureau chiefs at the federal level, and deputy commissioners on the local level, not to mention local and state legislators. On the federal level, district judges draw salaries of $40,000, while U.S. Court of Appeals judges make $42,500. The American Bar Association reported that the average salary for state trial-court judges in 1966 was $21,-030; in state appellate courts the judges averaged salaries of $25,115. Judges on both state and federal levels have ample opportunities to supplement their salaries with honorariums earned on the lecture circuit, although this means of deriving income has recently come under scrutiny by Congress and the organized bar as ethically questionable.

Rarely are judgeships included in the economy drives that reduce the pay of other public officials; in fact, judicial budgeting practices themselves are regarded by many critics of the system as examples of legislative favoritism. In New York State, for example, the judicial budget passes through the state legislature without having to submit to hearings. According to Mrs. Elizabeth Schack, who chairs the Judiciary Committee for the New York State Chapter of the League of Women Voters, each judicial district makes up its own budget, then sends in its request which passes almost automatically, enabling judicial salaries to climb without regard to wage-price guidelines or the fiscal health of the state. The governor includes in the state budget the requests of the courts without revision, then sends it to the legislature where it is passed by legislators, most of whom are lawyers by profession,[7] without question. Since so many state legislators have remained in private law practice, it is unlikely that they would cut the salaries of judges before whom they frequently appear.

This explains how one year in Erie County the judges raised their own salaries by $3,000 from $28,500 to $31,500. And in 1968, the New York State Legislature raised salaries for judges on the Court of Appeals $2,500, adding $6,000 in expenses for the Chief Judges, another $2,500 for judges on the Court of Claims, and $2,100 for Supreme Court justices, with $16,000 expense allowances for justices in the 1st, 2nd, 9th, 10th, and 11th judicial districts.

One especially lucrative state appointment to the Court of Claims in Saratoga County reported by the Albany *Knickerbocker News* yielded its beneficiary, Judge James H. Glavin, Jr., a Democrat, over $51,000 a year, which included his salary, plus other judicial benefits. In addition to his salary of $31,500, Judge Glavin was given an expense-and-travel "lulu"[8] of $4,500; his family law-practice office, designated his official residence, was paid for by the state (this came to $1,400); and he appointed his daughter-in-law his confidential clerk at an annual salary of $14,500.

Judgeships are also attractive to politicians who seek them for their short working hours, long holidays, and

[7] In New York State, approximately 71 percent of the state senators are lawyers; in the Assembly, about 56 percent of the legislators are lawyers.

[8] Money allotted for job-connected personal expenses.

exceptional retirement benefits. In striking contrast to
the hectic pace and killing hours of political life, the average judge's working day runs from about 10:00 A.M. to
4:00 P.M., often with long lunch hours and recesses in between. Judgeships are insulated from controversies which
so often rage around other public officials, and even when
a judge must submit to an election campaign, very few
judicial elections are actually contests. More often the
real struggle occurs for the nomination, which in many
areas of the country is tantamount to election. In New
York City and Chicago, for example, the judicial nominee
is virtually guaranteed the job; in fact, he will often receive bi- or tri-partisan endorsement. Parties agree beforehand on candidates, then parcel out the judgeships. One
Democratic district leader in New York City related his
abortive attempt to get the Democratic Party not to re-
endorse a notoriously inept Republican judge, most of
whose decisions had been reversed on appeal. Refusing
him, the other district leaders said: "That's their [the
Republicans'] problem."

To a lesser extent, the same situation holds true on
the federal level. Through the process of senatorial courtesy, once a senator has made up his mind to appoint
someone to a federal judgeship (even though the appointment technically comes through the executive branch),
only a major scandal or strong pressure behind the scenes
from organized interest groups or from the Justice Department will deter the appointment. It made no difference when Irving Ben Cooper was nominated for a federal
judgeship in New York that many citizens' groups—including the Citizens Committee for Children (Cooper
had been Chief Judge of the Court of Special Sessions),
the Association of the Bar of the City of New York,
and the New York County Lawyers Association—went

down to Washington to declare him unfit for the job;
Cooper was appointed anyway, his appointment ultimately approved by the Senate Judiciary Committee and
by the entire Senate.[9]

◖ How Judgeships Help the Party

*"No one knows how much judgeships go for, yet everyone
knows they go for a price."*

—a professor of law

*"Money is the criteria for judicial nominations . . . the
question is how much goes into the pocket of the district
leader and how much into party coffers."*

—a city councilman

*"At cocktail parties you can always hear judges' wives jok-
ing about their 'debt,' referring to the money their husbands
had to borrow to get on the bench."*

—a judge

The above quotations, from sources who prefer to
be anonymous,[10] tell the tale of how the party parlays

[9] The case against Judge Cooper was based on allegations that he
lacked judicial temperament, and lacked sufficient legal experience.
Witnesses testified that Judge Cooper called the youthful offenders
who appeared before him in open court "punks," "bums," "flotsam and
jetsam," "slime of the earth," and were told that they would "rot in
jail" if it were not for the candidate (Cooper). Cooper's name was
submitted to President Kennedy in 1961 through the good offices of
Representative Emanuel Celler, chairman of the House Judiciary
Committee, in the absence of any Democratic senators (senators customarily have the right of initiating nominations) from New York.
Mr. Celler wrote to the Attorney General: "I submit this name to you
because I believe him to be the best qualified. . . . I would be less
than frank if I did not tell you that I would be greatly disappointed
were he not nominated." See Joel B. Grossman, *Lawyers and Judges:
The ABA and the Politics of Judicial Selection* (New York: John
Wiley & Sons, 1965), p. 182n.

[10] Many sources in this chapter preferred to remain anonymous, owing
to the questionable legality of some of the information they revealed.

its judicial nominating power into a means of increasing its revenue. No one really knows in how many areas this practice prevails, although there exist many educated guesses. Only in New York and Chicago, according to an official from the U.S. Department of Justice, do judgeships go for a price: in New York, he estimated, the average judgeship costs $80,000, while in Chicago, where service counts more than money, judgeships extract only about $7,500. "Chicago bosses will only appoint someone who's safe as far as the machine is concerned—reliable in terms of giving patronage out—and they will even give a judgeship for service without requiring a contribution," he added. Of course, those judges who have arrived on the bench through the force of their own outstanding legal reputations have won their judgeships without having to contribute to any party organization or serve the party for any length of time.

In New York, the party relies on judicial "revenue" to finance its activities on the district level. Responsible for collecting the pay-offs, the district leader is then free to disburse the funds in whatever way he chooses. Of course, this leaves the more unscrupulous district leaders under considerable temptation to keep all or a goodly share of the funds. One newly elected State Supreme Court judge described how he paid for his judgeship: "First I needed the O.K. from my two district leaders. Then the county leader told me to pay the district leaders directly in cash . . . untraceable." This amounted, he said, to a shakedown by the district leader, with the approval and encouragement of the county leader. By opening this

---

In order to utilize their valuable data, these respondents will henceforth be referred to only by their respective roles in the judicial process.

source of revenue to the district leader, the county leader is relieved of channeling too large a share of the party's funds down to the districts.

The price tag on New York judgeships varies in accordance with a carefully worked-out formula based on the relative status and salary of the individual judgeship. In their encyclopedic study of New York City government, Sayre and Kaufman describe how this formula works.[11] The district leader decides whether to extract one or two years' salary from the judicial nominee, or relies on the method of charging $50 to $100 (probably higher today) for each election district within the judicial area. If, for example, the judicial area amounted to a municipal court district, encompassing between 145 and 180 election districts, the price would go up to about $20,000. Before inflationary tendencies set in, judgeships were cheaper; and in the early nineteen-thirties, the Seabury investigations reported, magistrates paid $10,000, while General Sessions or Supreme Court judges paid $25,000 to $50,000. "Payments were made in crisp, undeclared currency," wrote Herbert Mitgang, who produced the definitive biography of Judge Samuel Seabury.[12] During Boss Croker's time, before the turn of the century, judgeships cost even less, about $17,000.

Several judges denied having to pay for their seats on the bench; the act of paying for a judgeship is, after all, an indictable offense, though never enforced. One State Supreme Court judge, however, who denied having paid directly for his judgeship, admitted responding to a "dear

[11] Wallace S. Sayre and Herbert Kaufman, *Governing New York City* (New York: Russell Sage Foundation, 1960), Chapter 14, "Courts and Politics."

[12] Herbert Mitgang, *The Man Who Rode the Tiger: The Life and Times of Judge Samuel Seabury* (Philadelphia: J. P. Lippincott, 1963), p. 161.

friend" letter sent to him by his local party organization soliciting contributions.

When the party awards a judgeship without extracting payment for it, the organization is compensated in other ways for its financial loss. Certain that his was an unusual case, one Municipal Court judge reported that the party had awarded him his judgeship free of charge in order to lure him away from his seat in the State Assembly where he had been harassing party regulars on too many issues. Telling their maverick member that this was his last chance for a judgeship, party leaders were able to entice him away from an uncertain career in the Assembly to a secure seat on the bench.

For those denied top spots on the ticket, for officials embroiled in controversy, or for others just too inept at what they are doing, and too influential to be fired or quietly shelved, there are always judgeships, consolation prizes used by the party to escape further political embarrassment, and to cushion the harsh risks inherent in electoral politics. Former Mayors Hylan and Impellitteri accepted judicial posts after being denied the renomination for the mayoralty. Former New York City Controller Mario A. Procaccino accepted his party's nomination for controller, and resigned his sinecure on the Civil Court bench, only after being promised the consolation prize of a Supreme Court judgeship if he lost the race. Subsequently, Controller Procaccino ran unsuccessfully for mayor of New York, and may claim the party's previous offering in order to assuage the blow of his recent political defeat.

All too often, examples recur to show that the first rule for succeeding in acquiring a judgeship rests on how dismally one can fail in the political arena. Mayor Lindsay bestowed a judgeship drawing a salary of $30,-000 a year on William Booth in order to fire him gracefully as chairman of the City Commission on Human Rights, after repeated pressure from the city's Jewish groups who felt Mr. Booth was ignoring their needs in favor of black demands. In order to remove Frank O'Connor (former City Council President and unsuccessful gubernatorial candidate) as leader of the New York headquarters of Humphrey's presidential campaign, the Democrats handed O'Connor a judgeship.

As shown by the Booth and O'Connor cases, judgeships serve to neutralize the opposition: for surely Booth would have fought bitterly for his job, perhaps aggravating even further New York's worsening hostility between her Jewish and black populations; and firing O'Connor without a peace offering might have caused dissension between the local and national party organizations. "This is patronage in its worst form," charged Charles Chrisman, of the Committee for Modern Courts. "The courts are too important to be used in this way."

The party also finds judgeships a convenient means of showing publicly how it rewards, through recognition, dominant ethnic and racial groups. Intending to gain mileage with black groups, former President Johnson appointed the first black Supreme Court judge, Justice Thurgood Marshall.[13] President Nixon, in striking contrast, bowed to white Southerners of conservative persuasion with his abortive attempt to appoint to the Supreme

[13] Johnson's appointment of Constance Baker Motley to a federal judgeship recognized two groups traditionally short-changed where patronage is dispensed: Negroes and women. Mississippi Senator James Eastland, head of the Senate Judiciary Committee responsible for corroborating federal appointments, tried to block the appointment in order to stem the rising tide of black patronage at the federal level beginning about this time. Achieving only a slight delay, Eastland conducted his own investigation of Mrs. Motley, not willing, he said, to rely on the Justice Department's investigation.

Court G. Harrold Carswell, a Florida judge who had once made a campaign speech declaring his belief in the doctrine of white supremacy.

If all the candidates seem equally qualified, often the Justice Department, the President, and the senators involved will try to choose the man who is identified with a particular ethnic group. Clinching the appointment of Judge Thomas D. Lambros as a federal district judge was his Greek-American ancestry; not only was he the best of seven candidates, argued his supporters, but he would attract Greek-American support to the administration which appointed him. Often even the recruitment of judges will center around ethnicity. In the early years of the Kennedy administration, one official working on judicial selection for the President admitted: "We were hunting like crazy for an Italian."

Bitter fights have centered around ethnic considerations, particularly when seats have been held in the past by representatives of minority groups. When Justice Fortas' seat was vacated on the Supreme Court, widespread speculation centered around whether the seat would remain a "Jewish seat," that is, whether a Jew would succeed Fortas. Federal Judge Julius Hoffman, who presided over the famous political trial of the Chicago Seven in 1969–1970, was known to have remarked, "I am lucky to be Jewish," after receiving his judgeship, known as the Jewish seat in the district. New York Congressman Ed Koch recounted a meeting of district leaders in the process of deciding who was to fill a particular judgeship. Leader Louis De Salvio protested some of the suggestions on the grounds that "that's an Italian seat." The seat was eventually filled by a Jew, Harold Birns. According to Koch, judicial seats were often parceled out ethnically in this way. Justice Cardozo was known to have explained his first election to the lower-court bench "because I was taken for an Italian." (Benjamin Cardozo was Jewish.) Although most judicial fights over ethnicity occur privately, Congressman Adam Clayton Powell publicly called on Harlem voters to "spit on Ray Jones [Tammany Hall leader] should they meet him on the street for not putting a Negro on the ticket [nominating a Negro for a judgeship]." [14]

❦ The Nitty-Gritty of Judicial Politics: Courthouse Patronage

To the public, judicial patronage means doling out judgeships, while the less visible, more commonly dispensed patronage comes from the judges themselves, who issue patronage from the bench: receiverships, refereeships, guardianships, and trusteeships. "In the area of surrogate patronage alone," estimates Judge Daniel Gutman, formerly Dean of the New York Academy of the Judiciary, "the cost to the public each year runs to billions of dollars, while one good civil servant paid $20,000 to $22,000 a year in each city could do all the work."

An indication of how lucrative courthouse patronage can be is the estimate of a San Diego, California, Republican that his appraiser fees totaled $33,000 during one six-month period, according to Murray Teigh Bloom, an expert on probate practices. Reform attempts fail, Bloom said, because this is such an easy way to repay political

[14] Powell called for this at the New York State Constitutional Convention, held in 1967. See "Transcript of the Minutes of a Public Hearing of the Judiciary Committee relating to Selection of Judges," recorded in the Senate Chamber, the Capitol, Albany, New York, on June 6, 1967, at 10 A.M.

debts; after all, it's a "dead man's estate, who's to kick up a fuss?" [15]

In Connecticut, the probate judges have formed a lobby to stymie attempts at reform. "Many probate judges earn more than the Governors of their states—indeed one Connecticut judge has an income 20 percent greater than that of the Chief Justice in Washington," wrote Norman Dacey in *How to Avoid Probate*.[16] Similar to guardianships, added Dacey, appraisers—who estimate the value of an estate—often do little or no work; in fact, "in a closed session speech to the Connecticut Probate Assembly, a powerful 'union' of probate judges, a member from one of the larger districts acknowledged that 90% of the persons appointed as appraisers do not work at all." [17]

While probate patronage flourishes in the rich, populous states of Texas, Ohio, Illinois, and New Jersey,[18] New York offers the most colorful illustration of how this kind of judicial patronage works to the benefit of the party faithful. For only in New York is the court required to list not only the lawyers who are assigned the cases but their fees as well, through a new amendment, Section 35a of the Judiciary Act, the token outcome of an unsuccessful reform movement to abolish probate patronage.[19] Surro-

[15] Murray Teigh Bloom, *The Trouble With Lawyers* (New York: Simon & Schuster, 1968). See pp. 11, 233–263.

[16] Norman Dacey, *How to Avoid Probate* (New York: Crown Publishers, 1965), p. 7.

[17] *Ibid.*, p. 8.

[18] In California, although there is a rotating list of lawyers who are eligible for *guardian ad litem* business, surrogate patronage still flourishes through the appraiser system.

[19] It is interesting that there almost seems to exist a conspiracy of silence with regard to figures on courthouse patronage and surrogate patronage as well as receiverships, refereeships, and trusteeships. Nei-

gate patronage is said by some to rival the mayor's office
in both actual and potential patronage power, and some
reformers point to surrogate patronage as the main reason New York has never achieved really broad-based political reform. During the La Guardia administration,
surrogate patronage kept the Democratic Party alive,
leading the "Little Flower" to call the Surrogate Court
"the most expensive undertaking establishment in the
world." During his anti-Tammany administration, he
found himself unable to cut off that source of patronage
to Tammany lawyers. Georgia, in contrast to New York,
channels all its surrogate business to a salaried official
called an "ordinary," who also presides over traffic violations—an indication of the level of importance given to
the work of the surrogate. The ordinary doesn't even have
to be a lawyer. It must be noted, however, that the ordinary seldom deals with the complex legal documents or
estates of the size commonly seen in New York City, the
financial capital of the country.

A survey of Surrogate Court records in New York
reveals that public officeholders, relatives of judges, politically connected lawyers, and law partners of judges receive a large percentage of the work. Former Surrogate
Edward Silver, in Brooklyn, has parceled out patronage
to: Blossom Heller, Assistant District Attorney from
Brooklyn; Samuel Greenberg, State Senator; Gladys Dor-
man, member of the Board of Education; and City Coun-

---

ther the Justice Department, the administrative branch of the federal
courts, the local courts themselves, the Department of Commerce, nor
the Bureau of the Census were able to furnish any data either quantitative or qualitative in this area on a national level. Only in New
York, where Section 35a of the Judiciary Act has opened this information to the public, is there any opportunity to find out who gets
court business, how the recipients of courthouse patronage are connected to the political system, and how much they receive from this
business.

cilman Dominick Corso. Included in Bronx Surrogate McGrath's list were Democratic Congressman Mario Biaggi and City Councilman Bertram Gelfand.

Mr. Corso, a former councilman and now a Civil Court judge, won renown with his admonition to a young Reform Democrat after a heated council debate. "You think it takes guts to stand up for what you think is right?" he asked. "That doesn't take guts. What takes guts is to stand up for what you know is wrong, day after day, year after year. That takes guts."

Many former public officials also benefit from court patronage. To name a few New York examples: former Corporation Counsel Peter Campbell Brown; former Deputy Insurance Commissioner Arthur Lamanda—whose guardianships included one with a fee of $15,000, and one drawing a fee of $20,000; former State Assembly Speaker Joseph Carlino, who was paid $10,000; former Assemblyman Irving Kirschenbaum; and former Deputy Controller Abraham Doris.[20]

Probably the luckiest beneficiary of court patronage was the late Edward V. Loughlin, former Tammany leader, whose fees over the last ten years from court-issued guardianships and refereeships ran well over $100,000. As a going-away present before leaving to become Ambassador to Spain, former Mayor Robert F. Wagner, Jr., was given a guardianship from the State Supreme Court of an estate whose assets totaled $5.5 million.[21]

[20] Surrogate Court material gathered here was collected from the following sources: 1) Surrogate Court records made public under Section 35a of the Judiciary Act; 2) an excellent series of investigative articles reported in the *New York Post*, February 5, 1969, February 6, 1969, and January 4, 1968; and 3) *The New York Times*, July 5, 1966.

[21] The State Supreme Court has jurisdiction over "inter-vivos" or "living trusts," in which the donor has effectively given away property

In addition to its political uses, surrogate patronage can also be highly personal, especially when guardianships are given away to relatives, law partners, or friends —who may also double as party workers or heavy contributors. Surrogate Di Falco, whose Manhattan fief yields the richest harvest of guardianships, bestows the best of these on members of his former law firm of Di Falco, Field, Florea and O'Rourke, which prudently made Di Falco's son a partner. To Sidney A. Florea went one appointment for $12,500; to Arthur Field, another for $20,-000. One judge from the Bronx estimated that Di Falco's power exceeded that of his county leader, Frank Rossetti, whose son, Frank Rossetti, Jr., also figures prominently in the awarding of refereeships and guardianships.[22]

Like judgeships, guardianship patronage is often auctioned off as a consolation prize for political losers. Richmond Surrogate Paulo bestowed two awards to Vincent R. Fitzpatrick, unsuccessful Democratic congressional candidate, and to Joseph M. Leahey, who lost a race for County Court judge.

Safely removed from the realm of dishonest graft, guardianships are considered especially valuable patronage gifts, and politicians dole them out abundantly, despite numerous attempts to remove them from political control. Except for the few complicated cases, most guard-

---

during his life. Thus the trust must be administered before the donor dies. Where there are minor or incompetent heirs involved, a Supreme Court justice will appoint special guardians to protect their interests.

[22] Judges practice nepotism quite shamelessly in awarding courthouse patronage. After rewarding his county leader Moses Weinstein with three guardianships totaling $13,000, along with several to Mr. Weinstein's son, Jonathan, Queens Surrogate John T. Clancy turned toward judges' relatives as likely recipients of court patronage, bestowing guardianships on: Myron Beldock, son of Appellate Division Presiding Justice Beldock, and Francis Murtagh, brother of Supreme Court Justice Murtagh.

ianships involve very little work—considering the fees allowed for them. An attorney from Brooklyn admitted how minimal was the work actually demanded by guardianships:

"I was put on the middle list when I became active in the Liberal Party. I got four or five appointments a year in the mail. It took me an hour or so to go to the Court House, look at the will, then write a two-page report. This went on for five years and my fees ranged from $50 to $250 a case." [23]

The system conspires to keep surrogate fees high, despite the unfair cost to the estate, on the assumption that, after all, it only amounts to a tax on the rich for the benefit of the party and its faithful volunteers. Judge Dorothy Kenyon told of charging $300 for some surrogate work she had done as a young attorney, after which she was called by the Clerk of the Surrogate Court who berated her in a shocked tone: "Why didn't you call us first? You should have charged $3,000." Judge Kenyon added that she was given this piece of surrogate patronage as a reward for her help in writing a bill subsequently passed by the New York State Legislature.

And why not, party advocates ask? Workers put in hours, if not years, of service to the party with no immediate tangible rewards. No doubt, it constitutes a political pay-off, but unlike an illegal political pay-off of the tin-box variety, surrogate patronage is visible, a matter of public record, and the service for which the payment is rendered stands clearly within the confines of the law. New York newspaper columnist Murray Kempton quotes a young Brooklyn lawyer who does legal work for his party during its primaries and who justifies this view:

"I've been working hard for Stanley Steingut, so it's

[23] *The New York Times*, July 5, 1966, p. 1.

only right I got some specials [special guardianships].
They used to be little stinkers, $75 or $100, but now I'm
getting some dillies. I just got one on a $140,000 trust
. . . and my fee's going to be $5,000. Well, who's gonna
pay for my time in politics? What's wrong with my getting specials?" [24]

Although the best publicized (thanks to Section
35a of the Judiciary Act), surrogate patronage is only one
of many varieties of courthouse patronage available to
party leaders and party workers. On the federal level, politicians high in the ranks of the party get refereeships and
trusteeships in bankruptcy cases,[25] where fees can run
even higher than they do in probate court. Judge
Charles Metzner of the U.S. District Court, appointed
Herman Stichman, Governor Rockefeller's former Commissioner of Investigation, trustee in the case involving
the Hudson-Manhattan tubes, for which he received a fee
of $445,000 for seven years' work. The total amount of
legal fees paid out throughout the bankruptcy proceed-
ings amounted to about two million dollars. Democratic
national committeeman Edwin Weisl, Sr., Lyndon Johnson's chief party liaison man in New York, was awarded
a fee in the neighborhood of $250,000 as referee of the
Shubert estate. Mr. Weisl reported that he worked over

[24] *New York Post*, February 4, 1969.

[25] *Referee*—"A person to whom a cause pending in court is referred
by the court, to take testimony, hear the parties, and report thereon
to the court." Referees may also receive "references," "the act of sending a cause pending in court to a referee for his examination and decision." The "receivership" is also considered very good courthouse
patronage, bringing substantial fees to the beneficiaries of this kind
of legal business. A *receiver* is "an indifferent person . . . appointed
by the court to receive and preserve the property or fund in litigation,
and receive its rents, issues, and profits, and apply or dispose of them
at the direction of the court when it does not seem reasonable that
either party should hold them." Definitions from Black's *Law Dictionary*.

ten years on this case involving the well-known New York theater-owning family.

Referees, in turn, can dispense patronage in deciding where the assets of bankrupt estates are banked, according to former U.S. Attorney Robert Morgenthau. The banks chosen may be run by personal friends of the judge or of the referee, or they may be run by campaign contributors. Referees are often bound by the politicians who originally bestowed the refereeship on them, resulting in clear-cut conflicts of interest. Morgenthau recounted a case in which a union contacted him to investigate the peculiar behavior of the referee appointed in the bankruptcy proceeding against their employer. Interested in keeping its company solvent so its members would not lose their jobs, the union claimed it had evidence proving that the referee had not accepted the offer of the highest bidder. The result of the preliminary investigations, according to Morgenthau, showed that "Herbie [the referee] had a contract," meaning that the referee had made a deal with an unknown party deliberately to stall the case in order to force the company to go into bankruptcy.

In some cases, where awarding the refereeship is discretionary, that is, when the judge decides if there will be a referee at all, judges will appoint referees in order to cut down their own work load, as well as to increase the patronage available to them. As chairman of the trust committee of the Association of the Bar of the City of New York, Harold Klipstein complained to Surrogate Ed Silver about using 54 referees within a six-month period, compared with a total of two referees appointed by all the other surrogates in the state in the same time span. Klipstein charged that not only did these refereeships cost the estates more money, but the public was also being deprived of its constitutional right to have a judge, not a referee, try the cases.

Judicial patronage is no exception to the rule that the best patronage is subtle, hidden from public view, and protected from the difficulties that follow from public awareness. Almost impossible even to research, courthouse patronage (especially in the areas of refereeships and receiverships) remains so covert that its value as political gifts is unquestionably priceless. When rewards become opened to controversy, their value as political favors inevitably declines.

Surrogate Court patronage would still be tucked safely away in the far reaches of obscurity had it not turned out to be the issue on which the late Senator Robert F. Kennedy seized in his attempt to establish hegemony over New York's fractious Democratic Party. With remarkably keen insight and La Guardia's experience in mind, Kennedy knew that if he could deprive the party of its most prolific area of rewards—surrogate patronage —he would stand a better chance of exercising his own control over the party.

Presenting as his candidate for surrogate a colorless but widely respected state Supreme Court justice named Samuel Silverman (connected to the Reform Democrats through his previous law partner, former Tammany leader Edward Costikyan), Kennedy took on the organization's candidate, Arthur Klein, in a highly publicized primary fight geared to purge the party machine and to purify the Surrogate Court. After a dramatic campaign during which surrogate practices were bared repeatedly before the public, 27 percent of the city's enrolled Democrats—considered a high percentage for a party primary—turned out to elect Silverman judge of the Surrogate Court. Throughout the campaign, Kennedy, who appeared constantly at Silverman's side, monopolized most of the speeches and took full charge of the campaign. On primary night, everyone regarded the victory as Kennedy's victory over the bosses; and the public, who had hardly heard from Silverman before his acceptance speech that night, never heard from him again as the candidate settled comfortably into his forthcoming judgeship. Interviewed three years later about probate patronage, Surrogate Silverman declined to describe present conditions, much less comment on the lack of reform which followed the platform electing him.

Senator Kennedy won the battle, but lost the war. His attempts to reform the surrogate system failed when he discovered, as La Guardia had, how deeply surrogate patronage pervaded the system. He learned how intensely party leaders coveted its rewards, and how they feared the damage to the party that would be created were this patronage taken away. Mistakenly, Kennedy tried to take one area of patronage away from the party without replacing it with another.

Opposed from all quarters, Kennedy's proposals to merge the Surrogate Court with the Supreme Court and to establish a State Office of Public Guardian were flatly rejected by lawmakers offended by the senator's argument that surrogate patronage sustained "the worst elements in our political parties." Countering Kennedy's attacks before the Joint Legislative Committee on Court Reorganization investigating surrogate practices at the New York State Constitutional Convention in 1967, Judge Silver (former Surrogate of Brooklyn) defended the system: "Activity in politics is no indication of lack of ability or integrity, and as examples of that I give you the Junior Senator of our state, Robert F. Kennedy, and Judge Silverman." Silver added that in only 10 to 15 percent of estates were special guardians appointed, and that of the $350 million which flowed through the New York State Estate Office, the percentage of guardians' fees only came to .0006% of that figure. Surrogate Joseph Cox added to

Silver's testimony defending surrogate patronage, stating proudly that he had never had a guardianship modified by a higher court. Intended as a defense of the system, Judge Cox's testimony instead provided an interesting illustration of how firmly Surrogate Court practices were reinforced up and down the judicial ladder.[26]

Even the bar associations, usually in the vanguard of judicial reform, attacked Kennedy's proposal for a salaried public guardian, unwilling to allow surrogate patronage to be eliminated, although they might disapprove of the way in which it was dispensed. Charles Chrisman, of the Committee for Modern Courts, told how his committee, together with the League of Women Voters, had tried to abolish the surrogate system: "We got nowhere. We couldn't even research the issue before the records were made public by law. The system is just too tight, and the rewards are just too plentiful for the party to give up." Today, although surrogate patronage has been brought into the open, one can safely conclude that its value as patronage has declined only slightly. For despite periodic attempts by newspapers such as the *New York Post* to air the issue, too many groups and too many political leaders are co-opted into the system to effect real reforms.

[26] And the legislative ladder. Four out of the seven members of the legislative committee charged with investigating surrogate patronage were linked to Brooklyn and Manhattan surrogate patronage appointments. Committee chairman Henry Ughetta's brother had received a guardianship; Assemblyman Oreste Maresca had himself handled four cases which he received from Judge Cox; Judge Silver had awarded a $116,000 estate to State Senator Jerome Bloom; and Senator Sam Greenberg held three estates totaling $647,000. Even Assembly Speaker Anthony Travia, who had called for the investigation, had received appointments in the past.

❡ Judicial Patronage at the Federal Level

After both senators from Georgia had failed to get President Roosevelt to appoint a federal judge from their state, Jim Gillis went to Washington to see what he could do. Gillis, the President's chief patronage dispenser in Georgia, went straight to Roosevelt who told him to "send the man's name [Gillis' choice for a federal judgeship] to the Justice Department." As Gillis tells it: "I sent his name to the Justice Department and after four days there was no response. So I called them [the Justice Department] and said: 'Looka here. I'm the patronage dispenser in Georgia.' It was clear I just wasn't their kind. So I called Roosevelt again and got the appointment."

In his informal role as regional patronage dispenser, Gillis' clout with the President surpassed that of even the highest elected officials of his state. Gillis alone was responsible for carrying the only county in Georgia that went for Roosevelt in 1936, and he was not about to let the President forget that, especially when it came time to parcel out federal judgeships. Men like Gillis are not used to losing judgeships or anything else. Explained Gillis: "You don't go into the ring with someone like Cassius Clay. You go in with someone you can beat."

No one knows how often politicans like Gillis can circumvent custom and the Justice Department to engineer the appointment of their personal candidates. Traditionally, the Senate serves more often as the visible marketplace for bartering judgeships. "Everybody in the world makes recommendations to Johnson, then they [the senators] eventually negotiate it out after terrific squabbles," reported M. Albert Figinski, counsel for the Senate Subcommittee for the Improvement of Judicial Machinery, describing the process of judicial selection in the

Johnson era. "Usually the appointments are not too bad," he added, "since the senators know the appointments will reflect on them."

While the Constitution gives the President formal power to appoint federal judges, with the advice and consent of the Senate, the custom of senatorial courtesy has assigned the real patronage power to the individual senators working in concert with their colleagues. With the help of their local bar associations and party chairmen, the senators decide on candidates, and then present their selections to the President, who abides by their choice and presents the nomination as if it were his own—of course, after the candidates have already been screened and approved by the elaborate machinery of the Justice Department and the Senate. What this means is that if senators from the President's party nominate a candidate, the rest of the Senate will approve their choice, unless the organized resistance to the nominee becomes too embarrassing to carry through the nomination. With federal judicial selection decentralized in this way, the President's power of initiative extends only to federal courts within the District of Columbia, including the Supreme Court. More informally, the President can always exercise the option of influencing the senators' choices. Negotiating for the President vis-à-vis the Senate, the Justice Department screens candidates, and through the Attorney General and Deputy Attorney General in charge of judicial screening, attempts to dissuade the senators from appointments they regard as unsuitable, before the nominations are made public.

Often held up as the model appointive plan, federal judicial patronage ironically remains as blatantly political as judicial selection on the local level. Beginning with the President and continuing on to the senators, the partisan pressures for judicial patronage intensify to the point "that few presidents can completely withstand." [27] When President Kennedy assumed office in 1961, the federal bench was almost evenly divided between Republicans and Democrats, and there was considerable pressure on him from bar groups and Republicans to preserve the balance. Counterbalanced against these pressures was the fact that the Democrats had been out of the White House for eight years, two-thirds of the Senate was Democratic, and the Democratic congressional leadership had gambled in the 86th Congress and had not passed a new judgeship bill pending the outcome of the 1960 presidential election. Bending to these partisan pressures, President Kennedy appointed 84 Democrats out of his first 85 judicial appointments, and the 85th was a member of the New York State Liberal Party—at that time a close ally of the Democratic Party. Kennedy's 100 percent patronage average was atypical; usually the President appoints about 92 percent [28] of the judges from his own party.[29]

Also under heavy pressure, senators use their power to fill judicial vacancies in widely varying ways, according to Ernest Friesen, administrative director for the federal

[27] Joel B. Grossman, *Lawyers and Judges: The ABA and the Politics of Judicial Selection* (New York: John Wiley & Sons, 1965), p. 34.

[28] To the Court of Appeals and to the district courts. Supreme Court appointments, except in President Nixon's case, are not as obviously partisan.

[29] Professor Rita Cooley points out that despite President Eisenhower's promises of divorcing the federal selection process from patronage politics (she quotes Republican National Chairman Leonard Hall: "Federal judges are not a political patronage"), Eisenhower's nominations were "made largely from members of his own political party, a notable exception being his appointment of Mr. Justice Brennan, a Democrat, to the Supreme Court. It is extremely unlikely that any President can do otherwise to any appreciable extent." See Rita W. Cooley, "Judicial Appointments in the Eisenhower Administration (January 1952—January 1958)," *Social Science*, Vol. 34, No. 1, January 1959, pp. 10–14.

court system. Many senators, who find judicial patronage an embarrassment and a bother, approach the Justice Department privately and ask that they remove the onus by picking the judges for them. This leaves immense discretionary patronage power in the hands of the Attorney General, who is by tradition a political arm of the President. Other senators tell the Attorney General what candidates they have chosen, but request that he publicize that the initiative for the appointment came from the Justice Department, not from them. While reluctant to give up their power over judicial selection, these senators nevertheless fear that any hint of patronage might harm their carefully cultivated statesmanlike image. In the last category are senators who pick one man and tell the Attorney General and the President: "That's the one I want." When senators are very close to the President, this method works very efficiently, except in cases of notoriously poor candidates.

Senatorial courtesy ranges widely beyond judgeships to the fertile field of appointing U.S. attorneys and U.S. marshals. Top marshals' jobs pay about $15,000 to $16,000; U.S. attorneys' jobs vary from as high as $38,000 (in Washington, D.C., and New York) to $36,000 (in Chicago and Los Angeles), down to $25,000 for smaller districts.[30]

Jobs in the U.S. attorney's office represent very important patronage for party leaders who are willing to risk the replacement of highly qualified men in order to use the posts for their own party faithful. Shortly after the Nixon

[30] Technically under the jurisdiction of the Justice Department, U.S. attorneys and marshals serve only at the pleasure of the President. Appointed by him with the consent of the Senate, they serve for four-year terms as law enforcement arms of the Justice Department. There are 185 U.S. attorneys and marshals appointed for each of the 93 judicial districts in the country. Each district has its own U.S. attorney and U.S. marshal except for the Virgin Islands, which has no marshal.

administration took office, New York's Senators Javits and Goodell reportedly joined with the Republican State Committee in seeking to replace Robert M. Morgenthau, U.S. Attorney for the Southern District of New York, with Paul Curran, chairman of the New York State Investigation Committee and son of the late Thomas Curran, former Republican leader of New York. A Democratic appointee, Mr. Morgenthau is the son of the late Henry Morgenthau, Secretary of the Treasury under President Franklin D. Roosevelt.

Flaunting the patronage traditions by which he himself was appointed, Morgenthau refused to tender his resignation along with the country's 92 other U.S. attorneys when the Nixon administration took office. Armed with an excellent reputation for enforcing the law with scrupulous impartiality,[31] Morgenthau was backed in his actions by many powerful forces in the city, including *The New York Times*, whose editorial writers called the threatened replacement of Morgenthau "an ill-advised mixing of politics with law enforcement." Finally, after months of privately pressuring Morgenthau to step down, Attorney General John Mitchell publicly requested his resignation in order to appoint Whitney North Seymour, Jr., a Republican with impeccable credentials within the judicial reform establishment, in his stead. In addition to Morgenthau's job, Mitchell anxiously awaited the opportunity of dispensing the 70-odd jobs of "assistant attorney" within Morgenthau's district, also under the patronage wing of the Attorney General. By this time, the two Republican senators were forced to come out publicly against patronage and request that Morgenthau be allowed to complete

[31] Morgenthau was best known for uncovering graft in New York's Democratic as well as Republican machines, for prosecuting financiers with illegal Swiss bank accounts, and for his continuing war against organized crime.

his projects; but neither senator—and after all they, too, have patronage obligations to the party—pursued his support of Morgenthau with much vigor. In the end, Morgenthau resigned—he had made his point—on the grounds that he could not operate effectively as U.S. attorney without the backing of the Justice Department.

In practice a long, drawn-out procedure, senatorial courtesy gives its participants ample time and unlimited opportunities in which to trade judgeships (marshals, U.S. attorneys, etc.) for other favors in the legislative arena. If both senators from a state come from the opposite party, the President may give the patronage power to the leading congressman in the state, even if the governor's party affiliation is the same as the President's. In this way, senatorial courtesy serves a positive legislative function, binding the congressman to the President with the best political tape available: patronage. Giving a congressman judicial patronage allows the President another outlet for favors on which he can later capitalize when he needs the congressman's vote on a key bill, or the congressman's support in a re-election bid. In a state with absolutely no elected officials from the President's party, the President will go to the ranking committeeman, rather than relinquish his precious judicial patronage power to the opposition. This explains why President Nixon, acting through Attorney General Mitchell, was willing to risk severe criticism in the Morgenthau case when confronted with the loss of some judicial patronage.

In the Senate, when the nomination comes to the decision stage—and this is where the term "courtesy" originated—a blue slip is sent to both the senator of the state sponsoring the nomination and to the members of the Senate Judiciary Committee telling them when a hearing on the candidate will be held. Under the old rules, if the blue slip was not sent back, and the senator came from the same party as the head of the Judiciary Committee (currently Senator James Eastland of Mississippi), then the hearing was never held, and the candidate was considered to have been rejected. In reality, this virtually gave the senators a veto power over judicial candidates. Senator William Proxmire of Wisconsin described this as the "personally obnoxious" theme of judicial selection: if the senator found the judicial nominee "personally obnoxious," and stated this fact, the nominee would be withdrawn with no further questions asked. If the senator came from the opposing party, then a second blue slip was sent and if this was not returned, then the hearing would be held and the candidate appointed in spite of the opposing senator's tacit objection. Today, senatorial courtesy may —depending on the personal power of the senator involved—extend across party lines; and if a senator from the opposing party fails to send back his blue slip, the candidate may also be considered rejected.

When a senator is influential, his power extends to judicial appointments, no matter what party he represents. Republican Hugh Scott, for example, failed to send back his blue slip on the promotion of Judge Francis L. Van Dusen from the district to the circuit court until he received assurances that a Republican would be appointed to the district court. Scott, a key member of the Judiciary Committee, could not have held up this appointment without the courtesy of Senator Eastland. Eastland also honored Senator George Murphy's refusal to return his blue slip on Cecil Poole, a Negro from California. Robert Kennedy was known to have held up judicial appointments in order to consolidate his bargaining power over New York's divided Democrats. He knew that if he appointed his quota of judges early he would lose potential power within the party. Senator Jacob Javits agreed not to block the appointment of Anthony Travia, Democratic Speaker of the New York State Legislature, whose legal skills he questioned, in exchange for the appointment of a Republican "quality" judge, Orrin Judd.

Stalling judicial appointments for political purposes often occurs when the senators from one state come from opposing parties. Mr. Figinski estimated that "the Eastern District of Pennsylvania has lost twenty judicial years due to squabbling over who is to appoint the judges between the state's two Senators who could not agree on candidates." Figinski warned that the delay in appointing judges exacerbated the already serious problem of court congestion, particularly when these battles are waged in districts (such as the Eastern District of Pennsylvania) afflicted with overcrowded court calendars. "The Eastern District of Pennsylvania," he complained, is the "second worst district in the country."

The same problem occurred in filling vacancies in the District of Columbia. Senator Joseph D. Tydings of Maryland called on the President to solve the emergency created there, explaining how seriously court delay impeded the fair administration of justice: "There was a twelve-month delay in filling the last vacancy on the District bench . . . such lengthy delay impedes the administration of justice. Such delay impairs the recollection, and therefore the value of witnesses. Such delay forces innocent persons to suffer substantial and unnecessary distress while awaiting trial. Such delay increases the chance that a guilty person will profit from tardy court processes and, perhaps, commit additional offenses while awaiting trial."

Senators from the same party but from different wings of the party sometimes clash over judicial patronage. Choosing a U.S. attorney from the Chicago area pitted the late Senate Republican leader Everett Dirksen and freshman Senator Charles Percy against each other in an Illinois version of David and Goliath. Declaring Dirksen's choice, a man named John J. Bickley, Jr., "personally obnoxious" to him, Percy threatened to invoke the tradition of senatorial courtesy to block the appointment. Challenging Everett Dirksen, then the ranking Republican on the Judiciary Committee, took great courage on Percy's part. Not only was Dirksen considered the most powerful Republican on Capitol Hill, but he was known to have more patronage power than any other Republican regarding judicial appointments in the five courts in the District of Columbia. In addition, Dirksen controlled a large quota of appointments to the numerous quasi-judicial boards throughout Washington, patronage technically allocated to the executive branch but parceled out judiciously to cooperative legislators. Dirksen men populated such boards as the Interstate Commerce Commission, the Federal Trade Commission, the Federal Communications Commission, and the Subversive Activities Control Board, all agencies of government with tremendous patronage power in their own right. Dirksen's influence over judicial and quasi-judicial appointments proved significantly how closely federal judicial patronage correlates with legislative power and influence.

In contrast to Dirksen, many senators have very little judicial patronage. Senators from states like South Dakota or Rhode Island, whose populations warrant only two district judgeships apiece, must wait a long time before exercising their patronage prerogatives; and even in larger states, judgeships are few and far between. Senator William Proxmire of Wisconsin reported that he and Senator Gaylord Nelson were able to appoint only three federal judges within five years in Wisconsin. In contrast, states like California, with 27 district judges, and New York, with 33 district judges, have kept their patronage dispensers much busier.

States without exclusive judgeships of their own on

the Courts of Appeals are theoretically supposed to rotate when a vacancy occurs, but in practice political factors more often determine which state chooses the judge, according to the discretion of the President. When Judge Vogel stepped down, for example, North Dakota's Senator Quentin Burdick got the appointment even though it was South Dakota's turn to appoint a judge on the eighth circuit. The reason: Senator George McGovern from South Dakota had thrown his support behind Robert Kennedy's bid for the presidential nomination before President Johnson, a political enemy of Senator Kennedy's, had withdrawn from the presidential race.

Other than Supreme Court appointments, presidential judicial patronage gets little publicity, and is often used for necessary, crony-type patronage. (The President appoints judges to the five courts in the District of Columbia plus the Court of General Sessions.) Lacking visibility, "White House patronage in these courts is much less responsible than senatorial," said one Justice Department official. "Since the senators know the appointments will reflect on them, usually they're not too bad. It's better to have a senator worrying than the President."

Reminiscent of President Adams' attempt to rush through the appointment of the Midnight Judges [32] immediately before he left office, President Johnson appointed two of his political cronies to federal judgeships several months before he was due to leave the presidency:

[32] Resulting in the famous case of *Marbury v. Madison*, 1 CR. 137 (1803). Marbury sued Madison, Jefferson's Secretary of State, for his commission authorizing his judgeship which Madison had failed to deliver along with the remainder of the commissions belonging to the Midnight Judges—an early attempt to eliminate some of the patronage of the previous administration. Marbury won his lawsuit and claimed his judgeship, although the case is best remembered for Chief Justice John Marshall's doctrine of "judicial review," incorporated in the decision.

Harold Barefoot Sanders, Jr., a close associate and legislative counsel to Johnson, named to be a judge in the U.S.
Court of Appeals for the District of Columbia; and David
Bress, a political protégé of Associate Justice Abe Fortas,
former counsel for Bobby Baker, and U.S. Attorney for
the District of Columbia, chosen for federal district judge.
Rebelling against these lame-duck appointments, the Senate neglected to act on them, and as expected, after Nixon
was elected, he withdrew all of Johnson's appointments
(including Bress and Sanders) not yet confirmed by the
Senate.

Considering the power over life and liberty which
the state bestows on judges, the courtesy system affords
too many opportunities for senators, bowed under by political obligations, to exercise poor judgment. A striking
example of this tendency was Senator Edward Kennedy's
effort to nominate Francis X. Morrissey, an old political
helpmate of his family's, to a federal judgeship. All the
evidence pointed to Morrissey's poor reputation both as a
lawyer and as a judge, a clear case in which the Kennedys'
family alliances superseded their judgment. In a rare mo-
ment of rebellion, senatorial courtesy acted in concert
against a senator when the Senate refused to confirm the
appointment, forcing Kennedy to withdraw Morrissey's
nomination.

The extent to which the President controls coveted
appointments to the Senate Judiciary Committee affects
his influence over judicial patronage, for he can prevent
these committee assignments from going to senators who
may challenge his judicial influence, and direct them
instead to his supporters. Texas Senator Ralph Yarborough, testifying before the Rules and Administration
Committee's investigation of the Bobby Baker case, reported that he had unsuccessfully sought a seat on the
Judiciary Committee in 1961, and later learned that Baker,

Johnson's right-hand man in the Senate, had explained to friends: "We couldn't afford to let Yarborough have that seat. He would then be in a position to control Texas' judicial patronage, or would be in a position to prevent Lyndon from controlling it."

Ultimately the party, its judgment tempered by interest groups, decides who gets the judgeships, regardless of who appears to have the power of initiation. Despite Eisenhower's attempts to purify the system of judicial selection, he too often relied on the system of "party clearance" before appointing judges. In 1959, after the Ohio Republican patronage committee (which included the state's Republican congressional delegation and the Republican state party leaders) decided to back District Judge Cecil for a vacancy on the Court of Appeals for the 6th Circuit, the Eisenhower administration promptly nominated him for an appointment.[33]

Initiative often comes from the judges themselves, who start the ball rolling for their own promotions and appointments. Judge Irving Kaufman actively campaigned for his position on the Court of Appeals for the 2nd Circuit by getting Senators Styles Bridges and Estes Kefauver to lobby for him.[34]

Exercising a quiet influence on judicial appointments, the Justice Department acts as a pivotal force balancing the senators, the President, and the American Bar Association. Aided by F.B.I. files, the Justice Department checks out judicial appointments, often determining by its "judicious" use of confidential information the final choice from among several candidates. F.B.I. files have armed

[33] The *Cincinnati Enquirer*, January 13, 1959, cited in Sheldon Goldman, *Politics, Judges and the Administration of Justice* (Ph.D. dissertation, Harvard University, 1965).

[34] Goldman, *op. cit.*

judicial selection officials in the Justice Department with information regarding illicit affairs, marginal business ventures, and alcoholism on the part of prospective candidates. When the sponsoring senator is confronted with damaging information of this kind—even though the poor candidate is never given the opportunity to refute the charges—the senator usually withdraws the candidate's name from consideration, regardless of the patronage obligations involved. Often, the Justice Department can play off senators against each other in order to get the best man appointed to the bench. Senators Lausche and Young, reported one official from the Justice Department, submitted separate lists of unacceptable candidates. Playing them off against each other, the Justice Department encouraged them to submit better lists, privately encouraging each man that his chances to prevail would increase proportionately with the quality of the candidates he proposed.

Well aware of the political factors at play, Justice Department officials must tread carefully if they wish to have an impact on improving the quality of judges selected for the federal bench. Often bound, however, by the patronage obligations of the Attorney General, they can become a political force themselves, pressuring for judgeships instead of mediating the patronage battles they are called upon to solve.

❪ *Judging the Judges:*
Mutations of Judicial Selection

Deluded by the belief that politics on the federal level has been extracted from judicial selection, judicial-reform groups in many areas of the country have succeeded in wresting judicial patronage away from the local party organizations, and with their new power have changed the character of judicial selection from an emphasis on elective plans toward appointive selection procedures. The new appointive plans, the most common being the Missouri Plan, claim to replace old patronage practices with "merit selection of judges"—where the qualifications of judicial candidates are weighed on the basis of juridical strengths, rather than partisan obligations and prior political service to the local party organization.

Looking toward federal selection processes as their model, organized foes of party selection argue that contrary to the appearance of appointive plans, democracy still plays a vital role in the plans of merit selection. For although candidates are initially "approved" (really selected) by a supposedly neutral appointing authority, the voters are given the option of ratifying the candidates in a general election. In this way, according to the plan's proponents, plans like the Missouri Plan give the public better judges by eliminating the worst evils of patronage and party in the same way that the federal selection process—also a two-step appointive and ratification procedure—has produced a reputedly higher level of federal court judges.

Merit-selection plans did not really catch on in this country as viable forms of judicial selection until the 1960s, when they became controversial issues in many states. Over half the states have succeeded in enacting some variation of the merit plan, although over 80 percent of the state judicial positions still remain elective. In some states, such as Missouri, where the plan originated, it only operates in several areas of the state (Kansas City and St. Louis), while other states have adopted the plan for the entire state.[35] In thirteen states, some or all major

[35] The first plan (known as the Kales plan after Albert M. Kales) was formulated in 1913. Not until 1934 was the Kales plan adopted

trial and appellate court judges are appointed under some form of the merit plan. In New York City and Puerto Rico, nominating commissions have been instituted voluntarily, working with uneven results. In nine states, some or all major trial and appellate court judges are appointed by the governor with confirmation by a legislative or other body. In four states, some or all major trial and appellate court judges are appointed by the legislature. Although formal provision is made in 34 states for election of some or all major trial and appellate court judges, in practice a full 50 percent of the judges in these states first come to the bench through appointment from the governor to fill a vacancy.

Prepared and pressured through the legislature by the organized bar of Missouri, the Missouri Plan (although categorized as an appointive plan) tries very hard to combine the best features of election and selection, by providing for a carefully drawn-up commission to nominate the judges, after which the commission's choices are

---

by any state—California adopted a plan, differing substantially from the Kales plan but influenced by it, which set up a nominating body for judicial selection. Progress was slow, and in 1940 the Missouri Plan was adopted in Kansas City and St. Louis, since these two cities were the real trouble spots of the state with respect to selecting judges. After 1950, the plan became increasingly popular; in 1950, Alabama adopted a nominating commission for filling judicial vacancies; in 1956, Alaska's state constitutional convention adopted the merit plan; in 1958, Kansas adopted a plan similar to the Missouri Plan; in 1962 Iowa and Nebraska joined the trend, providing appointive-elective selection of judges of the supreme and major state trial courts; in 1963, the voters of Dade County, Florida (which encompasses the Miami area) adopted a merit plan for judges of their Metropolitan Court; in 1965, Utah instituted a merit plan for judges of the county courts, followed by the voters of Denver who adopted the plan for their city courts; in 1966, the voters of Kansas City extended the plan to municipal court judges; and in Vermont the voters approved a nominating-commission feature for superior- and district-court judges.

ratified (or rejected) by the voters at the polls.[36] Stressing its apolitical nature, Chief Justice Laurance M. Hyde, of the Supreme Court of Missouri, described the plan:

> "It is a plan for the maintenance of a thoroughly qualified and independent judiciary by taking the selection and tenure of judges out of politics. Selection is by appointment by the Governor, but from a list of three nominees named by a commission composed of both lawyers and laymen, who do not hold any public office or any official position in a political party. The Governor's appointment must be confirmed by a vote of the people at the next general election held after the appointed judge has served twelve months in office."

Judicial patronage does not hold a monopoly on the patronage market, yet reform has progressed in the judicial arena much faster than it has elsewhere, perhaps encouraged by the increasing level of public awareness. Far more visible than other forms of patronage, judicial patronage has led many substantial critics to attack judicial selection procedures for producing poor judges, particularly on the local level. "The problem is not corrupt judges," according to former Attorney General Herbert Brownell, but "mediocre judges . . . the gray mice of the legal establishment" that cause justice to suffer because "we are not getting the best qualified lawyers as judges." "Unfortunately," continued Brownell, "it is the vast number of 'small people' in our courts whom the mediocre judge hurts the most. Well-to-do clients have able law-

---

[36] The commission itself, with jurisdiction over the appellate courts (Supreme Court and three Courts of Appeals) has seven members, and is chaired by the Chief Justice of the Supreme Court. Three members of the commission are attorneys who are elected by the bar, one from each Court of Appeals district. Three lay members of the commission are appointed by the governor, each being a resident of the Court of Appeals district which he represents. The seventh member is the chairman.

yers to protect their interests. If things go wrong they can afford to appeal and get things set straight. For the client of modest means, any lawsuit is a financial hazard; he cannot afford to have things go wrong through the mistakes of an incompetent judge. This is particularly true in courts that deal with intimate family problems and in the criminal courts, where life or liberty is at stake."

The crisis over judicial mediocrity was expanded recently by the newly developed willingness of the media to expose abuses common to local courtrooms but for some reason previously relegated to private conversations among lawyers, court buffs, and other participants in the area of criminal justice. *The Wall Street Journal* recounted two incidents to illustrate the low caliber of Criminal Court judges. One article described how Judge Howard Gleidman, reluctant to try a defendant without counsel, took over the defense himself. After questioning the policeman, he turned and addressed the bench himself: "Defense makes a motion that the charge be dismissed on grounds of insufficient evidence." He then replied to himself: "Motion granted, charge dismissed." The other story quoted Judge Manuel Gomez addressing a tardy defendant: "Is this the idiot that's supposed to be in this case?" [37]

Blaming the abuses inherent in the patronage system for the low caliber of judges, the President's Commission on Law Enforcement and Administration of Justice gave final legitimacy to the advocates of merit selection: "The true judgemakers are the leaders of the dominant party. . . . Intricate bargaining may evolve and balances must be struck to reward the party's principal financial supporters or those who have labored for the party organization. All too frequently in this bargaining process, scant attention is given to the abilities of the proposed candidates.

[37] *The Wall Street Journal*, December 7, 1967, p. 1.

. . . In sum, merit-selection plans provide a more rational procedure for selecting judges than popular election alone." [38]

What advocates of judicial reform really fear is the great potential for conflict of interest built into the system of party-created judges. Thinking foremost of the party's security and maintenance of power, party leaders urge the appointment of judges who will continue to help the party even after they have reached the bench. What this means is that *some* judges continue to be influenced, if not dominated, by the men to whom they owe their good fortune. Incidents occur again and again which corroborate the dangerous potential for conflicts of interest. One former municipal court judge told how he had received a number of letters from district leaders "telling me a certain case was coming up." After making a habit of sending these letters to the district attorney (who did not act on them), the good judge was coincidentally not renominated by his party when his name came up for re-election! Sayre and Kaufman point out that in New York, judicial conflicts of interest appear quite clearly after studying the interpretations of election laws written by local judges. [39] In the interest of maintaining the party's organizational security, judges too often tend to remove insurgent groups from the ballot by declaring their nominating petitions invalid. Although the situation of judicial conflict of interest—as related to the party [40]—has not reached scandalous proportions, the potential and the tendency remain,

[38] President's Commission on Law Enforcement and Administration of Justice, *Task Force Report: The Courts* (Washington, D.C.: U.S. Government Printing Office, 1967), pp. 66–68.

[39] Sayre and Kaufman, *op. cit.*, Chapter 14.

[40] In 1969, following the Fortas controversy (Justice Abe Fortas was forced to resign his seat on the Supreme Court after disclosures that he had received excessively high lecture fees from a foundation under

leading one advocate of judicial reform to observe: "In New York, the reason most lawyers want juries is to make sure there is no fix."

❑ *The Flaw in Appointing Judges*

Whether judges have arrived on the bench through merit or elective procedures, in the last analysis someone has to pick who runs, who is appointed, and ultimately who will be ratified by the voters. Although reformers have succeeded in publicly identifying patronage solely with partisan activity, it seems reasonable to assume that nominating commissions claiming nonpartisanship have patronage power at least equal to those party organizations which have succeeded in retaining control over judicial nominations. In fact, nominating commissions probably have greater patronage power since their reform image helps them to avoid the kind of criticism which the party continually withstands. After all, how can anyone reform what has already been reformed; or challenge a system which claims to be based on "merit" alone? Luckily for them, the challengers chose all the right labels—"reform," "merit," "quality judges"—leaving their adversaries stripped of ideological ammunition.

On the surface, the contest over differing methods of judicial selection pits the philosophical aspects of each issue against each other, while the facts show a clear-cut, old-fashioned power struggle emerging between local party organizations and organized interest groups dominated by regional bar associations, both sides wrestling over the fruits of judicial patronage. Logically, there is no

---

federal indictment), many groups began studying the conflicts of interest which might possibly derive from ways in which judges made extra income—such as lecture fees.

really basic difference between appointing and electing judges; in fact, procedurally, the systems look identical when scrutinized closely. With elected judges, for example, the party decides in caucus who will be nominated in the same way that a small group of seven men working on the Missouri Plan commission choose a slate of judges which the governor will present to the voters. Except in those few areas where there is really a contest, party-chosen judicial nominees generally receive bipartisan endorsement, rendering their election identical with the ratification procedure set forth by the Missouri Plan. If the voter has no real alternatives—the case in elective and appointive systems—his vote constitutes a rubber stamp, ratifying decisions made long before by a small group of men.

Cognizant of these facts, party leaders have geared the full thrust of their opposition to merit selection on the question of *who* really selects judges, warning the public that if they submit to appointive plans they will be relinquishing their judicial selection power to the local bar associations and their allies, none of whom are accountable to the public in the same way that elected officials must respond to public opinion. Former Tammany leader Edward Costikyan, by far the most articulate spokesman for elected judges, warns that political factors operate more strongly within appointive systems than elective ones, adding that the only difference between the two is that "the appointive system tends to place greater weight on prior political service to the appointing authority." [41] Costikyan fears turning the selection process over to elites in the bar associations on the grounds that they would fail to respond as quickly as the party to public needs and demands.

Another common objection voiced against the domi-

---

[41] Edward Costikyan, *Behind Closed Doors: Politics in the Public Interest* (New York: Harcourt, Brace & World, 1966), Part 5.

nation of bar associations in judicial selection is that these groups will invariably ratify a "sitting judge" (a judge already on the bench who is up for promotion) whatever his level of competence, since members of these groups may have to try cases before these judges in the future. Many well-qualified judicial candidates smart under this form of discrimination. One New York State Supreme Court judge in his sixties, who was elected in spite of the local bar association's refusal to endorse him, indignantly described the degrading experience which he suffered when he appeared before the bar association's screening committee: "What were they? Boys, just young boys, judging me!" The judge claimed that the bar association would not lend him its endorsement on the grounds that he was not a "sitting judge." For their part, representatives of the bar contend that, in the selection of judges for the higher courts, legal and political experience do not compensate for the lack of judicial experience. In countries like France, where aspiring judges are apprenticed as young lawyers to sitting judges for a considerable part of their professional lives, this problem does not exist; once judges are appointed from the ranks of these apprentices, the public and the professionals can be sure that they have many years of judicial experience under their belts.

Aaron Broder, president of the New York Trial Lawyers' Association ("the only bar association that doesn't want the bar associations to select the judges") charged that his city's bar associations, dominated by aristocratic Wall Street law firms, discriminated against Jews in their preferences for judicial nominees, mirroring the inevitable discrimination of their own hiring practices. "In New York City," charged Mr. Broder, "bar associations represent WASP power, neglecting the needs of other ethnic groups." The preponderance of lawyers with large corporate practices in control of the bar associations, Broder added, also tended to prejudice these groups against trial lawyers in favor of attorneys involved in their own field of specialization.

To be fair, the Missouri Plan does not hand the bar associations *carte blanche* in selecting the judges; they must share their power with carefully selected laymen representing other interests within the community. Some jurists, however, including former Judge Bernard Botein, argue that the presence of lawyers on nominating commissions inevitably creates a situation in which laymen are overwhelmed by professionals, with the experts gaining almost total control over the selection process. According to Botein, the Missouri Plan leaves the voters without a voice in selecting their judges, and relieves their leaders of the burdens of accountability for appointments: "The Missouri Plan has kept judicial selection out of the best kind of politics—healthy, clean, responsible, competitive politics . . . the commission is not responsible to anyone . . . and cloaks his (the Governor's) responsibility to the electorate."

Ironically, the nominating commission, designed to remove patronage from judicial selection, constitutes an excellent patronage outlet for the political leader entrusted with selecting its members. In New York City, for example, when former Mayor Robert F. Wagner introduced the nominating-commission concept (for judgeships reserved for mayoral patronage), he reserved for himself the power to appoint the panel. The American Judicature Society credits Mayor Lindsay with improving upon the Wagner panel by giving away his own power to name the entire panel. Lindsay still names the minority of the panel, while two appellate-division judges name the majority of the 15-member panel. But he did not wait for the panel's approval before appointing William Booth to the Criminal Court, a political emergency that could not wait for the trappings of good government. The mayor also delegated to the panel the authority to recommend candidates for judicial office, not just to review the qualifications of those candidates already submitted to it as a *fait accompli*—as was the case with the Botein committee. The governors of Pennsylvania and Colorado have utilized similar nominating commissions. In many cases, the nominating commission insulates the governor (or mayor) from his patronage obligations; and while he may completely control the choices made by the nominating commission, its presence gives him a handy excuse for not coming through with his own political pay-offs. He can then tell disappointed judicial candidates: "You were my choice, but they said no."

What the fight over judicial selection shows is that in a small number of states, temporary mergers of interest groups—dominated by lawyers' interest groups—have successfully wrested some judicial patronage power away from the party. No empirical evidence has yet appeared to show that either the appointive or elective plan has produced a higher caliber of judges, or that appointive groups are any less politically motivated than political parties.

On the national level, the American Bar Association won a great patronage victory from the Nixon administration, which agreed at the ABA's 92nd annual convention in August 1969 to abide by its recommendations in refusing to appoint any candidates which the ABA screening committee found unacceptable. Prior to this, the ABA had sought to influence federal judicial selection in the same way that the Justice Department operates, by running its own checks on candidates and rating them within one of four categories: exceptionally well-qualified, well-qualified; qualified; and not qualified. Although the ABA professed to have only a ratification role, it is primarily an interest group, and in this capacity gained considerable power over the initiative in judicial selection, in the same way that its regional counterparts were able to modify local party patronage practices. Bolstered by its sturdy reform image, the ABA rating serves to add good-government-type legitimacy to judicial appointments; and usually both senators and presidents welcome its voluntary service. Although Presidents Eisenhower, Kennedy, and Johnson honored the ABA's recommendations most of the time, they never considered them binding; indeed, President Truman ignored them completely. Presidents have often used the ABA "not-qualified" rating as a convenience, the perfect excuse for refusing to appoint a political hack.

Given so much officially sanctioned power, it is no surprise that the ABA often exceeds its function of ratifying candidates in order to seize the initiative and promote candidates favored by the group's more influential members. For this reason, many critics have emphasized the impropriety of giving a pressure group—even one with the stature of the ABA—such immense power over selecting and vetoing federal judges. Describing his dealings with the ABA, a former assistant to Attorney General Ramsey Clark warned of the occasional improprieties practiced by this organization:

When you deal with the ABA, you have to deal from knowledge. . . . I gave a name to the ABA. They sent it back saying the man wasn't qualified; he had lousy grades in law school. I told them he was Phi Beta Kappa and Order of the Coif; they must have been misinformed. It just so happened that someone on the ABA committee had another candidate whom he wanted appointed and planted a false story. Heads of ABA committees occasionally give false information when they have their own candidates. The Department of Justice must have the capability of knowing as much as the ABA, and this should all be done privately.

❏ *Public Apathy and the Future of Judicial Patronage*

One of the reasons judgeships remain a most fruitful area of political patronage on the federal as well as local levels is that judgeships represent an area of politics least open to public scrutiny. Except for courthouse patronage, no conspiracy keeps judicial politics out of the public arena; but rather, the public just happens to be bored by judges, by judicial contests, and by the whole area of judicial selection.

"The public should be grateful for the party organization since they are so apathetic about politics themselves," said Marshall Korshak, City Treasurer of Chicago. "In Illinois, only 18 percent of the public turned out to vote for judge of the State Supreme Court . . . the public should care more."

A fascinating poll taken by Allen Klots for the Association of the Bar of the City of New York corroborated Mr. Korshak's complaint, revealing that well over 90% of the voters in his sample did not even know which judges they had voted for. Comparing judicial contests in New York City, Buffalo, and Cayuga, the poll recorded that only 1% of the voters in New York City remembered voting for Judge Albert Conway, a distinguished jurist elected to the Court of Appeals, endorsed by both parties; and only 19% could remember at least one judicial candidate. None remembered a candidate for whom they had not voted. In Buffalo, the percentages were higher: 30% remembered at least one name. Demonstrating that there is little difference between rural and urban judicial ignorance, in upstate Cayuga County the figures paralleled New York City: 1% remembered Judge Conway, and 4% remembered the name of one judicial candidate in the race. In all three localities, most of the voters were unable to name the court being contested: 80% of the voters in New York City; 86% in Cayuga; and 89% in Buffalo.

The study proved what it intended to show: that the public was not interested in the courts, much less in court reform. "A person doesn't give a damn until he's belted by them," said Charles Chrisman, whose Committee for Modern Courts is especially interested in public apathy toward judicial reform. Until the public demonstrates more of an interest in the selection of judges, judicial patronage will continue in much the same way it has proceeded before, with few modifications and uncertain results insofar as the quality of judges it has produced. Said Peter M. Brown, former president of the Federal Bar Association of New York, New Jersey, and Connecticut: "A judgeship is a political plum . . . and it's not practical to expect a man who has rung doorbells for 25 years to give up such a plum easily."

5

Patronage Politics in Congress: The Realities of Representative Government

In my thirty years of public office, nobody's ever asked me for a favor.

—Senator Abraham Ribicoff (Democrat—Connecticut)

I have a constant fight with Portland, but I get most of the projects in Seattle because these fellows have to come back to me for money.

—Senator Warren Magnuson (Democrat—Washington, and chairman of the Senate Commerce Committee)

❡ *The System*

"A Congressman has two constituencies," the late Sam Rayburn, Speaker of the House longer than any other man, told freshmen members. "He has his constituents at home, and his colleagues here in the House. To serve his constituents at home, he must also serve his colleagues here in the House." This advice was recently recalled by D. B. Hardeman, Mr. Rayburn's administrative assistant, along with Mr. Sam's admonition that "To get along, you have to go along. Anybody who tries will find a way to go

187

along with his leaders 60–70 percent of the time," the Speaker would say, and thereby obtain for his district the dams, defense contracts, tax advantages, architects' fees, model cities, job patronage, and other government largesse that many members say privately are more crucial to their careers than their voting records.

The Speaker's advice is based on mastery of a legislative system that contrasts sharply with the British system, whose classic tradition of representing the national interest was expounded in Burke's famous letter to his constituents back home in Bristol: "Parliament is not a congress of ambassadors from different and hostile interest . . . but parliament is a deliberative assembly of one nation, with one interest, that of the whole; where not local purposes, not local prejudices, ought to guide, but the general good, resulting from the general reason of the whole. You choose a member indeed; but when you have chosen him, he is not a member for Bristol, but he is a member of Parliament." [1]

At the Constitutional Convention, the Founding Fathers chose not to follow the British system, but instead to elect representatives of designated districts, on the theory that if everyone represented his constituency, together they would represent the best interests of the nation. A congressman thus has the constitutional obligation to promote the economic interests in his district. Subsidies to oilmen, homesteaders, railroaders, airlines, shipping interests, colleges, churches, and publications were all begun to promote the national economy. To settle the West, the government gave homesteaders free land, and railroad magnates virtual freedom from government control, just as today the oil industry benefits from generous subsidies

[1] Speech to the electors of Bristol, November 3, 1774, in *Burke's Politics*, edited by R. J. S. Hoffman and P. Levack (New York: Alfred A. Knopf, 1949), pp. 115–116.

on the grounds that the oil supply must be maintained for reasons of national security.

In the years since the founding of the Republic, the congressional bureaucracy has become so complex that a new member is virtually compelled to rely on his party leadership to become a knowledgeable and effective member. Similarly, it has become increasingly easier with the development of the committee system "to go along with his leaders" with impunity and without the knowledge of the constituents at home, since such a large part of government business is conducted behind closed doors in committee hearing rooms. In 1968, 43 percent of all committee hearings were conducted in secret.[2]

Even when a congressman's actions are public, they are often obscured by House procedure. The House rules are such that omnibus bills are submitted and voted upon, denying the members the opportunity to zero in on particular targets. "Do you know that we were not allowed to have a roll-call vote on whether to deploy the ABM?" asked an incredulous newcomer, Representative Allard K. Lowenstein, a Nassau County (N.Y.) Democrat, "And that on the Vietnam resolution the President wanted pushed because it was so vital to his plan for peace, there were no hearings, and discussion was limited to four hours —which averages out to 30 seconds a member—and there was no way to introduce reductions of dollars without having amendments explained, let alone discussed. If only the

[2] *Congressional Quarterly Almanac*, 1968, pp. 798–799. In the Senate, closed hearings accounted for 46 percent of meetings of the Foreign Relations Committee; 67 percent of the Armed Services Committee; 93 percent of the Senate Rules and Administration; 30 percent of Senate Public Works and 47 percent of Senate Labor and Public Welfare. In the House, closed hearings accounted for 44 percent of Agriculture, 100 percent of Appropriations (compared with 31 percent of Senate Appropriations Committee, 54 percent of Foreign Affairs, and 56 percent of Judiciary.

country understood what goes on. But the whole procedure is designed to make that impossible." [3]

Punishment for disloyalty, for "not going along" customarily involves withdrawing from the congressman his capacity to perform the services—both large and small —expected by his constituents, who soon angrily conclude: "Old Joe just doesn't seem to know his way around Washington." Conversely, the leadership's ability to help a compliant legislator runs the gamut of favors from the sublime to the minuscule. Harry S. Dent, former legislative aide to Senator Strom Thurmond of South Carolina (now patronage-dispenser for President Nixon), recalled that on several occasions Mr. Thurmond sought to leave the Senate chamber for a flight back home to address a local organization, but was fearful of missing an important vote. "He'd go to Lyndon [Lyndon Johnson, then Senate Majority leader] and ask him to either speed up the vote or hold it over until the following day. Lyndon would say that as much as he sympathized with Strom's problem, he didn't see what he could do. Finally, Strom would be practically on his hands and knees, begging, and Lyndon would say, 'Well, maybe there was something [he] could do,' and he'd order the vote and supply a Capitol limousine and police escort to take Strom out to the airport."

The fundamental question raised by our "representative," two-constituency form of government is the degree to which both the national interest and the public interest suffer because of a member's need to show his effectiveness by getting patronage for his district. To what extent, for example, is the nation's $80 billion defense budget dictated by national necessity, and to what extent is it the result of members' needs to obtain as many military instal-

[3] *The New Yorker*, January 10, 1969, p. 57.

lations and military contracts as they can, in order to increase government spending in their own district? To what extent has the Vietnam war been continued because members have been compromised by their patronage needs? To what extent has tax reform been evaded because of the patronage needs of the congressmen? To what extent has pollution been ignored because its foes lacked the patronage to dispense to congressmen? How much has the war on poverty suffered because the principal recipients of antipoverty patronage lacked the national clout to make themselves effective?

Representative Jamie L. Whitten, a Mississippi Democrat on the House Appropriations Defense Subcommittee, testified: "I am convinced that defense is only one of the factors that enter into our determinations for defense spending. The others are pump priming, spreading the immediate benefits of defense spending, taking care of all services, giving military bases to include all sections. . . . There is no state in the Union, and hardly a district in a state, which doesn't have defense spending, contracting, or a defense establishment. We see the effects in public and Congressional insistence on continuing contracts, or operating military bases, though the need has expired." [4]

Representative Whitten has not challenged Defense Department patronage politics lately, perhaps because he has been institutionalized into silence by another subdivision of the executive, the Department of Agriculture, which in 1969 was ready to underwrite a $265,000 loan to build a golf course in Representative Whitten's district. Anxious to please Representative Whitten, who chairs the Appropriations Subcommittee that approves Agriculture's budget, the department's decision would have enabled the

[4] Testimony before the Joint Economic Committee's Defense Procurement Subcommittee, January 29, 1960.

Natchez Trace Golf Club, Inc., in Lee County to buy land for a nine-hole golf course, and build an additional nine holes, a clubhouse, pool, and tennis courts.[5] The loan, one of approximately 500 made for golf courses since 1962, raises anew the question of government priorities. The decision to subsidize a golf course in Lee County, where 40 percent of the families subsist on incomes well below minimum poverty levels, shows how easily the public interest can be sacrificed for private patronage considerations. It also shows how congressmen decide just which constituents they will favor—a selection often influenced by the political clout of those benefited. A loan of $265,000 seems even more brazen in view of the paltry sum of $300,000 spent in 1968 by the Department of Agriculture for food stamps for 2,000 recipients in the county.

Federal agencies are not the only organizations that seek to service congressmen in return for the expectation of congressional favors. The favors showered on congressmen from the private sector also raise the question of the extent to which the national/public interest suffers from the obligations these favors extract. Representative Wright Patman, the Texas Democrat who is chairman of the Banking Committee, spoke of the seductive attempts of the large banks. "Freshmen members have been approached within hours of their arrival in Washington and offered quick and immediate loan service," Mr. Patman told the National Press Club. "Banks should not be allowed to dispense favors through their loan-making powers."[6]

Representative Seymour Halpern, a New York Re-

[5] The Bank of Mississippi at Tupelo would make the actual loan, but the golf club paid only 5 percent interest, with the government putting up the additional 3 percent interest to make the arrangement acceptable to the bank at the then current rate of 8 percent.

[6] Speech to the National Press Club, July 31, 1969.

publican and third-ranking Republican member of the Banking Committee, acknowledged debts totaling more than $100,000, including an unsecured loan from the First National City Bank of New York. All House members have been eligible to keep standing loans of more than $13,000 at lower-than-market interest rates, and at least 15 members of the 35-member Banking Committee owned stock in banks or mortgage firms. The major problem is not profiteering, but rather the impact of these favors on national policy.

Typical favors bestowed on congressmen by private groups include political and financial support at election time. "There's no secret about it, the companies do support candidates," said H. P. Newson, vice-president for public relations of the Forest Industries Association. "We are actively concerned with having representation in the Congress of the United States which understands the relationship between land and jobs, regardless of party. We urge our people to participate in political activities." The industry supported Wayne Aspinall, a Colorado Democrat and chairman of the House Interior Committee; Senator Wayne Morse, Oregon Democrat; and Don Clausen, a California Republican.

Through its political-action committees, labor has also constructed an elaborate set of mutual-favor relationships with Congress. "Members of Congress know that it is in their interest to vote our way to get help from COPE [Committee on Political Education]," said Ken Young, the AFL-CIO's legislative liaison man. In addition to garnering favorable votes, unions also claim they have been able to press many congressmen into service as quasi-lobbyists, acting as a ready-made intelligence network informing labor whether other members really mean what they are saying, or are just—as one lobbyist explained—"making noise." Cooperative congressmen also lobby on behalf of labor among their wavering colleagues, while committee chairmen, anxious to please the unions, often postpone or hasten hearings on crucial bills. In exchange for their cooperation, labor offers congressmen substantial campaign help—the Seafarers Union is especially noted for its campaign talent—supplying them with mailing lists, sound trucks, advice on what contacts to cultivate in their districts, and, more covertly, hard cash.

❈ *Patronage and the Power Structure*

"A good congressman sees to it that he's on a committee that can help his state," said Representative Thomas Rees, California Democrat, echoing a sentiment shared by congressmen interested in maximizing the political advantages available to them. Rees's own committee assignment, on the House Banking and Currency Committee, holds special relevance for his home state, California, whose expansion as an importing state depends on federal credit policies. An exporter by profession, Rees admitted that his special interest as a committee member was to protect his state by preventing credit from becoming too tight. Other congressmen try to get seated on committees that will bring federal offices to their districts. Considered particularly valuable patronage plums, federal buildings are valued not only for the federal jobs they bring permanently to the district but for all the contracts (architectural, engineering, and construction), employment, and business opportunities benefiting the district while the building is being constructed. Congressman Morris Udall, Arizona Democrat, explained that as a member of the Post Office Committee, "a committee riddled with gimmicks," he was able to put 30 to 40 post offices in his district, with one right in the middle of a shopping center, even though by rights his district was only entitled to half that amount.

Owing to the enormous number of rewards channeled through committees, the power to assign committee seats amounts to one of the major patronage-dispensing operations in Congress. Handled on a *de facto* basis by party leaders, committee assignments are technically parceled out through the Republican Conference Committee and the Democratic Steering Committee in the Senate; and through the Republican Committee on Committees and the Democratic Ways and Means Committee in the House. Although considerable jockeying goes on behind the scenes over assignments, little of this ever becomes public knowledge, with congressmen choosing to perpetuate the myth that committee work is strictly business, unaffected by patronage considerations, while they patiently wait their turn to be assigned to a fruitful committee.

This tradition of silence was broken by Shirley Chisholm, an outspoken Brooklyn Democrat who is the first black woman elected to Congress in the history of the country. Representing the decidedly urban district of Bedford-Stuyvesant, Mrs. Chisholm was given her first committee appointment to the Agriculture Committee. "Apparently, all they know about Brooklyn is that a tree grew there," protested the fiery politician who indignantly demanded another committee assignment. Mrs. Chisholm was taken off Agriculture and put on Veterans Affairs, where party leaders hoped she would remain at least temporarily obscured.[7] "She virtually has no committee assignment," noted Representative Jacob Gilbert, a product

[7] The customary silence was also broken during the hearings on the Bobby Baker case when more evidence of patronage factors relating to committee assignments was revealed. Senators Humphrey and Clark testified that Baker had appeared before the Senate Democratic Steering Committee in January 1961, and told it that Senators Young (Democrat—Ohio) and Burdick (Democrat—North Dakota) were no longer interested in assignments to the Judiciary Committee—a committee with considerable patronage power over judicial appointments.

of the Bronx Democratic organization. Mr. Gilbert's
party regularity was well rewarded by a seat on the politically lucrative Ways and Means Committee.

Mrs. Chisholm's experience was typical of freshman
congressmen and congresswomen, particularly those from
cities and other marginal districts, where the next election
might very well rout them from office. To party leaders, it
is rarely worth the investment of good committee seats to
promote the careers of those whose tenure is so insecure.
They also hesitate to delegate too much power to unproven
or unreliable representatives like Mrs. Chisholm, who may
be unwilling in the future to reinvest the party's favors
back into the party. In cases of congressmen who have already cast the party establishment in an embarrassing
light, committee assignments are purposely used as punishment. Representative Allard Lowenstein, best known
for his role in the "Dump Johnson" movement, was purposely assigned a seat on the Agriculture Committee
where it was thought he could do little for his district.
(Nassau County is primarily a suburban area, with very
little farming left.) But the resourceful Mr. Lowenstein

Acting on Baker's recommendations, the Steering Committee appointed instead two less-senior senators, Russell Long (Democrat—
Louisiana), who later became quite influential in the Senate as Majority Whip, and Blakley (Democrat—Texas), although later on it
was Senators Young and Burdick who protested that they were indeed
very much interested in Judiciary Committee appointments, and that
Baker had lied to get his friends appointed to the committee.

Another instance bared in the Baker investigation showed how
committee assignments used as patronage were also traded for votes
needed on close issues. Senator Moss (Democrat—Utah) testified that
Baker had told him he would be assured of seven Steering Committee
votes in support of his application for a seat on the Aeronautical and
Space Sciences Committee in exchange for his support on a close issue. Moss said he did not support the issue and subsequently lost the
committee assignment. (*Congressional Quarterly*, "Congress and the
Nation, 1945–1964," p. 1777.)

exploited the assignment through food-stamp programs for the poor and other unexpected projects.

"The standard Capitol Hill explanation of the senator's committee preference is 'political advantage,' " wrote Professor Donald R. Matthews. "The tendency of Senators to be attracted by committees of special importance to their constituents is well known." [8] Matthews notes that the postwar committee on Interior and Insular Affairs, for example, was overwhelmingly made up of senators from the public land states. There were about three times more members from Rocky Mountain and Pacific states than one would expect on the basis of chance, while the Senate Agriculture Committee consisted of nearly three times the proportion of senators from the Great Plains and one-half again as many Southern senators as there were in the Senate as a whole. The Committees on Labor, Commerce, Finance, and Banking held special appeal to senators from highly industrialized Northeastern and Great Lakes states.[9]

In the case of Senate committees,[10] where the temptation of instant publicity is always present, personal and

[8] Donald R. Matthews, *U.S. Senators and Their World* (Chapel Hill: University of North Carolina Press, 1960), p. 153.

[9] A typology constructed by Dwaine Marvick ("A Quantitative Technique for Analyzing Congressional Alignments," Ph.D. dissertation, Columbia University, 1950) divides up committees into categories: 1) prestigious committees, which include Foreign Relations, Armed Services, Appropriations and Finance; 2) special-interest committees, which include Agriculture, Banking and Currency, Interstate and Foreign Commerce, Judiciary, and Labor; and 3) "pork" or patronage committees, which include Interior, Post Office, Civil Service, and Public Works; and 4) duty committees, which include Government Operations, Rules and Administration, and District of Columbia. Cited in Matthews, *op. cit.*

[10] And occasionally in the House. President Richard Nixon first thrust himself into the national spotlight as a member of the House Un-American Activities Committee, which initiated his involvement in the Alger Hiss case.

political advantages may outweigh the importance of constituent favors; and the senator may instead prefer a committee seat from which he can more easily project a national reputation for himself. Contrary to other senators who might have attempted to change their appointments, Senator Abraham Ribicoff stayed on the Government Operations Committee, where he later conducted hearings which were to identify him closely in the public mind with the politically advantageous issue of auto safety. Ribicoff explained that he preferred a committee in which he did not have to compete with senators whose seniority gave them so much more leverage than he could hope to exercise. Senator Joseph McCarthy achieved national notoriety as a result of his Senate investigations into internal security, and other investigations have promoted John McClellan and Estes Kefauver, who ran for Vice-President in 1956, largely on the strength of his nationally televised hearings on crime. Although a place on the Foreign Relations Committee may constitute a liability for many senators, J. William Fulbright of Arkansas and Eugene McCarthy of Minnesota have profited considerably from such positions. Indeed, Eugene McCarthy rose from relative obscurity to build a reputation which enabled him to launch a highly effective bid for the presidency in 1968.

The bulk of committee favors rests solidly in the hands of committee chairmen, whose control over committee agenda is converted into the more basic power over the priorities of legislation. Since only one bill out of ten survives the rigors of committee,[11] the power of controlling the agenda in effect gives the chairman jurisdiction over whose bills will be allowed through the maze, and whose will not; and what issues will be covered and what issues

---

[11] Robert Bendiner, *Obstacle Course on Capitol Hill* (New York: McGraw-Hill, 1969).

will be ignored. Reaching the coveted post of chairman through seniority, not talent, committee chairmen remain in their posts as long as their constituents back home choose to keep them in Congress; neither their committee colleagues nor Congress as a whole wields any power over their tenure. Accountable to only one small district, committee chairmen hold a disproportionate amount of power over the national interest, which all too often, because of this system, takes second place to particular interests.

Most often associated with the bill-connected favors they can do, committee chairmen—particularly those on finance committees—also wield tremendous influence over private favors, which may mean millions of dollars to an individual, or to an industry. In the area of tax patronage, negotiated with the utmost privacy, the public sees only the results, without ever knowing who acted as the beneficiary's "good rabbi," or benefactor. The most famous example of tax patronage, the "Louis B. Mayer" amendment, saved $2 million in taxes for the former head of Metro-Goldwyn-Mayer studios, thanks to the good graces of the House Ways and Means Committee. The amendment enabled Mr. Mayer to retire with a lump sum, without paying the 91 percent tax rate, but allowing him instead to pay the far more favorable 25 percent capital-gains tax. Another private tax favor, the "Leo Sanders amendment," enabled its namesake to save taxes on $995,000 in government income.[12]

The House Ways and Means Committee, the tax-writing committee, derives its power from three main sources. Democratic members are endowed with the authority to grant or withhold politically vital committee assignments for their Democratic colleagues; the committee

[12] See Philip Stern, *The Great Treasury Raid* (New York: Random House, 1962), for further examples of tax patronage.

has jurisdiction over most political bills—tariff and social security fall under its jurisdiction; and it maintains a tight rein on the passage of all tax bills. By House procedure, no amendment to a major tax, tariff, or social security bill may be made during floor debate without the assent of Ways and Means; and by committee practice, any "minor" tax or tariff bill desired by a non-committee member to aid a favored constituent has little chance of passage without the active support—and preferably the co-sponsorship—of a Ways and Means member. At selected intervals each month, in a closed-door session and without public hearings, each Ways and Means member is allowed to call up a bill of his own choosing which, by gentlemen's agreement and in a spirit of mutual helpfulness, generally wins unanimous committee approval. Usually the bills spring from the tax problem of a lone taxpayer, and are generally opposed by the Treasury Department. All members' bills emerge anonymously as Public Law X, not under the name of the person they directly benefit.

Committee chairmen also control appointments to subcommittees carved out within their own committees; and the competition for these subcommittee posts is sometimes as intense as the race for valued committee seats, as congressmen recognize how often subcommittees influence the legislating out of important bills. In this way, the chairman can delegate out patronage to cooperative committee members, by giving them an independent power base of their own on a subcommittee. Senator Philip Hart's antitrust subcommittee, for example, which seats about 80 members, deals with so much business within its own confines that its parent committee chairman, Senator James Eastland of the Banking Committee, is forced to leave Hart relatively free to exercise total control over the subcommittee. The chairman still retains a certain degree of control through his power to shuffle subcommittee personnel at will, and through his privilege to name the floor manager for all bills reported to the floor from the committee. The chairman also controls and appoints the committee staff, although since the passage of the Legislative Reorganization Act in 1946, many committee-staff positions have developed tenure status. This still leaves the committee chairman many vacancies to fill, and a large staff, characterized by at times "excessive loyalty to the chairman." [13] Committee chairmen can also collect proxy votes from absent members and shower them on cooperative committee members as rewards for past favors.

Bowing to their power to delegate favors, key members of the executive branch of government very often direct projects to districts represented by committee chairmen as the best possible insurance for continuing congressional support. The Strategic Communications Command (Stratcom), planned for Virginia, was moved to Arizona because Carl Hayden then chaired the Senate Appropriations Committee. Chairman Hayden did not have to exert his personal influence to press for the project, as the proponents of Stratcom, anxious for his permanent cooperation, did his pressuring for him. Instinctively, executive agencies know the best methods for establishing permanent favor relationships with committee chairmen. The Army, for example, does not have to be told where to recommend locating new defense installations; they start their searches in South Carolina, home of House Armed Services Committee Chairman L. Mendel Rivers.

As suitable sites, Arizona and South Carolina already stand high on lists which have weeded out locations that fulfill all necessary rational criteria. When Congress announces the choice of a site for an army base, a space center, etc., it appears to the public fully justified by public

[13] Matthews, *op. cit.*

documents showing that the site has won out over several other sites by sheer virtue of its merits alone. This is rarely the case, however, since there might easily be six sites which fulfill the requirements about equally. At this point, where purely discretionary power determines the choice, patronage factors enter in, carefully covered up by layers of bureaucratic jargon. It is no coincidence, for example, that NASA, the National Space Center, was located at Houston at the same time that Representative Albert Thomas of Houston chaired the subcommittee of the House Appropriations Committee designated to rule on NASA's budget. Houston met all the criteria for site selection, but this was no surprise either, since Thomas is credited with having written the criteria himself. According to D. B. Hardeman, there were six sites equally qualified to house the projected Air Force Academy. All six boasted appropriate weather conditions for flying, and good flat land for landing fields. In addition, each had demonstrated the need for the economic infusion which would be produced by a new federal installation. Yet the Academy was eventually located in Colorado Springs, with Senators Edwin C. Johnson and Eugene Millikin [14] exerting the clout that brought the academy to their state.

Committee assignments and chairmanships also yield valuable opportunities for congressmen to develop expertise in politically lucrative areas. "Dick Russell's great strength comes in part from his expertise," said an aide to Lyndon Johnson. "He could glance at a Defense Department budget requisite that is sixty pages long, and in 30 seconds could pick up the tricks. Sometimes he would want them [the Defense Department] to get away with them. Knowledge is power." This is true, too, of positions on the

[14] Millikin chaired the Finance Committee; Johnson was the ranking Democrat on the Interstate and Foreign Commerce Committee.

Appropriations Committee, prized for the vantage point from which members of Congress can gain intimate knowledge of the inner workings of the executive branch.

The theme of cooperation, rather than conflict, dominates the day-to-day relationships between committee chairmen and their counterparts in the executive branch. Rather than supervising the executive—the intention of the Founding Fathers when they constructed a system whose branches would "check and balance"—the legislature finds itself with many more opportunities for mutual accommodations with the executive. The Army is always willing to accommodate Richard Russell and Mendel Rivers, for example, as insurance against retribution and as a guarantee of forthcoming favors, as Russell and Rivers show their appreciation by funding the defense establishment without pinching pennies.

In contrast to committee chairmen, whose patronage is reinforced by the system's uneven allocations of power, the patronage accorded other party leaders, such as majority and minority leaders in both houses, is often difficult to determine, and most often depends on the individual's ability to construct his own set of obligation-relationships. The former Speaker of the House of Representatives, John McCormack, lacks the formal power to make committee assignments, although his influence over them is widely recognized. McCormack has built up a reputation of following the President and the committee chairmen, instead of being a leader. "Rivers doesn't have to worry about whether McCormack agrees with him or not," said one of McCormack's numerous critics. "His biggest patronage favor is letting committee chairmen alone." [15] The Speaker has also been described as having

---

[15] The Speaker has been able to survive, a tribute to his use of binding his colleagues through the use of patronage, despite a recent scandal leading to the indictments of his legislative assistant, Martin

more power than one committee chairman, but not as much power as all the chairmen together. His patronage adds up to a wide range of small favors, along with whatever mileage he is able to develop on his own through the judicious use of these favors. The Speaker's recent patronage, for example, included the appointment of Bruce Bromley, a New York lawyer recently given a judgeship, to represent the House before the Supreme Court regarding the case of Representative Adam Clayton Powell. Mr. Bromley received a fee of $213,000, exclusive of his fee for appearing before the Supreme Court, although the legal work was minimal since much of the research had already been done by the select committee of the House investigating Mr. Powell.

Along with his more substantial powers, such as designating whom a bill will be named after, or who will preside over the House when bills come up (which may mean the difference between the life and death of a bill), the Speaker also controls a wide variety of prestige-type favors. He appointed Congressman Udall, for example, to represent Congress at the Mexican Interparliamentary Group, which meets once a year. "This was a big deal back home," Mr. Udall noted. "He won't pick me now," referring to his current opposition to Mr. McCormack's leadership. Other minor favors include deciding who will read George Washington's Farewell Address on February 22, and who will be assigned to prestigious commissions like

---

Sweig, and a close friend, Nathan Voloshen, who were accused of attempting to gain favors for friends and clients by using the Speaker's name, and in the case of Dr. Sweig, sometimes impersonating his voice. Recent opposition to McCormack by House reformers centered around the complaint that he was unresponsive to modern problems and had let his power erode to conservative Southern chairmen. A formal challenge by Representative Morris Udall, who ran for Speaker himself in 1969, was lost in the Democratic Party caucus.

the Warren Commission and the Kerner Commission. "This is all good for press releases back home," said Mr. Udall, who attributed McCormack's retention of the Speakership, despite the frequent and serious challenges to his leadership, to the wide range of favors, large and small, under the jurisdiction of the Speaker of the House.

The Speaker also appoints Capitol architects, which explains why a small group of architects have been responsible for almost all Capitol construction in the last 15 years. Since 1954, $250 million has been spent under the direction of former Representative J. George Stewart, formerly a landscape contractor with the firm of Dewitt, Poor and Shelton. The firm did the design work for the Old Senate and Supreme Court chambers, plans for the extension of the east and west fronts of the Capitol; and designed the James Madison Memorial, for a fee of $75 million. The east front was pushed through the legislature by the late Speaker Sam Rayburn, while the west front was lobbied by McCormack.[16]

Roscoe Dewitt (and friend Fred Hardison), both of Dallas, were friends of Mr. Rayburn. Jesse Shelton of Atlanta was a friend of Carl Vinson, the Georgia Democrat; and architect John Harbeson, a friend of Stewart's, performed the design work on the Rayburn building. The American Institute of Architects found a lack of long-range planning in the architecture, and Representative James H. Scheuer, a New York Democrat and builder, said that "an unspeakable monopoly" had done all the work, with results that were "uniformly dismal, a program of unplanned ugliness." [17]

Mr. Stewart also operates the Capitol cafeterias, which are $500,000 in debt every year, Representative

---

[16] *Congressional Quarterly Almanac*, 1967, p. 1031.

[17] *Ibid.*

Andrew Jacobs has charged. Management receives enormous salaries, but cafeteria workers do not receive wages which are set by the District of Columbia board because, it is claimed, there is not enough money. Representative Jacobs also accused Mr. Stewart of manufacturing makework jobs for Capitol architects. "There was a balustrade on top of the Cannon building, like a squirrel tail on a car. One day I noticed they were taking it off. When I asked why, they said that the stone was beginning to sugar, which means that a century from now it might weather. This means another job for them. Then another day, I saw them building another balustrade, colored white, which didn't even match the building, which was gray. It looked like tennis shoes and a tuxedo. The cost of the new balustrade was $500,000."

The "favor power" of the Speaker is very real, but is based in large part on the mythology that everybody is getting a favor, when in reality the favor may be a service to which the citizen is entitled, regardless of whether or not he stands in the good graces of the Speaker. A good labor lawyer, for example, who gets his name in the *Congressional Record Index* is made to believe that this constitutes a favor, even though he is fully entitled to this recognition for the role he played in drafting an important piece of labor legislation. Many critics feel that this practice should be treated more neutrally, as recognition accompanying a service, regardless of who performs it—and not to attract someone's loyalty and obligate him for an indefinite period in the future.

❡ *Yes, But What Have You Done For Me Lately?* [18]
Constituent Interests and Political Survival

A new, overly ambitious member of the House of Representatives worked especially hard to get a water project for his district. Unexpectedly, he achieved the unheard-of victory of getting the project authorized by Congress during his freshman term on Capitol Hill, instead of the customary 6 to 16 years usually taken to move a major project out of the maze of congressional-executive bureaucracy. A Southern committee chairman took the starch out of his victory, however, by suggesting that he'd gone about the whole thing in the wrong way. "You never get the whole project," the chairman advised. "You get one mile, and you go home and brag about that, and then you go to the next congress and go for another mile. That way

[18] From an old story, perhaps apocryphal, about the political career of the late Vice-President Alben Barkley, proving how ungrateful constituents can be, regardless of the favors bestowed on them. "Barkley began doing favors for Jones when he started out in 1905 as prosecuting attorney of McCracken County, Kentucky, and continued doing favors for him as a judge, United States Representative, and senator. Barkley . . . visited Farmer Jones in a hospital in France during World War I to console him; he interceded with General Pershing to get him home quickly after the armistice; he intervened with the Veterans Bureau to speed up his disability compensation; he helped him get loans from the Farm Credit Administration. On top of all this, he got Farmer Jones a federal disaster loan to rebuild his farm after a flood had struck, and he also got Mrs. Jones an appointment as postmistress. Then, in 1938, Barkley found himself in a close primary fight. To his astonishment, he learned that the man he had so often befriended, Farmer Jones, was going to vote for his opponent. He hurried to see Jones and reminded him of his many labors in his behalf. 'Surely,' Barkley said, 'you remember all these things I have done for you?' 'Yeah,' said Farmer Jones sullenly. 'But what in hell have you done for me lately?' " Cited in Donald Matthews, *U.S. Senators and Their World* (Chapel Hill: University of North Carolina Press, 1960), p. 219.

the project is good for five, maybe six terms. You've gone ahead and spent it all in one term, and now you'll have to wait for years for another project." The old-timer was right; and the congressman was retired by the voters after serving two terms, unable to satisfy their queries of "Yes, but what have you done for me *lately?*"

The moral of the story is cynical, but clear. Ignorant of the inner workings of Congress, the voters often appear insatiable, unpredictable, and ungrateful, regardless of the magnitude of past favors their representatives have been able to direct their way. The loyalty of an individual constituent, on the other hand, can be bought for a much longer period of time by a lucrative government contract, or a secure government job; but congressmen find that obligating constituents as a group is quite another matter, and far more difficult to accomplish. To survive politically, a congressman must convince the voters—both as individuals and as groups—that he is perennially engaged in doing favors for them; that he is better than his opponents in garnering for his district the benefits of power; and that he spends the major part of his tenure in office occupied with the business of government advantages. Many members of Congress say privately that bringing home the patronage is more important to their careers than their voting records. Indeed, some congressmen who are highly respected in Congress are unaccountably retired by the voters because they have lost contact with their districts and have ignored their patronage obligations.

Doing favors dominates congressional activity at all levels, and determines the power configurations of Congress itself. Most congressmen spend a good part of their day handling favors: special "cases" for their constituents; "issues" for their region; and favors for conglomerate interests within their districts or states. Individual constituents can expect their congressman to fight the executive

branch's intricate bureaucracy on their behalf—taking
their cases before the Veterans Board; expediting loans for
them from the Small Business Administration; or perhaps
getting them jobs with the Post Office. Regional and corporate favors include even greater returns: dams; farm
subsidies; new federal buildings which attract money and
jobs; military bases; defense contracts; purchasing contracts; etc.

Congress itself is structured around the process of
dispensing favors, with a lion's share of the rewards strati-
fied to coincide with the general power structure: committee chairmen, influential committee members, and party
leaders in both houses. A member's success in Congress
depends on whether he gets assigned to the right committee, a favor in itself dispensed by party influentials, and
whether he can stay in this niche long enough to accrue
substantial benefits for his constituency.

In the broadest sense, congressional favors include
an oil depletion allowance of 22.5 percent, after Congress
in 1969, under intense public pressure, reduced the allowance by 5 percent, which still gave oilmen $1.5 billion
annually. The reduction came on the wave of tax reform
after unsuccessful efforts that dated back at least to 1950,
when President Truman said there was no tax provision
"so inequitable" as the "excessive" oil-gas depletion allowance. Other federal subsidies include maritime subsidies in the form of $150 million a year plus cargo prefer-
ence for all military, AID, and Food for Peace shipments;
and farm subsidies of $4 billion. The average subsidized
farmer earns $20,000, with 68 percent of the subsidies go-
ing to the big farmers who comprise 16 percent of the
total farming group. Like the merchant fleet, the airlines
operate at a deficit, with the federal government picking
up the difference. Indeed, it is hard to find a business, profession, or group that does not receive federal subsidies,

either directly or indirectly. Airlines and their users benefit from $1.2 billion in federal grants; railroads, trucking firms, and motorists benefit from $5 billion for highway and rail construction; construction men receive $2 billion to build private housing; suburbanites write off interest payments on their mortgages as a tax advantage; and veterans receive $7.3 billion annually in federal funds.

Most of these subsidies are stated to be in the public interest, but legislators rarely think of balancing the national interest against constituents' interests, except in cases of national emergency; or in the rare instances when these two interests actually conflict; or when a senator or representative has built up so much security, seniority, and personal wealth to carry him through campaigns that he can afford to ignore his constituents' interests for a while. The average congressman, however, spends his political life revolving around the orbit of favors, busily negotiating with his constituents and his colleagues in Washington for his share of the booty, justifying his patronage actions with the theory that if he's really concerned about the public/national interest, then he'll do whatever is required of him in order to remain in Congress.

The resulting disparity is indicated, for example, in farm subsidies to middle-class and wealthy farmers that far exceed expenditures on such national problems as hunger, housing, urban transportation, or air and water pollution. These subsidies "have helped create a class of wealthy landowners while bypassing the rural poor, and that means 40 percent of the poor people in this country," according to C. E. Bishop, agricultural economist and vice-president of the University of South Carolina.[19]

Members of Congress find that the government rein-

[19] *The New York Times*, April 5, 1970, p. 1.

forces their ability to dispense favors by impressing them in the role of middleman between their constituents and an otherwise unresponsive bureaucracy, in very much the same way in which Mayor Daley's aldermen are empowered to expedite city services to the voters. In both cases, the net effect is intended to obligate the voter to his elected representatives, regardless of how he feels toward these men, strictly on the basis of past services rendered.

Personal intervention from a congressman, perhaps the most common (and least expensive politically) form of patronage, pushes a sluggish and unfeeling bureaucracy to provide justice, service, and equity to aggrieved citizens without the clout necessary to produce this reaction on their own. "The congressman is often a glorified messenger boy," explained Representative Jacobs of Indiana. "His chief function is raising hell if a person is entitled to something and doesn't get it. A call from a congressman will obtain equity."

Agreeing with the commonly repeated charge of bureaucratic insensitivity, Representative Ogden Reid, a Westchester Republican, recalled the case of a family that had come to him after the Army had refused to transport them to the funeral of their son, who had been killed when his helicopter caught fire over Vietnam. Due to a minor bureaucratic regulation, the Army customarily provides transportation only when there are remains, which were absent in this case. The Defense Department finally obliged the aggrieved family only at Congressman Reid's request. "A congressman can more effectively reach the bureaucracy," said Mr. Reid, who also described how he had expedited social security payments when there were clerical errors, and how he continually tried to obtain information on prisoners of war for anxious families who lived in his district.

Bureaucratic inertia was the reason most often given

by congressmen for their intervention on behalf of a constituent. Although they complained of the sluggishness ever present in the executive branch, congressmen seemed to welcome the opportunity to prove to their constituents that they were always working in their behalf. "This office handles 2,000–3,000 problems a year, mostly problems of people who are up against the federal agencies," said Elliot H. Stanley, assistant to Representative Chet Holifield, a California Democrat. "We've had many more military problems since 1965, although our success rate is only about 30 to 40%." The Pentagon has a quota system for filling congressional cases. Representative Thomas Rees, another Democrat from California, reported that his biggest load of cases were also draft cases, even though 80 percent of the youths in his district went on to college and were not subject (at that time) to draft pressures. Congressman Rees emphasized how he was able to help business interests, an important constituency in his district, to obtain financial equity from the government. Rees intervened, for example, on behalf of two Beverly Hills builders (Litton and Douglas) who were being victimized financially by bureaucratic inaction. The builders needed a decision from the Internal Revenue Service concerning a merger contemplated by the two businesses. If no decision was made, they would have had to spend an extra $100,-000 in legal fees to make up two merger plans. While the agency insisted that it would take eight months to make a decision, the company said it needed one in three months to avoid the extra fees. Only the intercession of Congressman Rees helped to cut through the dispute and bring the agency to a more timely decision.

Some congressmen seem less optimistic about their effectiveness vis-à-vis the bureaucracy. Representative John Anderson, an Illinois Republican, said he spent a lot of time on problems which involved his personal intervention, but doubted whether this made an impact on the final decisions: "I go with the Vets and hold their hand while they're appealing a case before the board. They think it helps." He also recalled the case of a constituent who was planting more than was allowed by the Agriculture Stabilization Commodity Service: "I went with him when he went before the board. Maybe it impresses them [the constituents]."

At times, a congressman may act on behalf of constituents whose philosophies may conflict with his own, in order to preserve the economic health of his district by keeping its jobs and credit intact. Although a pronounced dove on the Vietnam war issue, Congressman Rees intervened on behalf of several defense industries in his district when they found themselves in trouble with the Pentagon, even though the industries in question did not seek his help. Mr. Rees interceded for Hughes Aircraft when the Army suddenly canceled its helicopter order in favor of Bell Aircraft in Texas; and supported Douglas Aircraft in its fight to prevent the federal government from imposing tariffs on planes the company had leased to foreign governments.

Congressmen do favors for their constituents without erecting the clear-cut bridge of obligations possible with other forms of political patronage. Representatives may never know whether their beneficiaries have voted for them, but must bank on the notion that maintaining a perpetually high level of personal-favor activity will inevitably bring them added credit toward their next election. Indeed, many congressmen owe their long tenure in Congress to the reputation they have carefully developed of attending even to the most minute demands of their constituents—while burying themselves in the far reaches of obscurity on issues of national importance.

Less consciously, the government provides yet an-

other outlet for congressional favors by perpetuating a
relatively poor communications apparatus between itself
and the public. Considering this just a normal accompani-
ment to bureaucratic inertia, congressmen act as conduits
of information, bringing routine answers to aggrieved
citizens seeking responses from the government. Representative Rees pointed out that many of his constituents
get poor service from the executive branch simply because
"they don't know the traffic signals." During the recent
floods in California, he reported, one of his constituents,
whose motel had suffered a great deal of damage, came to
ask just how she could obtain a loan from the Small Business Administration. "Her motel," the congressman
pointed out, "was legitimately damaged, and she should
have gotten the loan when she applied by herself." Having failed by that method, the woman came to her congressman, who channeled her through the bureaucracy
and expedited the loan. "No matter how carefully you
write a law," said an aide to President Johnson, "there will
always be individual injustices . . . there is no place else
for the citizen to go but to his congressman." Representative Rees admitted that sometimes he has come to the
shamefaced conclusion, often too late, that his constituents
are in error. "I went to bat for a guy who was supposed to
supply refrigerators to the government, and then they
didn't pass inspection," recalled Mr. Rees. "This was bad
management. We ended up walking the guy to the bank
and advising him on management, like a Dutch uncle."
Even in a case like this, however, the congressman can
still emerge as a savior, doing the constituent a favor,
even though the voter has not gained materially.

Since no formal recourse from bureaucratic injustice
exists in this country as yet, the congressman finds himself in the role of perpetual ombudsman—perhaps even

more responsive than an ombudsman since his political survival depends on his accountability. Regarding their acts of personal intervention as essential, congressmen talked of how they were able to rectify many personal tragedies caused by computer-clerical errors involving social security payments, veterans' payments, loans, visas, army regulations, etc. Often it makes little difference whether the congressman succeeds in fighting the bureaucracy, for as long as he shows the constituent he has bravely exerted himself in his behalf, the citizen is obligated, whether the victory is won or not. The rule with political favors is that when the service is performed, the debt is contracted, regardless of what portion of the quid pro quo is later delivered.

In the case of private immigration bills, the process of constituent favors is often exploited, for personal and political profit. Representative Ogden Reid charged that many of his fellow congressmen used these bills for purposes of patronage exploitation, deluding the public into thinking that they will succeed, when they know in fact that their bills have little chance of passing through the Immigration and Naturalization Service. The sin is compounded, he added, by the practice, common among certain congressmen, of charging legal fees for introducing immigration bills. Mr. Reid recalled a constituent whose wife wanted to keep her Spanish maid. The maid was in this country on a visitor's visa, and he advised the constituent to send the maid back, then let her enter legally. Shortly thereafter, another congressman notorious for his activity in this area, introduced a bill for the same Spanish maid. The congressman who submitted the bill, Reid alleged, knew that it would not be approved, and that the maid would be ejected, with her chances for re-entry diminished. Nevertheless, the congressman submitted the bill on the theory that aside from the fee he probably collected, the constituent would be indebted to him whether or not the bill passed.

When a large corporation needs a favor to expedite its way through the bureaucracy, it may bypass the congressman in whose district it is located, and move strictly through the senator. This depends, of course, on the relative influence of each; if the congressman has already obtained seniority on a relevant committee, then it may be unnecessary to approach the senator. When Senator Hubert Humphrey of Minnesota sent letters and telegrams on behalf of Napco Industries, a corporation located in his state, to Under Secretary of State George W. Ball, to officials of AID, to the Development Loan Fund, and to the Indian Planning Commission, he portrayed his efforts on the industry's behalf as routine senatorial service for an important constituent. Following the senator's letters of introduction requesting prompt attention to the company's application, Napco received a $2.3 million loan to carry on its business activities in India. The letters and telegrams were later introduced by the Justice Department as evidence in a lawsuit for fraud brought by the government against the company.

Quietly serving constituent interests, however, will not substantially help a legislator's national reputation, although it may safely ensure him re-election in a favor-conscious state. As shown by the successful examples set by Senators Fulbright, Proxmire, and Kefauver—to name but a few—leading the attack in chosen issue areas brings substantial image gains to the politician seeking to broaden his base of political support. Of course, the battlefield must be situated far away from his district's own needs: Senator Proxmire is free to attack patronage in the Pentagon because there is no defense industry in Wisconsin; and the tycoons of the drug and crime industries were far away from the hills of Tennessee, home of the late Senator Estes Kefauver, who conducted widely publicized hearings on abuses in the drug industry and on organized crime.

If a legislator conscientiously fills his constituency's favor needs, then he is free to launch attacks in other issue areas, a practice which keeps American representative government from becoming totally absorbed in a revolving orbit of self-interest. Senator William Proxmire of Wisconsin, who took pride in his successful fight waged on behalf of American Motors, saw no inconsistency in attacking other congressmen's patronage activities on behalf of their own districts. Senator Proxmire championed a long and successful fight for tax advantages that meant life and death to the company, which found itself in danger of going out of business in the late 1960's, in spite of the large profits it had reaped in the early part of the decade. (American Motors has large plants located in Kenosha and Milwaukee, Wisconsin.) The senator also pressured the General Services Administration to purchase Ramblers from American Motors for the Post Office, and finally succeeded in getting Ramblers purchased for the F.B.I.

Yet Lockheed-Marietta, a company which manufactures airplanes, found itself in circumstances similar to American Motors, after Proxmire's attacks on the C5A [20]

[20] A controversial supertransport airplane, whose production was cut back by the Defense Department after Senator Proxmire, who chairs a Senate Appropriations Subcommittee, attacked the scandalous cost overruns of the original contract to build the planes by the Lockheed-Georgia Company of Marietta, Georgia. For Lockheed's argument, see Daniel J. Haughton, Thomas J. Haley, and Thomas R. May, "The Other Side of the C5A Story," *Statements before the Committee on Armed Services, United States House of Representatives*, Washington, D.C., June 17, 1969. (All three authors are officers of the Lockheed Company.)

airplane placed in jeopardy the company's defense contracts with the government. "One of the reasons I can attack the Pentagon is because there are no real defense installations in Wisconsin," said Senator Proxmire. "People don't regard defense as a giveaway, while the very nature of these programs is patronage. There are thousands of jobs in Marietta, Georgia, which depend on the C5A." Since there is also no shipbuilding in Wisconsin, which would be affected by the new supertransport airplane, Proxmire was left completely free to attack, a luxury he would not be permitted were any of his constituents to profit or lose by his public activities.

The Proxmire pattern of attacking defense spending in Georgia while defending auto purchases in Wisconsin recurs with great frequency and is regarded by other congressmen as an accepted norm of legislative behavior. Congressman H. R. Gross, who vociferously opposed government spending in all areas, didn't object when the Army Corps of Engineers put a flood-control project in his district of Waterloo, Iowa. Paradoxically, one of the most outspoken opponents of public power, Representative A. L. Miller, hails from Nebraska, a public-power state, forcing him into the untenable position of opposing all expenditures for public power except those allotted to his own state. Representative Mike Kirwan, an Ohio Democrat who chaired the Public Works Committee, once withheld all patronage from Miller's district with the comment: "The Congressman from Nebraska would support the second coming of Christ only if he came to Nebraska!" Given this pattern of staunch constituent favors, it was no surprise that when Representative Charles Joelson, a New Jersey Democrat, wrote a letter to each member of Congress asking "Where can we economize in your district?" not one reply was returned to his office.

In contrast to political patronage on the state, local,

and presidential levels, job patronage plays a relatively small role in Congress—where the real fruits of power derive from the government's ability to allocate its financial and technical resources. Although senators are luckier, "the number of jobs for congressmen is so small, it is not a factor," according to Congressman Morris K. Udall. "A congressman has a staff of 8–10 people in his office, and post office jobs are available when his party is in the White House." When his party fails to get itself reelected, as one congressman waggishly remarked, the new administration "fires on patronage, and rehires on merit." Congressmen are allowed a certain number of menial jobs—Capitol housekeeping jobs, Capitol policemen, elevator operators, etc.—which depend on his seniority. A Special House Patronage Committee determines how many of these jobs each congressman can dispense. A freshman congressman probably would get no housekeeping patronage; in his second term he may get one job, and so on.

Many congressmen find job patronage a bother, arguing that their constituents expect only good service from their congressmen, not jobs. "When Kennedy won, there was a Post Office slot open," recalled Representative Thomas Rees. "I went to Ed Day (then Postmaster General), and said: 'Please appoint a top man to the post.' I didn't want 10 people out of the Beverly Hills club vying for the job."

But representatives and senators augment their scarce job patronage by obtaining government-job contracts for skilled constituents such as architects and engineers in their districts. "When a Post Office building was to be located in my district, I was notified that I could pick the architect," recalled Congressman Udall. "The congressman is always asked which architect he would like. One of the local Democrats was asked which architect he would like, and got a $2,000 campaign contribution from the architect he eventually selected. Now that Nixon is in power, I doubt that I'd have much to say." When an especially ripe patronage plum is deposited in a state, the senator may dislodge a representative in naming the recipients of federal funds, leaving the congressman to the lesser glories radiating from expedited veterans' payments, flood-relief loans, or post-office jobs. Congressman Udall was lucky enough to have sufficient seniority in the state when the Democrats asked him to select architects; Congressman Andrew Jacobs (Democrat—Indiana) was less fortunate, noting that when a "federal facility was put in my district, both the architectural and engineering contracts were preempted by the Senators." Representative Jacobs, who believes in the positive uses of patronage, proudly admitted he would have nominated a ward chairman who was an architect for the job. Jacobs added that he also had some influence over government bank deposits, which he was able to turn to the advantage of his local party organization.

Constituent favors also include the ability of congressmen to help in the area of government contracts. The general rule in helping constituents to obtain federal contracts seems to be that the congressman can introduce the constituent seeking a contract to the agency with the power of letting the contract—on the theory that since Congress funds these agencies, they will be more responsive to the congressman than they will be to individual inquiries. The federal bureaucracy is also a good buffer for congressmen seeking to put the blame on someone else for the failure to obtain these contracts. Since the public is still unclear as to the extent of congressional influence over contracts—as are congressmen themselves—the bureaucracy, one step removed from public pressure, is still the best place to place the blame for all matters of patronage failures. Even the President sometimes uses bureaucratic resistance as an excuse for his own failures to deliver on political contracts.

The congressman with average influence can still be a great help to a constituent seeking federal contracts. Very often, individual businessmen ask their congressmen to get them the specifications for bids on contracts; and it is then up to the congressman to find out—even if he doesn't already know.

"When the Central Arizona reclamation project passed, everyone wanted to know how to get in the bidding," said Representative Morris Udall. Regulations prohibited anything but competitive bidding, but there were still ways in which a congressman could help the companies in his district. "I could refer them to the Reclamation Director who would give them hints on how to win a bid," he said, "[such as] 'Watch out for the price of steel,' or 'Save money on this.' I would alert the companies as to what contracts were coming up, which is of particular use to the small company that doesn't have a battery of lawyers to keep up with the current bids. He makes up for this if he gets in with the party."

Aware of the patronage needs of congressmen, as well as the plight faced by small businesses threatened with obliteration by industrial giants, the government leaves about 10 percent of its contracts free from restrictions, only on condition that these contracts go to small businesses. Since these contracts are parceled out on a discretionary basis, congressmen are allowed a large role in determining who will become the benefactors. "A sandbag company in our district wanted government contracts," explained Elliot H. Stanley, legislative assistant to Representative Chet Holifield. "The Corps of Engineers buys millions of sandbags each year. This company employed a large number of minority, unskilled workers. Under Defense Department regulations, it was possible to get a portion of funds because it met the criteria for set-asides [those defense contracts set aside for small businesses]. We wrote letters to the Defense Department and to the Small Business Administration to see if they met the requirements. We try to help by pressuring the government."

Ultimately, congressmen and senators get their power to give favors from the financial power vested in them by the Constitution; executive departments who hold the rewards of government must return to Congress for their funding. "I'm going to want to please the ranking member on the House Interior Committee more than a freshman senator from New York," said a top aide in the Department of Interior, describing the vast network of favors built up between himself and key congressmen. This leaves the congressman with a definite entrepreneurial function, and the bureaucracy with no real incentive to improve its communication and access routes to the public. All courtesies in government rest on power; and when the power base is removed, all patterns of behavior which might be considered routine suddenly become unpredictable: "Your phone calls are not returned, you wait an hour to see someone who was your best friend the day before, and an overwhelming amount of red tape confronts you which had never obstructed your path before," said an administrative aide whose boss, a senator, had suddenly died. An identical situation confronts the citizen in his dealings with the government, leading him to the conclusion that unless he enters and reinforces the established patterns of mutual obligation, he will not get proper access to the government.

❰   *The Horn of Plenty—*
Patronage "Boodle" as System Favors

Compared with the favors hidden in defense budgets and the lavish gifts which abound in the public sector, constituent favors seem minuscule. How effectively he can collect these discretionary gifts measures a congressman's influence in both houses of Congress. "System favors," in the form of reclamation projects, federal power projects, defense contracts, and defense installations which will bring funds, jobs, and an invigorated economy, will make a hero of the man able to muster these resources for his region.

The introduction of heavy federal expenditures throughout the country left vast areas highly dependent on the federal government for their economic sustenance and development. Economic necessity forces these areas to choose political representatives on the basis of their ability to get the most out of government for their regions; and particularly in depressed regions, political longevity is virtually guaranteed to the leader who can bring a dam, a post office, or a defense installation to his people. Political life in the West, for example, centers around the competition for publicly financed land reclamation—using government money and technical help to convert arid land into irrigable land through dams and other irrigation projects—leading political analysts to label Western-style politics as "federal politics that centers on relations with the federal government, rather than decisions to be made within the states." [21] In the South, defense installations and companies relying on defense contracts have revived sagging economies; and are now so crucial to local econ-

[21] Frank Munger, ed., *American State Politics* (New York: Thomas Y. Crowell & Co., 1966), p. 283.

omies that defending the defense industry has become as important a political question in Congress as the defense of the nation. Areas like Georgia, home of Senator Richard B. Russell, Democratic chairman of the Senate Armed Services Committee, and Charleston, South Carolina, located in the congressional district of L. Mendel Rivers, chairman of the House Armed Services Committee, have been so saturated with defense installations that many wryly believe them in danger of sinking from the sheer weight of these installations.

As examples of "system favors," prizes involving huge investments of government money virtually up for grabs, reclamation and defense projects proliferate— rarely challenged except when a public scandal is involved. Congressmen openly refer to large-scale government favors as "boodle," [22] a newer term for a more sophisticated form of pork barrel legislation.

The allocation of large-scale favors all too often bears no relation to rational planning, more often tying in with the political clout of the representative or senator than the area's need for water, defense installations, or a new post office. Representative Richard Bolling of Missouri pointed out that the most important factors enabling him to get federal boodle for his district were his close friendship with the late Speaker Sam Rayburn and his seniority within the party organization in Congress.[23]

The political success that has surrounded the victors in the race for boodle has made the sport itself attractive; and what began as economic necessity has ended up as a

[22] The mortar that binds the system consists largely of what has been called inelegantly but properly "boodle." . . . The boodle itself is legitimate and productive. The hitch is in the way it is distributed. See Richard Bolling, *House out of Order* (New York: E. P. Dutton & Co., 1964), p. 109.

[23] *Ibid.*

habitual form of political activity. Water resources, for example, which used to be a matter of life and death for the West, have become an autonomous feature of its political life. The survival factor is significant only insofar as it relates to the political survival of the leaders who have attached themselves to water issues.

The lavish congressional spending of the taxpayers' money has changed landscapes and shorefronts. Charles G. Schultze, former U.S. Budget Director and now with the Brookings Institution, speaks of the wastefulness of irrigating the lands of farmers who are paid not to grow crops. "Out in the arid west, they charge so little for water that a favorite crop is watermelons," said Mr. Schultze, not without a sense of outrage. "The last place you want to use water is on agricultural production, when you've got other programs trying to hold it down." Others who disagree with him argue that even though using water for agricultural purposes (as opposed to water for electricity, municipal uses, and industrial uses) has produced agricultural surpluses now, the expanding population would require the irrigable land ten, twenty, or thirty years hence.

Irrigation projects have included construction of Lake Texoma in Sam Rayburn's district—an artificial lake covering 149 square miles, with a 540-mile shoreline. Mr. Rayburn felt that he needed Lake Texoma to survive politically, but it was constantly turned down because it did not meet the cost-benefits ratio. At the time, a water project, to be approved by the U.S. Army Corp of Engineers, had to show that it would improve the economy by $4\frac{5}{8}$ percent a year over a 50-year period. Anxious to preserve Rayburn's political future, President Roosevelt asked the Speaker to request a new survey, which coincidentally was approved, and the lake was eventually built. Today the lake attracts over six million visitors a year.

What leaves reclamation wide open for such intensive patronage activities is the lack of centralized planning: there is no agency that coordinates water resources, and no long-range national policy concerning water.[24] A National Resources Planning Board, created in 1933, was killed by Congress ten years later by legislators who said publicly that they feared centralization of water planning within the executive branch of government while privately they worried about their potential patronage losses. Later on, another bill—sponsored by the Kennedy administration—to create a National Water Resources Council failed to pass the House of Representatives both in 1961 and in 1963.[25]

Administrative confusion invariably increases patronage opportunities—a condition encouraged by Congress and often by the President in the area of land reclamation. Water policy is so diffused that even the building of reclamation projects is divided between two jurisdictions, the Department of the Interior and the Army Corps of Engineers, which continually compete with each other for water projects. Acting very much like competing regions, the two agencies lobby independently for projects, aided by the contacts each has built up in Congress, in the Bureau of the Budget, and in the nation's major water pressure group, the National Rivers and Harbors Congress, whose membership includes state and local officials, local industrial and trade organizations, contractors, congressmen, and members of the Army Corps of Engineers. A former president of the "Congress," Senator John McClellan of Arkansas, was also a member of

[24] Arthur Maass, "Congress and Water Resources," in Alan Altschuler, ed., *The Politics of the Federal Bureaucracy* (New York: Dodd, Mead & Co., 1968), pp. 283–297.

[25] *Congressional Quarterly*, "Congress and the Nation, 1945–1964," p. 869.

the Public Works Subcommittee on Appropriations, which handles Army Corps legislation. Often accused of acting like a separate branch of Congress, the Army Corps has recently come under intensive scrutiny by the executive branch. Fearful of its intensive lobbying activities, its competitiveness with the Department of the Interior, its close relationship with Congress, and the numerous times it has been able successfully to ignore the recommendations of the President and the Bureau of the Budget, many Presidents have recommended divesting the Army of its rivers-and-harbors function, their recommendations being formalized in the Hoover Commission Report on the executive branch of government.[26]

On the surface, water projects appear to take on all the accoutrements of rational planning, even though former Secretary of the Interior Stewart Udall called water projects "purely congressional log-rolling operations, with the administration playing an important role." Kenneth Bousquet, an administrative aide to the Senate Appropriations Committee, described the technical factors involved in bringing a corps project through its executive-legislative phases:

> First, the local people have to see a need. Then they hold a public hearing, and notify their congressmen and the newspapers. Third, the Corps takes a survey. Fourth, a second public hearing is held, with possible plans for improvement. Fifth, the plans are submitted to a Board of Engineers for Rivers and Harbors —consisting of seven officers. Sixth, if the report is favorable (about 50%) or unfavorable, the other side can request a hearing. Seventh, the report is submitted to the chief of engineers, and a draft of the report is sent to the governors of all the affected states and government agencies, which are given 90 days to submit revi-

[26] Maass, *op. cit.*

sions; eighth, the report is sent to the Secretary of the Army and the Bureau of the Budget for approval; ninth, the report is transmitted to Congress, to the Public Works Committees; tenth, the bill is submitted to Congress; eleventh, Congress authorizes the project; twelfth, the Appropriations Subcommittee votes the funds.

From beginning to end, the average project takes fifteen years from the time the local groups request a survey to completion, if an immediate appropriation is granted. The survey takes three years, with one year lost before planning, then three years of planning, with one year lost before construction, and then seven years in construction. Appropriations are granted annually, but once the project has gone beyond the point of no return, the approval is almost perfunctory.

According to Stewart L. Udall, what happens in counterpoint to water projects at their political stages is really quite different, more hidden and less rational. At the lowest level of political activity, individual congressmen must apply pressure just to get resolutions passed expressing the need for water projects in their districts. After those congressmen without the clout necessary to carry the project through are weeded out, the next step is to determine who will get the surveys taken which will set at least the minimal standards for building the projects: Is the land irrigable, does it need soil analysis, what is the cost-benefits ratio? After the administrative barriers are overcome, the political ones loom into view, where key members of Congress, the President, and the Bureau of the Budget must be convinced of the political and economic necessities of the project.

The bare mention of the Colorado River Project, perhaps the largest land-reclamation project put through Congress in the last decade, evokes patronage memories from everyone questioned about it. Surrounded by controversy from its beginning stages, the project was far more costly and elaborate than originally planned, according to a legislative aide to former Secretary Udall, because of five additional projects the sponsors were forced to include as "boodle" in order to consolidate sufficient support to get the bill through its committee obstacles. As a member of the administration, the aide recalled, even he had to scout around collecting past favors on his own in order to increase congressional support for the bill. One Eastern Republican, he said, made it known that he intended to vote against the bill, arguing that when he had wanted a project of his own, and had approached his fellow Republicans, they refused him on the grounds that it was "uneconomical." "Well, I'll be damned if I'll help my brethren now," said the congressman. The aide then reminded him of past favors the department had done for him, and then asked him if he wanted to meet with Secretary Udall to "discuss" the Colorado project. Flattered by the suggestion and the subsequent appointment with the Secretary, while grudgingly admitting past favors he owed the department, the congressman finally voted for the project.

Even the name of the Colorado River bill involved patronage considerations. Originally it was named the Central Arizona Reclamation Project; but the bill's Colorado supporters (headed by Representative Wayne Aspinall of Colorado) insisted on changing the name as a major consideration in releasing the bill from committee. Representative Morris Udall, who co-sponsored the project in 1966, told how this occurred: "The committee approved my bill. This was a big deal back home. Then Colorado put the squeeze on . . . after it was sent to the White House, it became the Aspinall bill. This was not directed at me. Aspinall just wanted the folks back home to recognize his influence." Congressman Udall added that there

were no fewer than twenty identical bills for the project,
with each sponsor hoping to get the bill named after himself.[27]

Congressmen often promote other congressmen's patronage in order to boost the chances of getting their own
"boodle" through Congress at a future date. Former Secretary Stewart Udall admitted that when he was a congressman he supported the Upper Colorado River project
—which then only included Colorado, for strictly patronage reasons. If he supported Colorado, he reasoned, they
might feel obligated to support him when he pressured
for his own water projects. "I supported the Colorado
River project over the objections of the Sierra Club [a
conservationist pressure group] even though I had serious reservations. I swallowed my reservations on the assumption that Colorado and Utah would support Arizona
when we wanted a project." Since Arizona remained the
only state without a water project at the time, Udall relied
on the theory that the best tactic to help his state would
be not to block other states, on the assumption, later proven
correct, that they would eventually reciprocate. This differs from ordinary log-rolling (strict vote-trading among
congressmen—"you vote for my project and I'll vote for

[27] For more complete data on the Colorado project, see "Colorado
River Basin Project, *Hearings before the Subcommittee on Irrigation
and Reclamation of the Committee on Interior and Insular Affairs*,
House of Representatives, 90th Congress, 1st Session, on H. R. 3300
and Similar Bills to authorize the construction, operation, and maintenance of the Colorado River Basin project, and for other purposes;
and S. 20 and Similar Bills to provide for a Comprehensive review
of national water resource problems and programs . . . March 13,
14, 16, and 17, 1967. Serial No. 90-5. This project was intended to
solve the existing and potential water-shortage problems of central
Arizona and six other states in the 250,000-square-mile Colorado River
Basin. The largest reclamation bill ever approved, the Colorado Project included the following states: California, Nevada, Utah, Wyoming, Colorado, and New Mexico—as well as Arizona.

yours") because the congressman is trading on potential rather than actual favors.

Recently, the customary traditions of reclamation patronage met a curious twist when public opposition mobilized against constructing the projected Glen Elder Dam in Kansas—a classic example of bipartisan patronage. The politicians who expected plaudits were shocked by the farmers who flooded Congress with letters opposing the dam. Even though their lands were to be irrigated by the dam, the farmers resented having to share the dam's cost of $77 million, a tab they felt was not worth the benefits of irrigation.

Nevertheless, both Kansas senators supported the dam, on the premise that even though so many people opposed it, the political mileage gained from a reclamation project of this kind was great enough to overcome what they considered minor and temporary opposition. Senator Proxmire, who opposed the dam, said he spoke for ten hours in the Senate only to get 17 votes against the dam, corroborating former Secretary Udall's theory that going along with one's colleagues on reclamation is the best way of collecting your own patronage later. "Voting against Public Works just isn't done," lamented Senator Proxmire. "The fear of retaliation is just too strong. The motive here was to help the state get $77 million worth of spending money. The labor unions like it; so do the contractors." Senator Proxmire could easily attack patronage in reclamation projects as he could oppose defense spending, for Wisconsin, with its plethora of lakes and rivers, is as free from irrigation problems as it is empty of defense industries.

The Glen Elder example offered further evidence of patronage politics, according to those who claimed that Lyndon Johnson had engineered through the appropriation for the dam on the basis of support he had been promised at the presidential convention in 1960. And like other recent reclamation patronage, the outcome seemed to push all hopes of rational planning even further off in the future; the reasons given for its existence were ludicrous in the light of current needs. "This dam would have given us 20,000 acres of feed grain," former Secretary Udall noted, "and we had just taken land out of feed grain."

Despite all indications to the contrary, the tides of reclamation are slowly changing, due to the increasing public support gathering around the conservation issue. Before conservationists had become an organized constituency, patronage politics was freer to operate in the water-resources area, primarily because there never was much opposition to proposed projects. Powerful interest groups supported reclamation; and rarely did opposition in Congress crop up because of the eternally sprung hopes on the part of other congressmen for future "boodle." Now conservationists are occasionally able to convince the public that water projects are no longer the panacea they once were, and must be balanced against environmental considerations; they hope that some segments of public opinion can be mobilized to mitigate the patronage returns which propel congressmen toward reclamation. In 1969, the conservationists, led by the Sierra Club, won a landmark victory in reclamation history when both the governor and one senator from Kentucky requested that the government hold up construction of a dam already authorized and approved. The dam, planned for the Red River Gorge,[28] one of the most scenic gorges in the Appalachian range, would surely have ruined the scenery and killed off much of the wildlife of the area. Governor

[28] The dam was approved in 1960–61 as a water-supply reservoir for Lexington, Kentucky, to protect two towns that had foolishly been built on a flood plain. The Army Corps of Engineers had already spent $1 million of the $11 million needed for the project to survey the site.

Nunn of Kentucky ultimately recommended that the dam be moved downstate.

Similar to resource allocations in land reclamation, defense spending has also produced a situation in which patronage favors have flourished unencumbered by any legitimate opposition. Until recently, there existed no pressure groups (at least off the Attorney General's list) opposed to the wide range of purely discretionary defense expenditures; and most congressmen, fearful of attacks on their patriotism, were unwilling to upset the applecart of defense patronage. To those who opposed the secrecy in which defense allocations were made, the Pentagon answered: "We can't let the enemy know how much we're spending and where it is being spent, for security reasons."

Along with the country's increased involvement in the Vietnam war, however, opposition grew from legitimate quarters; and increasing numbers of congressmen, particularly those without defense installations in their states, have been willing to challenge defense expenditures and policies, often with politically advantageous results. Basing their opposition on a shift in priorities, these congressmen have supported a general shift in government spending away from the traditionally heavy emphasis on defense spending, focusing instead on increased domestic spending: for the cities; for antipoverty programs; for education, etc.

In effect, defense spending operated in an atmosphere uninhibited by the usual challenges of representative government. Even the President often confronted insurmountable difficulties when he attempted to exert his influence in this area, as President Eisenhower did when he unsuccessfully attempted to reduce the National Guard and Army Reserve manpower levels on the grounds that they were "unnecessarily costing the American people over $80 million annually and have been too long based on other than strictly military needs." [29]

Defense industries with sharp political intelligence units (and most large companies do include "political departments") make it their business to locate in areas whose congressmen can ensure them government business. The eighty-billion-dollar defense budget is spread through the United States, but there are concentrations in key areas, namely, states such as Georgia, South Carolina, California, Texas, and Massachusetts.[30] In South Carolina alone, there are two Army bases, ten Navy installations (including hospitals, a weapons station, a supply depot, a submarine base, and a missile facility), and two Air Force bases, compared to Wyoming, which only has one defense installation, or Maine (like South Carolina, a coastal state and much closer to Europe) with only three naval outposts.[31]

When the Pentagon closed the Marine Corps Transportation Shed (which employed three persons) as part of an economy move, the city of Charleston was assigned another squadron of Polaris Missile submarines with a complement of 2,200 men. The latest defense-construction bill approved by the Armed Services Committee contained $11.7 million in new facilities for bases in Charleston alone—which include the Charleston Army Depot, the

[29] In his now famous farewell speech on January 17, 1961, Eisenhower warned of the dangers presented by the nation's "military-industrial complex."

[30] See Office of the Secretary of Defense, Directorate for Statistical Services, *Department of Defense Prime Contract Awards by State*, March 1968, pamphlet; and *U.S. Military Prime Contract Awards by Region, State and Commodity Category, Fiscal Years 1962–1967*, booklet.

[31] Department of Defense, *Major Military Installations in the United States*, March 31, 1967, pamphlet.

Charleston Shipyard, Naval Hospital, Naval Station, Naval Supply Center, Naval Weapons Station, Navy Fleet Ballistic Missile Submarine Training Center, Polaris Missile Facility, and Charleston Air Force Base.

The state of Georgia, home of Senator Richard B. Russell, has also been amply provided with defense installations. Senator Russell is chairman of the Senate Armed Services Committee and occupies the seat second in seniority to the chairman of the Senate Appropriations Committee—an unbeatable combination of committee assignments. Nevertheless, the dispute over the C5A transport jet which pitted Senators Russell and Proxmire against each other, in a battle not unlike David and Goliath's, eventually led the Defense Department, yielding to public opinion, to curtail the program. The outcome of Senator Proxmire's investigations into the C5A cost-overruns, which disclosed that costs of building the transport planes had soared from $1.9 billion for 115 aircraft to $3.2 billion for only 81 planes, led an ad hoc committee of 45 congressmen (nine senators and 36 representatives) to recommend more stringent review procedures over military budgeting practices, with the long-range goal of reasserting "congressional control over the nation's military industrial establishment." [32] Senator Proxmire charged that "one of the great and tragic issues of defense" involved patronage considerations, particularly "the question of friends getting defense contracts." He noted this practice was made easier by the process of awarding contracts: "only 11% of the Defense Department's contracts are competitive and advertised, while the remaining 89% are negotiated procurements," a term which means virtual discretionary power.

Originally used by President Eisenhower, the term

[32] *Congressional Quarterly*, "Fact Sheet," June 5, 1969, p. 1.

"military-industrial complex" never included the word "political," even though evidence keeps appearing—such as the relationship between the location of military installations corresponding to the districts of key congressmen —to indicate that political factors often take precedence over technical considerations. The contract award for the TFX aircraft (later renamed F-111) revealed in investigations conducted by the Senate Government Operations Committee in 1963 what were the significant patronage factors affecting a decision of this kind.[33]

The TFX contract, involving more than $6.5 billion, 20,000 jobs, and 1,700 airplanes, was awarded to General Dynamics for the purpose of building the largest tactical airplane ever built. The question quickly arose as to why General Dynamics got the contract despite the unanimous endorsement by military, financial, and technical advisers from the Air Force and the Navy of the plans submitted by the Boeing Company. The answers were slowly uncovered when it was learned that General Dynamics planned to build the TFX at its Convair plant in Fort Worth, Texas, and at the Grumman Aircraft Engineering Corporation in Bethpage, Long Island, while Boeing, with headquarters in Seattle, would have built the aircraft at its plant in Wichita, Kansas. Pressuring for the contracts were representatives of competing regions—Lyndon Johnson, then Vice-President, and the Texas delegation, versus Senators Henry Jackson and Warren Magnuson of Washington.[34] The dispute was further complicated by the existence of interlocking relationships of mutual obligation among key personnel in the Defense Department and top executives from General Dynamics. Roswell Gilpatric,

[33] Congressional Quarterly, "Congress and the Nation, 1945–1964," pp. 1766–1767.

[34] *Ibid.*

then Deputy Secretary of Defense, had previously acted as General Dynamics' legal adviser, and his law firm was still counsel to the corporation; his former law partner was on the board of the company. Navy Secretary Fred Korth was formerly president of a Fort Worth bank that had loaned money to General Dynamics. Testimony showed that he had been in contact with representatives of General Dynamics sixteen times during contract negotiations, while meeting only twice with representatives of Boeing. He also was accused of "indiscretion" for entertaining "extra good customers" of his Fort Worth bank on the Navy's official yacht.

General Dynamics proceeded to build the plane while the investigation was underway, under a "letter contract," a common Defense Department procedure for permitting a contractor to get his project started, leaving the details of the more complex, formal contract to be settled later. In this way, the material effects of a controversy are minimized; for by the time the issue is resolved, if ever, even the antagonists are unwilling to waste what money has already been spent. Many considered the competition for defense contracts itself a source of patronage, with ten companies each given $1 million grants to submit proposals.[35]

Except for the patronage features illuminated by its disclosures, the TFX controversy never became more than a convenient issue valuable for its prolific production of political ammunition. Charges of political pressure were made by Representative Stinson, a Washington Republican, in whose seventh district Boeing was located, who called the TFX the "LBJ aircraft." Later, similar charges

[35] The cost estimates of both General Dynamics and Boeing were called unrealistic by Defense Secretary Robert McNamara. Later, the costs were to become even more of an issue when construction far exceeded the estimates.

were incorporated into the 1964 Republican platform to the effect that the Democratic administration "permitted non-military considerations, political as well as economic, to reverse professional judgement on major weapons such as the controversial TFX, the X-22 and the nuclear carrier." [36]

The vast defense apparatus leads congressmen to protect existing installations and to seek new ones. "It's harder on you to lose something you have than fail to get something new," D. B. Hardeman observed. He recalled an antiquated Veterans Administration hospital in Mr. Rayburn's district that should have been closed: "This was a very important payroll in that county. Politically, he had to keep it open, and he did." The threat to close the Brooklyn Navy Yard in 1966 brought Representative Celler, Chairman of the Judiciary Committee, in whose district the yard was located, and the entire New York congressional delegation to Washington. Navy Secretary Paul H. Nitze made two trips to inspect the installation, and gave guarded assurances that some parts of the yard would remain open. Eventually, it was entirely closed, leading to the widespread realization of the collective political impotence of the New York congressional delegation.

Similarly, Senator Albert Gore, the Tennessee Democrat, wrote to then Secretary of the Air Force Eugene Zuckert about reports that the Stewart Air Force Base at Smyrna, Tennessee, might be closed, and received assurances that no changes were contemplated. Senator Olin B. Johnston, South Carolina Democrat, called on President Kennedy to receive assurances that the future of Fort Jackson, in Columbia, South Carolina, and Donaldson Air Force Base, in Greenville, South Carolina, would be

[36] "Congress and the Nation, 1945–1964," *op. cit.*, pp. 1766–1767.

carefully considered. Representative Samuel S. Stratton, New York Democrat, wired Secretary Zuckert about reports concerning the transfer of certain operations from Griffiss Air Force Base at Rome, New York: "It is fantastic to learn that once more the Defense Department is considering recommendations which would have the effect of increasing unemployment in upstate New York, already hard hit by layoffs." [37]

Citizens across the country seem to feel they hold a vested interest in the production of armaments, and expect their congressmen to intercede whenever possible to cull the benefits of armament production for their regions. Already dramatized by the TFX issue, the widespread acceptance of unchecked armaments production woven tightly into our political culture undoubtedly has increased the country's receptivity to entering military conflicts, and prolonged the war in Vietnam. Congressmen, conditioned by this national mania and fearful of the unproven assertion that defense industries cannot convert to peacetime purposes, beg for defense contracts, rarely considering the effects. Representative John R. Foley, a Maryland Democrat, offered an amendment to the defense bill in 1959 to add $10 million to Air Force funds to buy 10 F-27 transports from the Fairchild Aircraft Company of Hagerstown, Maryland, in Foley's district. This failed, but the Senate came through with $11 million. When House conferees refused to go along, Senator J. Glenn Beall, Maryland Republican, begged the Senate to insist, saying that of the $4 billion to be spent on aircraft, "all we ask for Fairchild is $11 million." [38]

The Army's Nike-Zeus anti-missile system was enthusiastically supported by congressmen whose states

[37] "Congress and the Nation, 1945–1964." *op. cit.*, p. 1582

[38] *Ibid.*

were to get the money—Representative George Miller, a California Democrat; Senator Strom Thurmond, a South Carolina Republican; Senator B. Everett Jordan, a North Carolina Democrat ($36 million); and Representative Daniel Flood, a Pennsylvania Democrat ($10 million). Representative John McCormack, the Massachusetts Democrat and long-time Speaker of the House, urged that the United States "close the gap in our military posture; muzzle the Mad-Dog Millie threat of the Soviet Union; loose the Zeus through America's magnificent production lines, now." Massachusetts was earmarked for $1.5 million.[39]

Members of Congress also show a great solicitude for military reserves—reflecting to some degree the widespread local interest in the payrolls, armories, and other benefits involved. Among the 40 reserve officers in Congress are Senator Barry Goldwater, Arizona Republican (Brigadier General, United States Air Force Reserve), on the Armed Services Committee; Senator Strom Thurmond, South Carolina Democrat (Major General, United States Air Force Reserve), on the Armed Services Committee; Senator Howard Cannon, Nevada Democrat (Brigadier General, United States Air Force Reserve), on the Armed Services Committee; and Representative Robert L. F. Sikes, Florida Democrat (Brigadier General, United States Air Force Reserve), on the Defense Appropriations Subcommittee.

Perhaps one of the most successful recipients of government favors has been Senator Warren Magnuson, Washington Democrat, and chairman of the Commerce Committee, who says that he fights for everything that is earmarked for the West Coast. "Maggie [Senator Magnuson's nickname] gets everything that isn't nailed down,"

[39] "Congress and the Nation, 1945–1964," *op. cit.*, p. 1583.

noted one of his Senate colleagues rather ruefully. "I have a constant fight with Portland," Mr. Magnuson said. "I get most of the projects in Seattle because these fellows have to come back to me for the money." But Mr. Magnuson insists that the supersonic transport (SST) contract went to Boeing on its merits: "Ninety percent of the contracts would be where they are if there were no Congress." His other achievements include the Bonneville Power Administration, the Hanford Atomic Project, a $9 million federal appropriation for Seattle's 1962 World's Fair, as well as government contracts for Seattle's Boeing Plant, for the Puget Sound Naval Shipyard and the Sands Point Naval Air Station. Indeed, he speaks of the vast Columbia River Basin reclamation project as though he had built it himself, boasting that "this year I put up the Glen Canyon Transmission lines."

At the other extreme are senators like Abraham Ribicoff, from Connecticut, who says with pride that he does not consider economic rewards at all; in fact, he recalled working against his state's economic interests, as he has done when he voted against Connecticut's tobacco interests. Senator Ribicoff noted that he could retain this independence, this freedom from entering the nasty business of culling rewards for his state, because he does not have to rely on industry to finance his campaigns. "My money comes from what I call emotional money," said the senator, "wealthy Jewish liberals from New York who like to see a good Jewish boy in the Senate."

❦ *Eve and the Apple:*
Conflicts of Interest Arising from
Congressional Patronage Opportunities

A combination of factors, including the abundance of government rewards, the lack of supervision and control over dispensing these rewards, and the increasingly high cost of campaigning, weaves together congressmen, lobbyists, industry, and interested citizens in a curious web of favors, many of which could be considered substantial conflicts of interest. Congressmen own bank stock, practice law, own real estate, invest in the defense industry, at the same time that they enact banking legislation, regulate the real estate industry, or belong to law firms which represent clients in litigation before government agencies.

Representative Emanuel Celler, for example, belongs to a New York City law firm that has erected an elaborate façade of separating its clients. One front door of Celler's law office identifies the firm of Weisman, Celler, Allan, Spett and Sheinberg, while the other door omits Celler's name. All cases involving the government are assigned to the firm without his name—as required by federal law which prohibits congressmen from taking fees in federal cases. But both firms have the same telephone number, the same furniture and fixtures, and the same staff. Indeed, federal officials are undoubtedly aware of Mr. Celler's interest in a client even though his name is omitted from the stationery of the firm that handles government business.[40]

The Florida law firm of Senator George Smathers lists clients including Pan American World Airways, Standard Oil, and the Home Insurance Agency,[41] a con-

[40] Drew Pearson and Jack Anderson, *The Case Against Congress* (New York: Simon & Schuster, 1968), pp. 118–119.

[41] Senator Smathers' law firm of Smathers & Thompson, located in Miami, Florida, includes in its roster the following clients: *Representative Clients:* Seaboard Air Line Railroad Company; Pan American World Airways, Inc.; Lineas Aereas de Nicaragua (LANICA); Western Union Telegraph Company; United States Aviation Underwriters; Lloyd's of London; Chubb and Son; Appleton and Cox; W. H. McGee and Company; American International Marine Agency; The Home Insurance Company; Union Marine and General Insurance Company;

venient combination that jibes aptly with Smathers' combined committee memberships which include: Finance, Small Business, Judiciary, and Joint Internal Revenue Taxation. A survey of House and Senate members who filed very limited financial disclosures in reports made available to the public revealed that twenty-four House members who are lawyers said they received at least $5,-000 in 1968 from the practice of law. Senators declined to report their income from law practices.[42] The same survey revealed that sixty-one representatives owned stock in companies ranked among the nation's top defense contractors—including four members of the House Armed Services Committee; ninety-four representatives owned an interest in banks, savings and loan associations, or bank

---

General Accident, Fire and Life Insurance Company; W. J. Roberts and Company; Atlantic Mutual Insurance Company; Insurance Company of North America; Gulf Oil Corporation; Standard Oil Company; Anheuser-Busch; McKesson & Robbins, Inc.; Tropical Gas Company; Winn & Lovett Grocery Company; Commercial Bank of Miami; Merchants Bank of Miami; Phillips Petroleum Company; American Mercury Insurance Company; New Amsterdam Casualty Company; Walson and Company; *General Counsel:* for the McKinley Group Marine Managers. The firm also has a Washington, D.C., office (Smathers, Merrigan and O'Keefe). See *Martindale-Hubbell Law Directory*, Volume I, 1969, pp. 2432B–2434B.

[42] *Congressional Quarterly Weekly Report*, Volume XXVII, No. 21, pp. 746–795, May 23, 1969. In 1969, both houses of Congress required members to make limited financial-disclosure reports, with the rules for each chamber differing considerably. Complete financial reports were kept confidential, to be opened only by a majority vote of the Senate Select Committee on Standards and Conduct, and the House Committee on Standards of Official Conduct. House members were ordered to disclose publicly the source of any income for services exceeding $5,000 and any capital gain from a single source exceeding $5,000. Senators were also asked to list publicly the source amounts of political contributions in excess of $50, but the information produced was very sketchy. Sixty-one senators reported income from honorariums, but little else; while 158 House members filed blank statements.

holding companies, including twelve of the members of the House Banking and Currency Committee; thirty-nine House members owned stock in oil or gas companies, with three of these members on the House Interior and Insular Affairs Committee; thirteen members said they owned stock in commercial airlines, with two of these serving on the House Interstate and Foreign Commerce Committee; and thirty-seven House members reported owning stock in ten companies receiving the largest contracts for the Sentinel ABM (Anti-Ballistic Missile) system, with two of these serving on the House Armed Services Committee, three on the Joint Committee on Defense Production, and one on the Department of Defense Subcommittee of the House Appropriations Committee.[43] Could this have affected their view of defense spending?

Even though it is difficult to prove specific quid pro quos that show that direct relationships between government decisions and congressional influence related to outside professional activities do, in fact, exist, the behavior of professional favor-seekers shows that the possibilities envisioned are not entirely imaginary. It is common practice, for example, for politically aware industries to hire law firms with congressional connections in anticipation of needed clout, whether or not this clout ever materializes, just as industries seeking defense contracts place retired generals, admirals, and other high-ranking defense officials on their payrolls. The Hebert probe revealed at the time that it was made that 1,400 retired officers in the rank of major or higher were employed by the nation's top 100 defense contractors. The company employing the largest number of military men was General Dynamics, winner of the controversial TFX contract, where 187 re-

[43] *Ibid.*

tired officers, including 27 generals and admirals, were listed on the payroll.[44]

Congressmen also derive outside income by remaining on the boards of their companies, and by accepting honorariums for speaking engagements. "Most do this ethically; people trade on the expectation of contact," said Representative Ogden Reid. "The honorarium begins with a speaking engagement, and the sponsoring group often says 'bring your wife.' They pay for the accommodations at a local motel, where the couple spend the night. The company says 'I'll fly you down,' on the company plane, and the congressman returns with a campaign contribution."

Representative Reid co-sponsored (with the then Congressman John Lindsay of New York) legislation to raise congressional salaries to $50,000 with full disclosure of income.[45] The legislation would ban outside employment, and elevate the job of congressman to full-time status. "Congressmen must cope with a conflict of time, if not of interest, if not both," Mr. Reid said. Congressman Reid also submitted another bill to curb what he regards as excessive conflicts of interest, requiring that written or oral communications between congressmen and members of regulatory agencies be part of the public record. "A congressman might contact the FCC if he felt a program was not in the public interest," charged Congressman Reid. "But he might also call for a TV license for himself or for someone he owes a favor." At present, congressmen earn $42,500 a year and still find it difficult to meet the

---

[44] Conducted by Representative F. Edward Hebert in 1959 under the auspices of the House Armed Services Special Investigations Subcommittee. "Congress and the Nation, 1945–1964," *op. cit.*, p. 1579.

[45] See Appendix A.

rigorous expenses entailed by frequent visits back home, entertainment, campaigning, etc. It is unlikely, however, that a hike in salary without effective enforcement of the ban on outside employment would work since Congress has shown in the past that it is unwilling to enforce even the most minimal codes against offending members.

Many regret the high costs of campaigning which keep congressmen (as well as the President) in economic bondage. To survive politically, most congressmen must overlook the Corrupt Practices Act, which places a ceiling on campaign expenditures, and pretend ignorance on the subject of where their money originates. Often, campaign managers, who handle the shadier side of campaign contributions, receive the contributions in untraceable cash deposits, while the congressman, aware of the practice but not the details, concentrates on loftier issues. After his victory, campaign aides slide easily into positions as legislative and administrative aides, more aware than their employer where the debts lie and thus more capable of redirecting future patronage favors. Congressman Reid, who is independently wealthy, recalls being called to the floor of the House one day by a union representative, who tried to give him a check for $500. The congressman sent it back to the dumbfounded lobbyist, who said he had "never had his checks refunded by anyone before." Speaking at a company dinner in Westchester, Reid also told how he was met at the door by a vice-president who handed him a check. The executive had dunned all his fellow executives for one percent of their salary for this contribution, which Reid also returned. It is against the law for candidates to accept contributions from corporations, although it may be accepted from a political education fund, or from individual executives of a company.

Sometimes senators, aware of the great potential of financial obligation, enhance their power by steering contributors to other senators, as in the case of Senator Russell Long, the Louisiana Democrat who is chairman of the Finance Committee. The senator's office has helped direct campaign contributions from the oil industry to friendly senatorial candidates suggested by Mr. Long, the *Los Angeles Times–Washington Post* reported in September 1969. Michigan Oil Executive Harold M. McClure, Jr., president of the Independent Petroleum Association of America, said he had sometimes consulted with Long's administrative assistant, Robert Hunter, about "who is good and who is bad" before writing contribution checks. Both men acknowledged that McClure gave Hunter a $2,000 contribution to be distributed to candidates of Long's choosing. A federal grand jury in Baltimore investigated the contribution, which records showed was made by McClure to former Maryland Senator Daniel B. Brewster. The money actually went from McClure to Long's office to the Maryland Democratic central committee, which was financing Brewster's unsuccessful re-election effort.[46]

The classic case revealing the opportunities for illegitimate congressional patronage, especially in the area of politically connected government contracts, was the Bobby Baker case, opened to public scrutiny by Senate hearings conducted by Senator John J. Williams, Republican, of Delaware. The Baker case demonstrated how crucial the secretary to the Senate Majority (1955–1963) was in the delegation of favors. The investigation of Mr. Baker, who was Senator Lyndon Johnson's right-hand man, was conducted by the Rules and Administration Committee. The committee did not initiate the investigation—an interesting indication of Mr. Baker's power—but rather acted after the Senate itself adopted through a

[46] *Washington Post*, September 5, 1969, p. 34.

voice vote a resolution offered by Senator Williams, after a civil suit had been filed charging Baker with using his influence to secure government contracts.[47] The Senate was embarrassed by the widespread publicity in the press into taking action, but was unwilling to investigate itself. In a stormy session the Senate, by a 42–33 roll-call vote, rejected a Republican resolution to broaden the inquiry to include senators and former senators. The Republicans alleged that the Democrats were trying to inhibit the investigation. Three senators on the Committee asserted: "The full story has not been disclosed concerning Bobby Baker and those associated with him, including present and former Senators and Senate employees. It has not been told because the majority prevented the investigation from proceeding"—a form of patronage in itself.

Subsequent investigations showed that the ingratiating young man from Pickens, Georgia, had always extracted a kickback for himself while furthering the business interests of others. A civil suit brought by a competitor, Ralph L. Hill, president of Capitol Vending Co., alleged that Baker had used his influence to obtain contracts in defense plants for SERV-U Corporation. Hill said that Baker accepted $5,600 for getting a franchise for Capitol with Melpar, Inc., and a subcontractor to North American Aviation Corporation on the Minute Man Missile. The suit, settled out of court for $30,000, also charged that Baker had told a consultant for North American that he was in a position to help obtain government contracts —in return for which North American installed SERV-U vending machines in its California plants. Baker was a partner in SERV-U. Baker obtained favorable rulings from the Internal Revenue Service for the Mortgage Guarantee Insurance Corporation of Milwaukee, in which he

---

[47] "Congress and the Nation, 1945–1964," *op. cit.*, pp. 1773–1778.

had built up sizable holdings which enabled the company to grow far beyond its original dimensions. Baker's holdings amounted to stock worth $217,000. Baker's partner, Fred B. Black, said that he, Baker, and SERV-U had borrowed over $500,000 from the bank of Senator Robert Kerr, Oklahoma Democrat.

Congressional attitudes toward patronage seem to encourage such lapses, but the real problem is not the dishonest or venal lawmaker, but rather the congressman who is merely trying "to go along" and serve his two constituencies. There are many who doubt that a man can serve two masters—or three or four, including the lobbyists and the executive branch.

"There is nothing inherently immoral about trying to succeed," Representative Lowenstein noted, "and in politics this society's idea of success is to get yourself elected. But once that has become the goal, all the other values and goals can be forgotten." [48]

[48] *The New Yorker, op. cit.*, p. 3.

6

Where the Clubhouse
Meets the White House:
Presidential Patronage

*If Lyndon found out somebody really wanted something
very badly, he would hold it up until he could trade it off for
something he really wanted.*
— Stewart L. Udall, Secretary of the Interior in the
Kennedy and Johnson administrations

*You can't use tact with a congressman. A congressman is a
hog. You must take a stick and hit him on the snout.*
— A Cabinet member to Henry Adams, in *The Education of Henry Adams*

❡ *From the Victor: The President's
Obligations as Party Leader*

"You can't keep an organization together without
patronage," advised former Tammany leader George
Washington Plunkitt. "Men ain't in politics for nothin'.
They want to get somethin' out of it." [1] At the peak of his
party's organizational pyramid stands the President, ulti-

[1] William L. Riordan, *Plunkitt of Tammany Hall* (New York: Alfred
A. Knopf, 1948), p. 51.

250

mately responsible for ensuring that his party's faithful have not entered politics for 'nothin'. How well he separates the cream of his patronage for the nourishment of the party determines his effectiveness in his loftier, constitutionally protected roles as: commander-in-chief; chief legislator; chief executive; and chief architect of his country's domestic and foreign policy. For the party which elects him and maintains him in power expects the fruits of power to flow its way, to keep alive past relationships founded on mutual obligation. These appointments also determine the President's future effectiveness, and the course of national policy.

The myriad ways in which the President can help his party through federal patronage were never better demonstrated than the way in which President Nixon showered his discretionary favors to aid the Republican primary prospects of John V. Lindsay. Mr. Lindsay had pocketed a Nixon IOU at the Miami convention by seconding the nomination of Spiro T. Agnew and by discouraging those who had urged Mr. Lindsay to contest the vice-presidential nomination. The Nixon administration directed every relevant federal agency to make a public contribution to New York City during the eight weeks before primary day. With much showmanship, Vice-President Agnew began the flow of favors by announcing the long-sought purchase of the Brooklyn Navy Yard by the city at an advantageous price. Then the Commerce Department announced grants for job training at the Yard; the Defense Department announced the lease of the Brooklyn Army Terminal; the Interior Department announced a new federal park in Breezy Point, the Rockaways; Health, Education and Welfare announced new narcotics projects; and the Attorney General announced aid for the city's "war against crime." "Agnew was interested in Lindsay," Harry S. Dent, President Nixon's special counsel and patronage overseer, said in his soft South Carolina drawl. "The Vice-President brought him here [Washington] and helped him with exposure. In the South, it means more to have a political leader who can bring home the bacon and outsmart those Yankees." But all to no avail. Mayor Lindsay lost the Republican primary to a Staten Island conservative, State Senator John J. Marchi. Mr. Lindsay went on to win re-election by forming a fusion campaign, soliciting endorsements from name Democrats, and staying as far away as possible from the White House. Indeed, Lindsay went so far as to attack the White House and Vice-President Agnew during the 1970 congressional elections, expressing his regret at having seconded Agnew's nomination. He noted that the Vice-President's attacks on "radical-liberals" had the blessings of the White House, and denounced the President for spreading "a cloud of suspicion and mistrust across the nation." After the campaign, Mr. Dent was asked if Lindsay would lose some of the federal programs designated for New York City. "Punishment is counterproductive," Mr. Dent replied. "It creates sympathy for a man"—although he added that new federal aid would now be channeled exclusively through Governor Rockefeller and Senators Javits and Buckley.

Mr. Nixon's rise from the political ashes was based in large part on his indefatigable campaigning for local candidates while out of office. The future president was photographed with Republicans across the length and breadth of the country, and was a frequent speaker at Republican fund-raising gatherings. The Nixon style was described by Governor Rockefeller in 1970, who told a dinner meeting of the Governor's Club that the President had personally promised him full support in his re-election bid. "Confidentially," the governor related, lowering his voice, the President promised: " 'I will campaign for

you in any way that will help, and I'll not hurt you.' " [2]
And for his part, Governor Rockefeller told the group, he
would continue to support the President's policies "in
every way I can."

To help Mayor George Seibels of Birmingham, Alabama, Republican mayor in a Democratic state, to stay
alive politically, Nixon sent federal aid, cutting through
the usual time-consuming red tape characteristic of government spending. Mayor Seibels told how he, along with
five aides, flew to Washington with the express purpose
of obtaining the federal aid which would enable them to
turn a large area of parkland into a recreational area for
camping and water sports. Meeting with representatives
from the Departments of Labor, Agriculture, and Housing and Urban Development, Mayor Seibels' group gave
a 12-minute presentation, and "within 48 hours," reported
the mayor, "the Labor Department gave us 500 Neighborhood Youth corps jobs; HUD gave us a matching beautifi-
cation program totalling $195,000; and we got 65 jobs
from OEO." Mayor Seibels added that it "helped to have
John Sparkman [senator from Alabama] as chairman of
the Banking and Currency Committee." Mayor Seibels reciprocated the President's shower of favors; and at the
Mayors' Conference in Pittsburgh in May 1969, he fought
valiantly with his colleague mayor J. Palmer Gaillard,
Jr., of Charleston, South Carolina, to defend the President's ABM program before a hostile group of big-city
mayors who were attempting to pass a resolution asking
the federal government to reorder its priorities away from
defense spending and into the cities. "It won't help to have
good housing and schools if we eliminate defense spending," argued Mayor Seibels. "What do we do if every-

[2] *The New York Times*, January 15, 1970, p. 34.

thing is blown up because we can't defend ourselves?"

Balanced against the high expectations of presidential patronage teeter the realities of what concrete forms of patronage are actually under the President's control. In the area of job patronage, for example, his resources are steadily depleting, as Civil Service "blankets in" more and more categories of federal service, without many allowances to compensate for the attrition of patronage. Whatever their private feelings, presidents publicly applaud the "blanketing in" process, having learned the public relations value of supporting this policy. New administrations are always surprised to find how little federal job patronage exists, and presidents must look elsewhere in order to even out their patronage debts. Compared to the governor of Pennsylvania who controls approximately 50,000 jobs, there are only 6,500 patronage jobs (with a total minimum annual salary of $106.4 million) open to a new President, out of three million civilian employees in government. Even of these 6,500 "exempt" jobs, many are filled by persons with "status," which protects them from summary removal, but who may nevertheless gracefully retire lest their professional lives be made too uncomfortable by the new administration. The posts filled by the President range from the $60,000-a-year Cabinet positions down to lesser jobs paying $6,000–$7,000 a year; these jobs are left free from civil service control theoretically to give the new administration its own loyal organization and flexible policy-making apparatus. Although modern presidents no longer throw everyone out of office to make room for their own supporters, as Andrew Jackson did, transition jitters still afflict Washington on the eve of an incoming administration, and even many of those who do have job protection—such as assistants to the assistant deputy secretary—show anxiety, wondering if they will be downgraded or shorn of responsibility by a new layer of government coming into office.

Despite all rhetoric to the contrary, all federal job patronage bears a direct relationship to the President's primary obligation to his party, and his entire patronage operation is based on that premise. President Kennedy, for example, received 15,000 to 20,000 job applications from individual job seekers, from Democratic leaders out across the country, and from Democratic members of Congress. The independent job seekers were quickly brushed off, while only party-connected candidates—required to submit proof of their fitness and their political "reliability" —were given serious consideration. Loyalty was at a premium in the Kennedy patronage-dispensing procedure; and if a candidate could offer strong evidence that he had supported Kennedy before the party's nominating convention in Los Angeles, his chances of federal employment were increased. Theodore C. Sorensen, a Kennedy aide, recalled how prior to the convention he had told wavering party leaders that President Kennedy would have to rely on a great deal of new talent, and that those who had supported him earliest would be the first to be considered. Politics was back in style, rejoiced the Democrats, thrilled that Kennedy took his responsibility to the party seriously, wasting little time on antipatronage rhetoric.

President Nixon, who did expend a great deal of energy on antipatronage rhetoric, set up an even more elaborate screening process designed to weed out the political faithful from among the thousands of applicants for patronage jobs. In contrast to Kennedy's patronage prerequisites, Nixon did not demand preconvention loyalty for many top-level jobs, owing perhaps to his need for talent, his own uneven party career, and his desire to unite the Republican Party. Nixon installed Robert L. Kunzig as

Administrator of the General Services, and Henry Kissinger as Assistant to the President for National Security Affairs, even though both men had supported Nelson Rockefeller very shortly before Nixon won the presidential nomination. Nixon's patronage process was described by George Bell, who ran the program, as a six-step filter process, ending with a security check, and divided into distinctly political categories which ranged from "U" ("failure to appoint would result in adverse political consequences to the administration") to "Z" ("applicant not compatible with the Nixon administration and should not be appointed to public office"). Categories in between included "Y" ("no political importance to the administration") and "V" ("played a prominent role in the campaign; recommended in the highest terms by a member of the House or Senate leadership").

The elaborate nature of the screening process itself showed how valuable were these patronage jobs to the administration in terms of unifying the party at its local and legislative levels. If a candidate opted for a job with the Department of the Interior (important also because of the patronage that department controls), a White House aide would telephone the ranking Republican on the corresponding committee in both the House and the Senate—Senator Allott, on the Senate Interior Committee; Congressman Saylor on the House Interior Committee—to corroborate the candidate's acceptability with them. If the job was important enough, the aide might continue his check with the House and Senate Interior Appropriations subcommittees, with the checking process also serving the useful purpose of increasing the contacts between the President and key legislators, who might regard as patronage the President's willingness to check with them before making patronage appointments within their jurisdiction. Once a candidate reached the stage in which he was seriously considered for a top-level government patronage job, such as civil service classification G.S. 16, then additional members of the White House staff would run further checks on him before he was actually appointed.[3]

Pressed by the decreasing number of jobs at their disposal, some presidents quietly attempt to augment their job patronage by creating new government agencies—secure in the knowledge that by the time civil service "blanketed in" the jobs, they would no longer be in office. One little-known reason President Roosevelt created all the new federal agencies born of the New Deal, according to James L. Rowe, a top White House aide at the time, was to deliver on his patronage obligations—an interesting historical sidelight adding political significance to the social rhetoric accompanying the innovations of the New Deal. The Federal Trade Commission, a more notorious example than most agencies, was run by Tennessee machine politicians, partly because Senator Kenneth McKellar chaired the Appropriations Committee.[4] "FTC was loaded up with layers and layers of Tennessee lawyers," Mr. Rowe recalled. Similarly, the Justice Department was overwhelmed by Montana lawyers, although Senator Burton K. Wheeler was not consulted over the appoint-

[3] For an excellent breakdown of current presidential patronage, see *Congressional Quarterly Weekly Report*, Vol. XXVIII, January 3, 1969, pp. 15–31.

[4] See Edward F. Cox, Robert C. Fellmeth, and John E. Schulz, *"The Nader Report" on the Federal Trade Commission* (New York: Richard W. Baron, 1969), which reported: "During the pro-business days of the Republican administrations of the 1920's, the FTC . . . became a dumping ground for political patronage." Roosevelt's attempts to reform the FTC failed, and he eventually "used it to his political advantage by granting it as a political dukedom to Senator Kenneth McKellar of Tennessee. The dukedom was managed for McKellar and 'Boss' Crump's Memphis political machine by another Tennessean, Commissioner Edwin C. Davis, from 1933–1949," pp. 140–141.

ments. "That's what turned him against the New Deal," said Mr. Rowe. Although he never admitted it publicly, realizing that it was good politics to support civil service, Roosevelt welcomed the opportunity the New Deal agencies offered him to administrate without accommodating to all the cumbersome procedures civil service inflicted on all the other agencies of government.

Reminiscent of Roosevelt's socially motivated ideologies for creating the New Deal agencies was Kennedy's initiation of the antipoverty program, which served noble social ends while it also opened up an entirely new area of federal patronage to the Kennedy administration.

In contrast to Roosevelt, Kennedy, and Nixon, Presidents Eisenhower and Johnson found job patronage a colossal nuisance, with Eisenhower publicly disavowing any relationship with what he considered an illegitimate function of the Presidency. Tending to ignore the clubhouse level of the party, Eisenhower made his appointments from among the larger constituencies within the Republican establishment: the large Wall Street law firms; the Chamber of Commerce; the Council on Foreign Relations; and the Ivy League universities.[5] Johnson, paradoxically, who mastered legislative patronage, considered job patronage bothersome, finding the visibility of job patronage and its accompanying publicity exceedingly uncomfortable. While he handled the private agreements of legislative patronage with extraordinary finesse, he lacked the resources to find highly qualified, yet politically acceptable men for government positions. In fact, Johnson

[5] He also turned over the task of patronage-dispensing to Sherman Adams, the somewhat puritanical former governor of New Hampshire, whose fall from power coincided with published reports that he had accepted gifts from Bernard Goldfine, a New Hampshire industrialist. For a brilliant analysis of Adams' role within the Eisenhower administration, see Louis Koenig, *The Invisible Presidency* (New York: Rinehart & Co., 1960).

offended many of his party colleagues on Capitol Hill, according to an assistant, because he had appointed political enemies to career positions, in preference to more politically sensitive candidates. Another aide [6] recalled an argument he had had with Johnson, warning the President that if he persisted in picking career men, he would have to "pick his own workers for the 1968 campaign." Johnson countered with a memo, arguing that "if we pick career men, or military men, we won't get in trouble. Every time we've gone outside we've gotten into trouble." Johnson went on to cite the problems he had met in staffing the regulatory agencies with men who had earned the confidence of industry and labor, yet were not at the same time owned by the private sector: "I needed an appointee for the Federal Power Commission. Because I'm a Texan, I had to get a fellow who couldn't spell oil. I finally found someone, a solicitor for the railroads from Illinois. After I appointed him, the newspapers charged him with sitting in on a segregationist meeting back in Illinois regarding real estate."

The higher the public official, the more vehemently must he protest patronage practices in any form in order to win the respect of the public, whose mental set rests firmly against the realities of American politics. In effect, this forces the politician to pursue a schizoid policy, leaving an enormous gap between theory and practice. If he wants his party to allow him to continue in politics, he must honor his debts, and disperse the rewards of government to those who in effect gave him the opportunity to

---

[6] In contrast to public officials in other branches of government, most of the politicians connected with the executive branch who were interviewed for this chapter—even those whose government service is past history—declined to be quoted for attribution, extremely fearful of the sensitivity and vulnerability of the office of President. Henceforth, they will be identified only as "aides," qualified only by the President under whom they served.

govern; yet if he wants the public to vote for him, he must disclaim any relationship with the tawdry practice of politics as it is.

The Nixon administation provided a perfect example of how this dichotomy, refined to its most ludicrous by 1970, works in the dispensing of federal job patronage. At the same time that Nixon aides in one wing of the White House were in the process of carefully screening all job applicants to weed out those with the wrong political complexion, in another section of presidential offices more aides were conducting a "national talent search," dispatching inquiries to the notables in *Who's Who* for the purpose of constructing their own federal patronage "merit" system. In keeping with his publicly projected good-government image, the President also announced that he would be taking the Post Office out of politics, thereby removing some 67,000 positions for postmasters and rural mail carriers from their traditional congressional controls. To cool down the patronage dispute which angrily flared up from this announcement, Winton M. Blount, Postmaster General, was forced to call leading congressmen to reassure them that reform would begin with the scrapping of the current list of eligibles (mostly Democrats) and the replacement of some of the 2,200 acting postmasters appointed by Kennedy and Johnson.[7]

At the same time that he shunned patronage publicly, Nixon appointed an all-Republican Cabinet and a White House staff whose major common denominator seemed to be that they had all worked for Nixon during one of his numerous political campaigns.[8] John Twiname, the Nixon appointee as head of the Social Security Administration,

[7] *Newsweek*, March 10, 1969, p. 28.

[8] See Appendix B.

was previously a successful salesman of hospital equipment. Mr. Twiname, an Illinois Republican who looks and talks very much like the actor James Stewart, talked of his difficulty in recruiting fellow Republicans to HEW: "The Republican Party was never overloaded with the socially conscious, liberal-oriented people who are concerned about HEW," he said. Customarily at least a few Cabinet jobs are given to members of the other political party, to create an aura of bipartisanship, intended to promote national reconciliation after the damages caused by a savage campaign. In this connection, presidents often have turned not to political men with political ambitions, but to private men who happen to be affiliated with the opposition party. President Kennedy turned to Robert McNamara, a Republican who was president of the Ford Motor Company, and to Douglas Dillon, an investment banker who had served under Eisenhower. President Johnson selected John W. Gardner, whose life was spent in universities, foundations, and in writing, to be Secretary of Health, Education and Welfare. President Eisenhower selected Robert B. Anderson, a Texas Democrat who earned his reputation in business, not politics. President Franklin D. Roosevelt chose Henry L. Stimson, a Yankee Republican with a lifetime of public service in the broadest sense, but no elective hopes.

President Nixon broke this pattern with an all-Republican Cabinet, partially because he considered only Democrats who had political ambitions. The three Democrats whom he pursued most ardently and to whom he made all but final offers were men who had served the Democratic Party in elective office, or who possessed future political ambitions. They were former Vice-President Hubert H. Humphrey, Senator Henry S. Jackson of Washington, and R. Sargent Shriver, Jr., who was finally named ambassador to France. The appointments of Humphrey and Jackson never materialized.

The Nixon Cabinet had an unusual number of past political allies—and the Cabinet posts may have been rewarded as much for past political service as for the level of competence offered by the men chosen. Robert Finch, Secretary of HEW, managed Nixon's unsuccessful 1960 presidential race. When Nixon lost the 1962 race for governor of California, many former Nixon supporters drifted away, but Finch remained loyal and confident.

John Mitchell, who became Nixon's Attorney General, managed the President's successful campaigns for the presidential nomination and election, and was a law partner of Mr. Nixon's in the firm of Nixon, Mudge, Rose, Guthrie, Alexander and Mitchell. After Mr. Finch's fall from grace, Mr. Mitchell was regarded as the President's most influential adviser, but he seemed to have lost some of his power after advising the President to pursue the nominations of Clement Haynsworth and later of G. Harrold Carswell for Supreme Court justices despite the storm warnings rumbling against both nominations. Aware of the enormous amount of job patronage (U.S. attorneys, assistant U.S. attorneys, marshals, and federal judges) at his disposal, the President is careful to select highly political men for the post of Attorney General. As was the case with Nixon's choice of Mitchell, this policy was true of President Warren G. Harding's selection of Harry Daugherty, who was Harding's campaign manager in 1920, as Attorney General. It was also true of Homer Cummings of Connecticut, a former Democratic National Chairman, appointed to the Roosevelt Cabinet; of J. Howard McGrath of Rhode Island, Democratic National Chairman, in the Truman Cabinet; and of Herbert Brownell of New York, a top official in three Republican campaigns, in the Eisenhower cabinet.[9] Robert F. Kennedy, who served as his brother's Attorney General, also took charge of patronage-dispensing. The Attorney General also decides whom to prosecute, and whom not to prosecute. In cases involving graft, the Attorney General often attacks officials of the opposite party and seldom officials of his own. Hence, the Nixon administration through the U.S. Attorney in New Jersey went after Mayor Hugh Addonizio, a Democrat, of Newark. Addonizio and his administration had been protected in the past by two Democratic presidents who used their discretionary power not to prosecute.

Winton Blount, the Postmaster General, was a wealthy Alabama contractor who headed Volunteers for Nixon-Lodge in the South in 1952. He said that his position as head of the United States Chamber of Commerce prohibited political activity during the 1968 presidential campaign. Walter Hickel, Secretary of the Interior, was a moderate Republican and co-leader of Nixon's presidential campaign in the Western states. George Romney, Secretary of Housing and Urban Development, threw his support to Nixon after his own unsuccessful bid for the nomination.

Secretary of State William Rogers, a close personal friend of Mr. Nixon's, headed the list of those selected for personal and political reasons. Melvin Laird, Secretary of Defense, was an influential House leader who promoted the Rockefeller presidential bid. David Kennedy, Secretary of the Treasury, was chairman of the board of Chicago's largest bank, the Continental Illinois National Bank and Trust Company.

[9] Richard Fenno, *The President's Cabinet* (Cambridge: Harvard University Press, 1959), p. 70.

Although Nixon rewarded top-ranking campaign aides, he seemed to shun the local organizations, who expected him as party leader to deflect federal patronage back to their clubhouses. Representative John Anderson from Rockford, Illinois (newly appointed leader of the House Republican Conference Committee), recounted how his efforts to obtain a job for a mayor in his district who had lost his bid for re-election were unsuccessful along with many other efforts to collect jobs for his constituents. "I can tell you this," said a disgruntled aide at the 1969 Governors' Conference at Colorado Springs, Colorado: "We're in trouble back home. There are a lot of unhappy Republicans out there." The unhappy warriors included the New Jersey State GOP, whose patronage committee met privately in Newark to plan an effort to open the jobs pipeline from the White House. The meeting was called by Republican State Chairman Webster Todd, who acknowledged that many party leaders in his state were "not happy at all" with the patronage situation, especially since New Jersey, the only Northeastern state carried by Nixon, had not as yet received one major patronage appointment that was considered political.

What party chairmen found most galling was that the Nixon administration allowed them to starve for patronage while it busily sent out computerized inquiries to names listed in *Who's Who*. Intended as an antipatronage public gesture, the inquiry not only brought more political crises than it was worth, but turned out to be an administrative disaster as well, according to an aide who claimed he "was the computer," programmed to process the reams of answers flowing in from the questionnaire. "They thought it would be good public relations," he recalled. "One day I walked into a room, and there was just paper. Thousands of sheets of paper . . . most of the letters were eventually lost, without ever being processed." Continuing to lament what he considered a political disaster of monumental proportions, he added: "The Democrats handle patronage so naturally; I don't know why Republicans always want to be 'statesmen.' "

Despite his steady flow of antipatronage rhetoric, Nixon met his patronage obligations on higher levels (White House staff, Cabinet appointments, Supreme Court appointments, and ambassadorships) very swiftly, demonstrating once again the harsh dichotomy between the President's conception of moral leadership and the realities of his patronage obligations. Nixon as President did not really feel that he had to identify his administration with low-level patronage politics; and was content to allow this operation to run itself into the ground, with jobs as high as assistant secretaries unfilled as late as three to four months after he took office.

Each President chooses his own patronage styles, and Nixon's willingness to support local candidates stands out as being unusual in view of the traditional reluctance on the part of presidents to enter local primary contests and local elections. Ever since Franklin Roosevelt's ill-fated attempt to unseat Senator Millard Tydings in the Maryland Democratic primary of 1937, presidents have been notably reluctant to involve themselves publicly in their party's primary contests. Either way they lose, when they take into account the resentment felt by local citizens who feel they have enough sense to choose their own candidates. Faced with a divided party following the New York mayoral primary, the President would not have been able, nor would he have been expected, to travel to New York to campaign for the mayor. In William Cahill's bid for New Jersey's governorship, on the other hand, the President did not hesitate to enter the state to campaign for a candidate with the party's full backing.

As party leader, Nixon has been very cooperative in

appointing men for the purpose of keeping them alive politically. His appointment of John H. Chafee to the post of Secretary of the Navy was seen as an effort to give Chafee visibility until such time as he chose to wage a campaign against Senator Claiborne Pell. (Chafee had been defeated for the governorship of Rhode Island.) The appointment of Chafee took great political generosity on Nixon's part, and a willingness to place his party over his personal feelings, for Chafee was an old political antagonist of the President's. Dickering between Mayor Lindsay and the Nixon administration, also unlikely party bedfellows, in the event that Lindsay chose not to seek re-election in 1969 ended in a stalemate, but there is evidence that the President was unwilling to allow New York's mayor a position within his administration. Mr. Lindsay apparently was negotiating for a State Department under-secretaryship, which was not offered.

The President often finds himself in the uncomfortable position of facing conflicting patronage obligations within the party. Among the complications faced by Kennedy's patronage-dispensing team (Lawrence O'Brien, Kenneth O'Donnell, John Bailey, and Robert Kennedy) were conflicting nominations and endorsements for the same jobs, especially in states whose party leadership was fragmented among several factions. In Ohio, for example, party leadership was fractionated among a Democratic governor, two Democratic senators, and the State Democratic Chairman, all of whom pressured the President for their share of the state's federal patronage. Only in cases of judgeships can patronage conflicts of this kind be solved promptly and arbitrarily by the traditional discretionary power of the senator. The Kennedys also found themselves embroiled in a knotty patronage problem in New York State, whose party structure was far more fragmented than Ohio's. Deeply obligated to New York for its help in the campaign, the Kennedy administration nevertheless had to face the difficulties presented by the harsh contrast between the bright image projected by the New Frontier and the shady reputation attached to the old-time "pols" (led at that time by Tammany Leader Carmine de Sapio) who dominated New York politics. When New York's Democratic forces finally resolved their differences and submitted their patronage list to Washington, Robert Kennedy was forced to confront them with the ultimatum of either introducing a more qualified set of alternatives, or losing the patronage.[10]

Nixon found himself enmeshed in conflicting patronage obligations involving the party and its related pressure groups over the appointment of Dr. John Knowles, the administrator of Massachusetts General Hospital, as Assistant Secretary for Health and Scientific Affairs. Indebted to Secretary of Health, Education and Welfare Robert Finch, the most liberal cabinet member, who wanted Knowles and had made the issue public, Nixon knew that his failure to appoint Knowles would embarrass if not humiliate a trusted friend, as well as undermine Finch's prestige and power in the new government. Finch had stood by Nixon throughout the President's long and uneven political career, not leaving him after crushing defeats had led many others to declare him politically finished. At the same time, Mr. Nixon also owed some deference to the American Medical Association, which had contributed heavily through its Political Action Committee to the Nixon presidential campaign. In deciding against the Knowles appointment, Nixon leaned

---

[10] Hugh Sidey, *John F. Kennedy, President* (New York: Atheneum, 1963), pp. 86–92.

in favor of the AMA and the Senate Republican leadership, perhaps regarding his debt to Finch as already paid off with a Cabinet appointment.

The AMA in the Knowles affair sought power similar to that wielded by the American Bar Association, to which the Nixon administration had already given a veto power over the selection of federal judges. The AMA wanted power to appoint the Assistant Secretary for Health and Scientific Affairs, and was said to "feel that its political contributions gave it the right to control the appointment and it had its own list of candidates which did not include Dr. Knowles." [11] Congressional opposition to Knowles was led by Everett Dirksen, then Senate minority leader, who threatened to generate votes against the White House-sponsored surtax bill. Other pressure came from Senator John G. Tower, the Texas Republican, and Representative Robert Wilson, California Republican, both chairmen of the Republican campaign committees for their respective houses of Congress. When the President ultimately rejected Knowles, who was well known for his interest in expanding federal health projects, the rejection was seen as a victory for medical conservatives. Ironically, the President replaced Knowles with Dr. Roger Egeberg, another liberal physician critical of the AMA and not on the list of six candidates submitted by the AMA for the post. The President apparently decided that it was more important to yield to the conservative members of Congress, upon whose votes he had come to depend for support on such controversial issues as the tax surcharge, defense budget, Haynsworth nomination, and the Anti-Ballistic Missile System.

[11] *The New York Times*, June 29, 1969, pp. 1, 42.

❡ The Power of the Purse: Contracts, Patronage and Party-Financing

American patterns of patronage politics sharpen the contrast between the President and his counterparts in totalitarian regimes, since such a large part of his discretionary power is already spoken for when he arrives in office. Bound to the exigencies of political quid pro quo inherent in democratic politics, American political leaders find that their power is checked before they even begin to govern—a factor which renders them less able than dictators to exercise their power arbitrarily.

At times, the President's patronage obligations seem overwhelming. Party leaders stand under the horn of plenty expecting to be showered with jobs, easy access to the White House, federal grants, contracts and franchises, as well as substantial White House support at election time. Traditionally, the really substantial party contributors—known as "fat cats"—expect their rewards straight from the President in the form of ambassadorships, although lately political ambassadorships appear to have dwindled in favor of assigning the posts to career diplomats. President Kennedy began the trend by giving only seven out of the first twenty-seven non-career jobs as Chiefs of Foreign Missions to men who had contributed over $500, a policy which Johnson followed [12] and Nixon continued by appointing a career diplomat, Charles Yost, to the post of Ambassador to the United Nations. In view

[12] Of some 35 similar appointments by President Johnson during 1964–1965, only 10 went to large contributors. See Herbert Alexander, "The Role of Money in the Political Process," unpublished paper prepared for the National Commission on Law and Law Enforcement and Prevention of Violence, October 1968.

of America's delicate position regarding its foreign policy, there remain very few ambassadorships subject to the chicaneries of political rewards. Political contributors still desire ambassadorships to Rome, London, or Paris, but these are "very expensive," according to presidential sources, although they are still given out on a financial basis. Walter Annenberg, a wealthy newspaper publisher from Philadelphia who contributed very heavily to the Republican Party, was named ambassador to London after Nixon became President. Others who have not contributed enough to rate ambassadorships can still hope for some government-financed travel in the form of State Department junkets (also used as congressional patronage) to foreign ceremonial festivities.

If contributors invest heavily enough to warrant presidential patronage, they probably cannot afford to leave their own business ventures to accept what by their standards amount to low-paying government jobs. Even so, they expect other forms of White House patronage in return for the patronage they have bestowed on the President in his candidacy. Many contributors welcome what may seem to be nonmaterial types of presidential patronage, such as an appointment to a nonpaying government advisory board, task force, or presidential commission, for these appointments offer wide visibility, free publicity, and lofty status to their beneficiaries, while usually involving very little work. Best of all, appearing on a presidential board makes a man look "plugged in," with channels to all the right contacts in Washington, an image which often materializes into substantial business gains. Many supporters of the President also prefer advisory board appointments because of their generally noncontroversial character. Unlike the appointment of a Supreme Court justice, the public scarcely cares who populate these boards, unaware that many of their decisions affect government spending and the public interest. The American Revolution Bicentennial Commission, for example, had to recommend where the next World's Fair would be located, a decision that would mean millions of dollars to whatever area of the country was finally chosen. The commission decided to recommend Philadelphia to the President, who chooses the final site—an important patronage decision on his part.

Financial supporters may be honored with other minor forms of presidential patronage: an autographed picture of the President; an invitation to a White House dinner, tea, or prayer meeting; or a picture taken with the President in the White House Rose Garden, always good for a press release back home. To help him out with these ceremonial patronage obligations to the party, the President frequently uses Cabinet members or the Vice-President, who are dispatched on trips throughout the country. Before they arrive, advance men contact party chairmen so that when the dignitary's jet lands, the local leaders can be on hand for pictures, speeches, and all the public-relations fanfare so important to the maintenance of the party system. "This is a time of lending public persons," said a Nixon aide. "This is very good patronage because local politicians can be visually identified with important national figures. When you're right there at Dubuque International Airport, it seems as if you've come just to visit the guy." In Great Britain, where the web of obligations between politicians and their supporters is far less elaborately woven, the royal family assumes many of these ceremonial duties, leaving the real head of state, the Prime Minister, free to concentrate on government business. Unlike the President, the Prime Minister is not as burdened with rapidly increasing campaign costs (his campaign time is restricted by law to three weeks, whereas the President often spends as long as two years campaigning for his office), whose excesses serve to bring the American chief executive under obligation to considerably more people.[13]

The President's prestige makes obligatory his presence at state and local party dinners designed to attract the party's "fat cats" to $100-a-plate (and over) dinners. Held to finance the party debt and to raise money for the future, these functions leave a large amount of money within the states to be used at the discretion of the party chairmen, whose effectiveness is often judged by their ability to attract officials like the President to state fundraising functions. Remaining a functional part of the party's fund-raising apparatus is expected of the President, who has already spent a large segment of his political career at party fund-raising functions. Since part of the proceeds from these functions carried him into the White House, it is likely that he will continue aiding the party in its financial efforts.

While ceremonial patronage appears relatively easy to discern, presidential favors which involve preferential treatment (such as delegating contracts, grants, and other material benefits channeled from executive departments) remain obfuscated. During the Johnson administration, the GOP House leadership revealed the existence of a President's Club, designed to facilitate the passage of material favors between the White House and wealthy contributors to the Democratic Party. Membership in the club

[13] In 1968, over $100 million was spent to elect a President, including the preconvention expenses of all candidates for presidential nominations as well as the cost of the conventions to the major parties and their delegates. A total of $300 million was spent on all levels during the 1968 campaigns. The 97 Democratic committees officially reported receipts of $20 million and expenditures of $19 million. This included $12 million spent by Hubert Humphrey. The Republican committees showed receipts of $29 million and expenditures of $29 million. See Herbert Alexander, *op. cit.*

could be purchased for $1,000 or more, with those 6,000 members fortunate enough to enter its elite corps guaranteed immediate access to the White House upon receipt of a spanking-new red-white-and-blue wallet-sized card designating their full-fledged privileges. "The President's club is . . . very exclusive," said Clifton Carter, formerly executive director of the Democratic National Committee. "Its members are assured of a direct relationship with President Johnson. Members who want to talk to the President, Vice-President, or one of their assistants, have only to contact my office. Members will immediately be put in contact with whomever they want to reach." [14]

The club was founded by John F. Kennedy in 1960 to help pay the party's campaign debt, and collected $4 million from 1964 to 1966, when it dropped out of sight, confronted with embarrassing evidence proving that card-carrying members of the club had gained not only access to the White House but lucrative contracts, grants, and control over several vital law-enforcement functions as well.

In 1966, for example, the Justice Department dropped an antitrust suit against Anheuser-Busch, the largest beer-producing company in the country, under very mysterious circumstances involving membership in the President's club. It was no coincidence, charged House Republican leader Gerald Ford, that the Justice Department dropped its suit against the company as "not warranted" scarcely less than one month after eight individuals associated with Anheuser-Busch had contributed $10,000 to the President's Club.

The opponents of the President's Club offered abundant evidence of patronage in government contracts, a

[14] Republican Congressional Committee, "Where the Action is. . . . The President's Club." Mimeographed pamphlet, Washington, D.C., 1966.

subject traditionally kept under wraps by both political parties anxious to keep these opportunities for political favors alive and well. Although difficult to implement, "contract" patronage is protected from public scrutiny by its very complexity, with bidding procedures couched in such incomprehensible legalistic language that determining the areas of discretionary power becomes virtually impossible. Defense contracts, for example, are practically all discretionary. Leading members of Congress who have mastered the technicalities and the jargon also control the vital patronage involved in defense contracts.

The political planners of the antipoverty program made sure that the contracts as well as the jobs created by the bill be allocated on a discretionary basis. Curiously, the patronage in the antipoverty program involved in the letting of contracts has virtually escaped the notoriety attracted by the numerous scandals surrounding the program's job patronage.

Representative Charles Goodell [15] (later the junior senator from New York) reported that one lucrative antipoverty contract was won by a member of the President's Club, over other contenders who had bid much lower than the victor. Late in 1964, said Goodell, OEO announced it was seeking a qualified engineering firm to provide guidance in selecting Job Corps sites and to furnish engineering services to Job Corps centers. Two weeks later, the contract was awarded to Consolidated American Services (Con-Am), a firm with a one-man office in Washington, which did not meet even the minimum requirements set up by the Chief of OEO's Job Corps Installation and Logistics Division, Mr. E. Hunter Smith, Jr., and was not among the firms his office recom-

[15] Mr. Goodell was a representative when the charges against the President's Club were publicized.

mended to OEO's chief contract-procurement officer. It turned out that the senior vice-president of Con-Am was W. C. Hobbs, who, according to Goodell, "contributed $1,000 to the President's Club on September 28, 1964, $1,000 to the Democratic National Committee on May 4, 1965, and $1,000 to the President's Club on March 11, 1966. Con-Am personnel informed our investigators that they had not done this type of work for the Government prior to the OEO contract." [16]

After George Brown (along with numerous members of his family) contributed $25,000 to the President's Club, his Houston-based firm of Brown & Root won a lucrative contract from the National Science Foundation to conduct a study of deep-sea exploration, known as Project Mohole. Brown & Root won the contract despite the fact that the firm's bid doubled the lowest bid submitted; and a grateful President Johnson prophesied that "The Project Mohole will provide the answer to many basic questions about the earth's crust and the origin of ocean basins." [17] Not limited solely to deep-sea exploration, the firm of Brown & Root also belongs to a consortium of four firms which have combined to build airfields and other military installations in Vietnam.

Links to the President's Club were also established in the awarding of architectural and engineering contracts, a form of patronage more commonly seen at the state and local levels.[18] What infuriated the House Republican leadership most was that the President's Club's records re-

[16] Republican Congressional Committee, "Where the Action is. . . . The President's Club."

[17] Press release, May 18, 1966.

[18] Reinforced by the firm resistance on the part of professional architectural and engineering societies against putting these contracts on a competitive basis.

vealed contributions from prominent Republicans, who not coincidentally had received architectural and engineering contracts from the Johnson administration. Two months before the November 1966 congressional elections, House Republicans charged that the architectural and engineering firm of Albert C. Martin & Associates had received contracts drawing a fee of $700,000 to $875,000 for modernization of a Veterans Administration hospital in California, following the contribution of $12,000 to the President's Club by Martin's brother and business partner, J. Edward Martin, a former Republican Party official and chapter leader of the John Birch Society. Maintaining that architectural and engineering contracts were awarded arbitrarily without legislative or public oversight, the Republicans resented the opportunities for patronage which cut so deeply into the structure of the Republican Party. What motivations existed for maintaining party loyalty, they asked, in the face of such overwhelming patronage bait dangled so flagrantly from the executive branch of government?

The effectiveness of the President's Club depended, it was seen later, on actual patronage, rather than merely the promise of future favors, for when Hubert Humphrey tried to resurrect a President's Club from Johnson's list, he met with meager success. About half the members from Johnson's list joined Humphrey's Club, and of these, nothing is known about the amounts they contributed. Perhaps, too, with Humphrey already acknowledged by many analysts as the losing candidate, politically acute contributors saw little chance of promises of potential patronage being actualized.

The President's Club revealed what is often difficult to prove but is generally known as fact: that there exists a definite relationship between presidential favors, political support, and the eventuality of material quid pro quos. Political support in exchange for executive favors turns up more often, and can be pinpointed with more accuracy, than favors which involve the flow of money between the government and the private sector. The fundraising efforts of the President's Club also show how ineffective the Hatch Act is in preventing the conflicts of interest arising from presidential favors in return for campaign contributions. While the Hatch Act forbids direct corporate contributions, there is nothing to prevent a corporation executive—or members of his family—from making individual gifts to the President, or to any other elected official with discretionary favors at his disposal.

❲ *The Carrot and the Stick: Controlling the Legislature through Patronage*

Senator Ralph T. Smith of Illinois arrived in Washington as the battle over the confirmation of Clement Haynsworth as Supreme Court justice neared its climax. Mr. Smith, a Republican and former Speaker of the lower house of the Illinois Legislature, was appointed by Governor Richard Ogilvie to fill the seat of the late Senator Everett Dirksen. He opposed the appointment, but reversed himself two weeks later, still smarting under the impact of the President's clout. "We did some checking, and our understanding is that if he didn't support Haynsworth, he would have a primary opponent, no support within the Illinois Republican party, and no money," said Kenneth Young, AFL-CIO congressional liaison, and a leader of the forces marshaled against Haynsworth, whom they considered a segregationist and guilty of judicial conflicts of interest. Smith could not reasonably be expected to have acted otherwise, in view of his tenuous political position both within his party and with the voters of Illinois, who had yet to grant him a mandate to govern. Similarly, it was believed that Senator James Pearson's support of Haynsworth was the price of his continued membership in the Kansas Republican Party. "I don't consider this to be dirty pool; this is the way the game is played," said Mr. Young.

As leader of his party, the President has unlimited opportunities to influence legislators through their local organizations. In the Haynsworth and ABM issues, Nixon reached downward into the local organizations as the most effective way he knew of pressuring from the top. The timing was perfect, as the White House proceeded to contact state chairmen and their major financial contributors at a time when Republican Party leaders around the country awaited their allocations of federal patronage. Senator Saxbe of Ohio quoted a Republican county chairman from western Ohio to show the kind of heat ignited under him over the Haynsworth vote: "Believe me . . . if you flub this opportunity to unite behind the administration, I and thousands like me promise we will never forget it." [19] To achieve this kind of clout, the White House asked state chairmen to lead telegram campaigns, flooding undecided senators with pressure emphasizing the importance of the installation of ABM or of Judge Haynsworth. "We went to the money people to lean all over them [the undecided Senators]," reported a former Nixon White House aide. "Pressure from the money people was the biggest thing we had. With Haynsworth we concentrated on lawyers. We asked other senators to talk to recalcitrants, who received poor service at the White House in connection with appointments, and got people in the states to start talking about supporting other candidates. Most people invited to the Presidential prayer meetings were unde-

[19] *Washington Post*, November 20, 1969, p. A19.

cided senators, who were then hustled in for coffee with the President."

What Nixon attempted to achieve by this method of patronage pressure was the direct identification of the legislator's loyalty to his local party organization with his loyalty to the White House. In this way, instead of allowing the congressman to draw strength primarily from his home base, as the Founding Fathers intended when they separated executive from legislative power, the legislator is left quite alone, stripped of a power base from which he can assert his independence from the President.

The "stick" approach to presidential power [20] also offended many senators whose patronage expectations, personal pride, and swollen egos conflicted with the heavy-handed approach used by the White House. The patronage pressure brought to bear on Senator Pearson of Kansas, a Republican who broke with Nixon on the ABM issue, covered still other fronts, quite different from the party pressures more commonly used in the Haynsworth nomination. First, an army general informed a plane manufacturer in Senator Pearson's state that the Pentagon might not be able to go through with an airplane contract if the administration's Safeguard ABM system was not approved by Congress. Then, the White House failed to notify the senator that it had decided in his favor against moving some regional federal offices from Kansas City to Denver, in order to prevent him from claiming credit for the decision—a customary form of executive patronage. And finally, the Department of Agriculture, having already given its private blessings to a rural job-development bill sponsored by the senator, decided at the last minute that it could not endorse the project after all.

---

[20] As opposed to the "carrot," to borrow President Theodore Roosevelt's term, as it was applied to foreign policy.

ABM managed to pass with a margin of 53–45[21] votes, while Judge Haynsworth's nomination was defeated 55–45. Both votes corroborated a favorite theory used by working lobbyists, relating Senate head counts to presidential patronage: When a Senate head count at the beginning of a controversy reveals a margin of two-to-three votes, then the White House will win, regardless of whether the "carrot" or the "stick" is used, largely because the President has at his disposal a sufficient store of patronage favors and threats to make the difference; when, however, the head count reveals a larger margin, an element of uncertainty appears, clearing the way for the opposition to prepare itself for a realistic onslaught.

Such an onslaught was mounted against the Haynsworth nomination by a coalition of liberal groups, led by the AFL-CIO, after early head counts revealed a wide margin of undecided votes. Deciding to fight White House patronage pressures with its own patronage resources, the opposition selected those senators whose political positions were relatively insecure; and then applied the heat, by getting its own local branches to threaten a similar withdrawal of support and money that Nixon was able to extract from his own party's chairmen. "It all depends on when the guy is up for election, what his pet projects are, and what his needs are," said lobbyist Kenneth Young. "To persuade Senator Hugh Scott [Senate Minority Leader from Pennsylvania] to oppose the Haynsworth nomination, the AFL-CIO sought to counterbalance White House pressure by going to the unions in Pennsylvania to make sure they let Scott know of their strong

[21] The Senate vote on ABM, taken on August 19, 1969, constituted an amendment to a military authorization bill that would have barred the Safeguard system, but permitted other antimissile research.

feeling—by phone, visit, personal letter. Scott was up for re-election, and he didn't win by a great deal last time." Despite Scott's power base as Senate Minority Leader, he lacked the strength within his own state (Pennsylvania is a very important labor state) to risk losing the favor of the unions, even at the expense of opposing the President's wishes.

Nixon's actions in the Haynsworth nomination demonstrated that presidential patronage power can often be effective in the form of threats, but that the threats are more effective when implied rather than publicly imposed, and even more useful to the President when judiciously applied, not rained down on the legislature all at once. While it is acceptable for the President to threaten to withhold a dam from a recalcitrant senator, when the threat emerges as a public issue and challenges the senator's power within his own fiefdom, then the threat power often boomerangs, as it did in the Haynsworth case: at this point it becomes a matter of personal pride and public face-saving for the senator to stand up to the President for what has by this time been elevated into an issue of right versus wrong. Witness the highly unorthodox revelations of presidential patronage pressure made public by Senators Saxbe, Pearson, and Jordan, senators known among their colleagues as regular party members, not as political mavericks. Significantly, the President knew that when he could no longer reach his own senators directly, the logical alternative was to turn to party leaders, whose egos were not at stake, and whose patronage needs were far more immediate than the senators'.

President Nixon lost the Haynsworth nomination, with many wondering just why he used up valuable presidential patronage resources in suffering such a humiliating defeat over one mere judgeship—rather low stakes by modern patronage standards. Since Nixon never articulated his reasons, it remains a moot question as to whether he would have laid his patronage resources on the line had he known how expensive the Haynsworth lesson would prove to be. The sole explanation justifying Nixon's actions by reasonable, pragmatic criteria can be found within the confines of his current policy, popularly known as the "Southern strategy": that the President, having committed his patronage thrust to the South, would stand bravely by the South in implementing the delivery of executive favors.

What the Southern strategy amounted to in concrete terms was a massive payment, on a kind of patronage installment plan, of what Nixon considered his major political debt: his election to the Presidency. With the help of the skillful Republican senator from South Carolina, Strom Thurmond, Nixon was able to collect a crucial 228 votes out of the South's total 310 votes at the Republican nominating convention, leading him to win 86 electoral votes from the South out of his total of 301 electoral votes in the presidential election. In an election regarded as extremely close, Nixon's Southern victory provided him with the margin of votes needed to beat Hubert Humphrey, no mean feat, indeed, from an area traditionally favoring the Democratic Party.

Having already lost one presidential contest by a frustratingly close margin,[22] Nixon felt deep gratitude to the South and its leaders, gratitude that he consistently expressed through political favors. The correlation between what Nixon promised the South and what he was able to deliver, was very high, peaking with his "fight to

[22] In the 1960 presidential election, John F. Kennedy polled 50.08% of the popular vote, while Nixon drew 49.92%, causing Nixon to lose by .16%. The difference in the electoral vote was much greater (Kennedy, 300 votes; Nixon, 219 votes).

the finish" efforts to force Congress to accept his appointment of Clement Haynsworth to the Supreme Court, an appointment designed to convince the South that Nixon's promise to shape a less innovative Supreme Court was sincere.[23] After Haynsworth's defeat, Nixon introduced yet another Southerner, G. Harrold Carswell, a federal judge from Florida, whose record and segregationist views appeared even more conservative than Haynsworth's. In Harry Dent's view, the concept of the "Southern strategy" was inspired in part by the neglect of the South by the Democratic Party in the 1968 election campaign. "Here was new ground," he argued, "because the Democrats had made the mistake of writing it off to Wallace. President Nixon would not make that mistake. He wouldn't write off any section of the country."

To a South resistant to integration, Nixon promised an administration more sympathetic to its school problems, one that would ease rather than intensify the crush of federal government seeking to enforce its civil rights laws. True to his word, the President delivered; under his dicta, federal officials began to operate under what they termed a more "realistic timetable" for integration; and subsequently he refused to support a five-year extension of the Voting Rights Act which had extended Negro registration in the South. To abate the resentment the South felt at having been singled out for its segregationist practices, the Nixon administration promised that its energies toward integration (if any) would be directed toward everyone, just as it intended to press for "national" changes in voting procedures and enforcement.

Many allege that Nixon's real patronage commitment to the South rested not with judges or with segregationists but with textiles, one of the South's major

---

[23] Before Haynsworth, Nixon had appointed Warren E. Burger, a federal judge known for his moderate views, to the post of Chief Justice.

industries. In one of his first acts as President, Nixon sent Secretary of Commerce Maurice Stans on a trip to Europe and Japan during the spring of 1969 in order to negotiate treaties more favorable to the textile industry. Although the treaties failed to materialize, the money invested in Nixon by the textile industry during his presidential campaign more than doubled as textiles took its place as the most favored industry at the White House.

If the South ever doubted its faith in Richard Nixon, it saw his final proof of loyalty in his unwise fight with the Senate over the appointment of Clement Haynsworth, a federal judge from South Carolina, and protégé of Senator Strom Thurmond, whose record on racial segregation and willingness to adjudicate cases involving companies in which he held a financial interest put many senators in the uncomfortable position of choosing between the President and the increasingly intense (and often conflicting) pressures back home. In his efforts to force the Senate to approve Haynsworth, Nixon unintentionally illuminated the otherwise shadowy area of presidential patronage in relation to the legislature, widely recognized as a legitimate tool of presidential power,[24] although

[24] In 1934, Professor E. Pendleton Herring introduced the idea of a President's legitimately using patronage to influence the legislature in reference to President Franklin D. Roosevelt: "His control of patronage was the only means that he had of touching individual members of Congress directly. The President could defy pressure groups and appeal to the country over the radio. But when he wished to marshal Congress behind his program and to persuade congressmen to risk the displeasure of important interests in their districts, he needed some means of strengthening their position at home . . . the consummation of a national program of legislation is greatly aided by transmuting through patronage the localism of our politics into support of the Chief Executive." "First Session of the Seventy-Third Congress," *American Political Science Review,* Vol. 28 (February 1934), pp. 82–83.

harshly criticized by moralists, such as former President Woodrow Wilson.[25] By publicly withdrawing presidential patronage from those who opposed the nomination while increasing rewards to his supporters, Nixon employed patronage as both "carrot" and "stick," with an emphasis on the "stick" in issues he considered especially important, such as the Haynsworth nomination. Nixon used the same tactics over the deployment of a national Anti-Ballistic Missile System (ABM), also taking into account Southern patronage in view of the preponderance of military bases located in states such as Mississippi, Georgia, and South Carolina.

The Nixon patronage approach leaned more heavily on threats than on guile, and helped explain why Nixon sustained such a crushing defeat in the Senate's rejection of Judge Haynsworth, while he squeaked through to a narrow victory over ABM. Franklin D. Roosevelt also withdrew patronage from senators who had opposed his court-packing plan, a policy which many of his advisers deemed regrettable in view of the animosity generated by imposing sanctions of this kind. The "stick" approach to patronage recalled a conversation between Henry Adams and a Cabinet officer. Responding to Adams' appeal to show patience with congressmen, the Secretary replied: "You can't use tact with a congressman. A congressman

[25] Wilson strongly disapproved of legislative patronage, writing: "There are illegitimate means by which the President may influence the action of Congress. He may bargain with members, not only with regard to appointments, but also with regard to legislative measures. He may use his local patronage to assist members to get or retain their seats. . . . Such things are not only deeply immoral, they are destructive of the fundamental understanding of constitutional government, and therefore, of constitutional government itself." See Woodrow Wilson, *Constitutional Government in the United States.* (New York: Columbia University Press, 1908, 1918), p. 71.

is a hog. You must take a stick and hit him on the snout." [26]

To Nixon's political advisers, the South and its leaders represented the best, most viable patronage risk, both in Congress and at campaign time. Bolstering the South, they felt, would bring greater returns than would similar efforts to construct relationships of mutual support in other areas, for Southern politicians are far more loyal than leaders from more heterogeneous sections of the country where party loyalties are not valued so highly as they are in the South. In Congress, for example, Southerners from both parties rarely break party ranks, and when appointed to committees will remain there until they build up sufficient seniority to dominate the committee. From this vantage point, they find themselves in better positions to cull more bounty for their region than representatives from other areas, who move more frequently among committees, and not entirely by coincidence move more frequently in and out of office. Coming from safer districts, Southerners are not threatened with removal as often as are more marginal representatives, whose districts are fragmented by a variety of pressure groups, greater demographic variety, and a wider spectrum of political threats.

As long as the rewards Nixon sent southward remained diffused, his Southern strategy might have worked with one hundred percent effectiveness. With Haynsworth, however, he gave the opposition forces an object on which it could concentrate its efforts in an attempt to turn the patronage tides. "Presidential power," concluded Richard Neustadt, "is the power to persuade," [27] a power

[26] Henry Adams, *The Education of Henry Adams* (Cambridge: The Riverside Press, 1918), p. 261.

[27] Richard Neustadt, *Presidential Power* (New York: Signet, New American Library, 1964), p. 54.

which he (the President) derives from "bargaining advantages," the numerous favors available to him as President. How he uses the advantages open to him determines his ability to control his party and pass his legislative program. Nixon placed too much confidence in the "threat" side to persuasion, especially risky in his case as a Republican President, elected by an uncomfortably small margin, and presiding at a distinct disadvantage over a legislature dominated by the Democrats.

In striking contrast to Nixon's public use of patronage as a "club" over the legislature, Lyndon Johnson was known for his more subtle approach, aware of how expensive carrying a grudge could become. "Patronage was very important to him [Johnson]," recalled Senator William Proxmire. "He didn't retaliate. He knew that a man who opposed you on some issues might turn up as your useful friend in others; Nixon is not as responsive as Johnson." A master of legislative politics (Johnson spent 12 years in the Senate, 6 years as Majority Leader and one year as Minority Leader, and 12 years in the House), Johnson was able to engineer through Congress many of the New Frontier bills formulated by his predecessor, President John F. Kennedy, taking great pride in delivering the nation's first strong civil rights bill, a strong housing bill, meaty social welfare legislation which included Medicare and Medicaid (federally supported medical care for the aged and the indigent), and a Model Cities Act.[28] Working on the theory that you build up favors for

---

[28] Unlike Nixon, Johnson worked with the marvelous advantage of a Congress not only heavily dominated by members of his own party, but many of whose members were freshmen, elected to office on Johnson's coattails, and deeply grateful to him (at the outset anyway) for carrying them through to political victory. With Johnson's victory in 1964, the Democrats picked up 38 new seats in the House of Representatives, giving them a majority of 155 seats. In the Senate, the Democrats only gained two seats.

future use, Johnson piled up the patronage chips slowly, without immediately stating the quid pro quo, so that at any one time when he decided he needed to "collect" on his due bills, he could draw on the huge reservoir of congressmen already under obligation to him for past favors. Nixon, on the other hand, believed he could rely on the promise of future favors (and the threat of their withdrawal) to bring congressmen into line, a theory which he found worked with uncertain results. Johnson's technique did not imply that he used patronage without threats, or that his relationship with Congress was strictly a cooperative venture; indeed, when Senator Frank Church cited an article of columnist Walter Lippmann's to explain his opposition to the war in Vietnam to Johnson, the piqued President countered with: "All right, the next time you need a dam for Idaho, you go ask Walter Lippmann." On the contrary, threats were just as real in Johnson's dealings with the legislature; the difference was that his threats were implicit, rarely carried on publicly, and thereby more effective, leading one of his former aides to describe patronage politics under Johnson as "war carried on by nonviolent means . . . with never an end to the conflict." "Johnson," the aide continued, "exercised dominance over legislators primarily through cooperation —a series of temporary accommodations—but the conflict continues."

One of the best examples of how Johnson structured a network of mutual cooperation among legislators was offered by the passage and execution of the Model Cities Act, whose grants were delegated not on the basis of need but of political criteria, formulated to reward towns which key committee chairmen happened to represent.

The original sixty-three cities chosen for initial grants varied in size from Smithville, Tennessee (population 2,300) to New York City (population 8,000,000).

New York City received three grants, but neither Cleveland nor Los Angeles received grants even though both had experienced serious racial disturbances. Since the purpose of the plan was to provide additional federal money for a coordinated attack on the social as well as the physical causes of urban blight, the inclusion in the program of Smithville, Tennessee, appears baffling until one realizes that the city is represented by Representative Joe L. Evins, a Democrat who is chairman of the House Housing and Urban Development Subcommittee on Independent Offices Appropriations. Four other cities whose representatives supported the program in a crucial subcommittee vote were also immediately rewarded by the program: Texarkana, Arkansas (population 21,000) represented by David Pryor, a Democrat; Manchester, New Hampshire (90,000), represented by Louis C. Wyman, a Republican; New Haven, Connecticut (151,000), represented by Robert N. Giaimo, a Democrat; and Springfield, Massachusetts (166,000), represented by Edward P. Boland, a Democrat. President Johnson also rewarded with Model Cities funds two House Democrats who had played major roles in salvaging the administration's antipoverty program. These were Pikeville, Kentucky (5,000), represented by Carl D. Perkins, a Democrat who is chairman of the House Education and Labor Committee, and Tampa, Florida (166,000), represented by Sam M. Gibbons, a Democrat.

Not forgetting his original constituency, President Johnson gave Model Cities funds to four communities in his home state of Texas: Eagle Pass (14,000), San Antonio (645,000), Texarkana (32,000), and Waco (105,-000). Two of these cities were represented by the chairmen of House committees—Texarkana by Wright Patman, chairman of Banking and Currency, and Waco by W. R. Poage, chairman of Agriculture. The President attempted to give the program a nonpolitical cast, however, by funding Charlotte, North Carolina, which was represented by one of the most vigorous House opponents of the Model Cities program—GOP Representative Charles Raper Jonas.[29]

At the presidential level, collecting on patronage debts means more than the simple exchange following a private, political contract. Legislators have constituencies and obligations of their own; and only occasionally can the President reasonably expect them to vote for or against issues which will cause them trouble back in their districts. Moreover, the President most often finds it in keeping with his own interests to help cooperative legislators from his own party to remain solidly entrenched politically, not only to ensure their re-election, but to free them from the rigors of party warfare so that their energies can more constructively be channeled back into legislative business. Nixon expected the impossible from senators, especially those from states with large constituencies of blacks and labor groups, when he demanded party loyalty above political survival. Johnson, on the other hand, understood the dangers inherent in forcing congressmen to commit political hara-kiri, and preferred other methods of arm-twisting instead. Perhaps this explains why Johnson, in spite of his well-known deficiencies, was so frequently hailed as a "parliamentarian." When Johnson wanted a congressman's vote on an issue he knew would be political suicide for the man back home, he would proceed to set up the issue to make it more palatable, enabling legislators to vote for the bill, yet still be able to justify their vote and return home without having to face retribution. As Majority Leader, for example, Johnson man-

---

[29] *Congressional Quarterly,* "Fact Sheet on Model City Grants," November 27, 1967, pp. 1–4.

aged the tricky feat of engineering through the legislature a public housing bill for the construction of 250,000 units. Homer Capehart, an Indiana Republican, knew he had the votes for an alternative bill allowing for the much lower figure of 35,000 units requested by President Eisenhower. But Johnson simply set up the bill's wording so that congressmen committed to voting against public housing could vote for the bill, yet save face at the same time. What Johnson did was to talk the Southerners, who were all against public housing, into voting against the Capehart amendment, so that they could all go home and say they had voted against public housing. Without the help of the Southerners, the Capehart amendment lost, and the Johnson bill went through with its original high public housing figure.

"Parliamentarians" know they have a better chance of persuading a congressman to vote against his constituency by promising him something concrete to neutralize his political losses back home. "It is very much like a ballet," said James L. Rowe, now a Washington attorney, who has served two Democratic presidents, Franklin Roosevelt and Lyndon Johnson. "When FDR was looking for votes, certain Senators said that the legislation was against their constituents, but said that they would go along if they could have something to show for it." One example was the 1940 vote on the extension of the draft, which was carried by a single vote, the most expensive vote Mr. Rowe said he could recall in all his years of government service: "Rayburn and McCormack yelled for help, and the vote turned on Representative Levy of Spokane, Washington. He had lots of problems, he told us. One thing he wanted was a judgeship. He also wanted a military airport in Spokane. I got Justice [the Department of Justice] to offer him a judgeship, which he took. We called Harry Stimson [Secretary of War] and Hap Arnold [general of U.S.

Army Air Force], and they said, 'You can flip a coin. You can put it in Spokane or someplace else.' I said, 'Mr. Secretary, the coin just came down Spokane.' "

The keynote is cooperation. When conflict enters into the patronage relationship between the President and the legislature, it indicates that obstacles have cluttered the channels which normally connect these two branches of government. "When a President makes appointments with an eye to winning support for some part of his legislative program, he is not doing something *sui generis*," wrote Professor Stanley Kelley, "the trading of favors is a practice that pervades the legislative process. Members of Congress, heads of administrative agencies, and lobbyists continually do unto others in the hope that others will do at least as well by them. The president as a manager of patronage is simply one trader in a market system." [30]

Equipped with a wide range of patronage tools, the President is able to increase or decrease his patronage over the legislature by: including items in the budget; ordering the actual spending of appropriated funds; authorizing studies of postal services; deciding on the location of government installations; interpreting civil service regulations; granting audiences to important constituents of legislators; and lending his status to cooperative legislators at campaign time.

Each President adds his own variations on the same theme. President Kennedy initiated the practice of giving advance notice to legislators in the awarding of defense contracts, a welcome change from the Eisenhower years, when many legislators from the President's own party often first learned of government contracts awarded to

[30] Stanley Kelley, Jr., "Patronage and Presidential Legislative Leadership," unpublished paper, Princeton, 1968.

their areas in the local newspapers. Lyndon Johnson apparently ended the practice of advance notice to everyone, and sought to plug bureaucratic holes through which news of federal projects had been leaked to politically undeserving Republicans who promptly claimed all the credit for the projects. A protégé of FDR's, Johnson intended to follow his mentor's example, keeping this important area of presidential patronage within party ranks. "In our day, we didn't tell the Republicans when we opened a dam," recalled James Rowe, speaking of the Roosevelt years. "If you didn't have anyone, you told the committeeman."

Considering it beneath the dignity of the office of chief executive, the President does not often handle his patronage tools directly: instead, he has built up both formal and informal liaisons, set up with the implied function of wielding the potent instruments which control discretionary favors. Although presidential staff aides have always retained this function, not until the Truman administration was this formalized with the appearance of White House staff personnel specializing in handling congressmen's requests for favors. Once the latter became legitimized, succeeding administrations have allowed their congressional liaison staffs jurisdiction not only over "favors" but also over the content of legislative proposals—a natural quid pro quo with which to follow up congressional favors. Under President Kennedy, it was highly significant that his chief special assistant for congressional affairs, Lawrence O'Brien, was also cast in the role of patronage-dispenser. Kennedy worked out an elaborate scheme whereby John Bailey (then Democratic National Chairman) was given official responsibility for patronage, while O'Brien took charge of actually dispensing the patronage. In this way Bailey could take the blame, while

O'Brien got the credit, enabling O'Brien to further the President's legislative interests as freely as possible.[31] O'Brien expanded the practice of allowing congressmen to announce federal grants and contracts in their districts, while letting the blame fall on federal agencies whenever pet projects failed to materialize.

In addition to his own formal liaison staff, the President builds up patronage relationships with selected interest groups, who then in turn serve him as extra channels to Capitol Hill, adding their own valuable clout to the President's. Understood in the patronage agreement Lyndon Johnson had forged with the AFL-CIO was that in exchange for presidential support for its legislation, the union would refrain from attacking the President, except under extreme circumstances. Staff members from the AFL-CIO routinely went over head counts with Johnson to see if they, through their political arm COPE (Committee on Political Education), could work with the more marginal members of Congress to bring them around on important votes. Few consider this a conflict of interest, but rather a normal outgrowth of the President's relationship with extraconstitutional powers, such as interest groups and political parties. In effect, when a President aligns himself with a group, lends his status and support to its legislation, and extends his patronage to them, he expects a substantial return—as he would from his own political party. What he is saying, though never directly, is: "We're going to help you because you're going to help us." On lower levels of government, lobbies lend their resources to print campaign literature, provide sound trucks, and otherwise help candidates to win elections, always with the expectation that their help will be reciprocated in the future. For cooperative congressmen, with

[31] Hugh Sidey, *op. cit.*, pp. 86–92.

whom they have developed a patronage relationship, lobbies lend their research staffs, ostensibly in order to provide understaffed congressmen with the help they need to "understand" legislation.

Thrust by patronage relationships into an entrepreneurial role between the President and the legislature, many interest groups have developed power comparable to that of party whips [32]—a function our own parties have all but abdicated—bringing recalcitrant members of Congress into line on crucial votes when the President has used up his own and his party's clout with them.

Presidential patronage power over the legislature must be played far more subtly than the patronage games worked out on other levels of government, for the President stands out as the most visible public official, more subject at any time than any other elected official to scandal and public humiliation. For this reason, favors must be traded in the shadows of government, their very success dependent on the loyalty of the participants and, more pragmatically, on their desire to consummate the bargains under consideration. According to Stewart L. Udall, who served both Presidents Johnson and Kennedy as Secretary of the Interior, the standard patronage agreements in which a legislator supported the President in exchange for some patronage "boodle" of his own were worked out privately, with the President speaking with the in-

---

[32] From the English term "whipper-in," used in fox-hunting to refer to the practice of keeping the hunting dogs in line. In Britain, the formal party whip wields the power to force members of Parliament to vote on important issues against their will. Backed by a party structure more disciplined and more centralized than that in the United States, the "whip" carries with his edicts the threat of withdrawing party support from the member of Parliament should he bolt the party too often on crucial issues, a threat which could cost him his political survival in a country where candidates have no recourse to open party primaries.

dividual senator. In this way, if a snag occurred and one party decided to publicize the event, then the other could always deny that it ever occurred, and claim the other had only himself as witness. "If Lyndon found out somebody really wanted something very badly," said Secretary Udall, "he would hold it up until he could trade it off for something he really wanted; the congressman's chances of getting something through were much better if he supported Johnson on something specific." Johnson, according to Udall, was much more thoroughgoing than Kennedy in these legislative patronage details, although Kennedy paid much more attention to patronage in its relationship to local party-building. Well aware of Johnson's caginess about legislative boodle, smart congressmen played it cool with the executive when they really wanted a project passed for their district or for their state. Of course the reverse was true as well: "If you let Lyndon know that you were really interested in a project, it was the best way to guarantee that it would be held up," said one legislator. "It was like playing poker. You had to act disinterested if you really wanted to win."

It was Johnson whose presidential career presented such an apparent paradox. A master of patronage politics, Johnson was clearly the master of his administration, of his congress and of his party; as such he brokered into legislation the domestic programs of John F. Kennedy, programs that many politicians believe Kennedy would not have been able to secure had he lived. How, then, could such a political master be driven from office over an issue like the Vietnam war? Johnson's downfall derived not from his inability to control his own political arena, but from his inability to understand a foe like Ho Chi Minh, whose outlook as a revolutionary was unfamiliar to a patronage-oriented politician like Johnson. Ho Chi Minh could not be put off by the promise of a dam—a

Johnson tactic that had worked successfully since his Senate days, and one which he had used, in fact, on the North Vietnamese leader. Johnson thus found himself unable to understand an alien political culture—in good company with the nation's foreign-policy apparatus, which has always found it easier to deal with traditional regimes which speak the language of political rewards than with revolutionary ones.

Few consider patronage politics illegitimate, particularly those circulating around the calm eye of the executive-legislative hurricane. If the game is played right, the opportunities for political enrichment (not to mention personal enrichment) are unlimited; those who lose either bid different hands, or try to reform the system. The game most often boomerangs, however, when the President's expectations grow too great, when he expects more loyalty than he actually gets, and places too much stock in his own patronage power. Too many variables affect the successful application of patronage, not the least of which occurs when a congressman's obligations toward his constituents (and correlatively their expectations and pressures on him) overwhelm both his loyalty and sense of obligation to the President. Nixon learned this lesson very early in his presidential career by his experience in the Haynsworth affair, while Johnson discovered too late the limitations on his patronage power. As he lost support for his policies in Vietnam, Johnson grew more and more confused, expecting the patronage obligations he held over Congress to stem the tide of resistance against the war— at least the resistance from Congress. Unlike the knottiest domestic problems, however, the war issue could not be contained in normal political vessels; it overflowed to force Johnson—in spite of his successes in other areas of presidential power—from seeking another term in office.

7
Patronage and
Political Change

"I felt after Chicago that there was no longer any hope for the American electoral system . . . that real democracy and real justice lay with the radical movement."[1] This bitter reflection by an 18-year-old high school senior reflected the alienation generated by the Democratic national convention toward blacks, students, and opponents of the Vietnam war. Many who came to Chicago hoping to reverse national policy and end the war discovered how delegates were bound to the national leadership by the lifelong, invisible threads of patronage loyalties. An overwhelming sense of futility led to mass demonstrations on the streets of Chicago (where demonstrators came face to face with the raw political power of the Chicago police) and later erupted in demonstrations on college campuses, in black communities, and in courtrooms across the nation.

Unable to influence decisions, alienated groups rarely even attempt to work within the system, aware that they cannot compete with patronage ties forged long before they entered the political arena. These frustrated and dis-

[1] David Romano, "I Saw America in the Streets," in Marc Libarle and Tom Seligson, eds., *The High School Revolutionaries* (New York: Random House, 1970), p. 9.

affected groups have turned from apathy to confrontation, which has become increasingly violent.

Some extremists among the alienated pose still a further problem. They would not accept patronage favors even if they were offered them, they claim, because their approach is basically ideological, and they cannot conceive of cooperation with the pragmatic grantors of these favors. Ideologues in general find European politics more congenial to their style, while American ideologues have been flattened by the steam roller of American pragmatism, which has co-opted into the system all manner of ideologues from Progressives to Greenbackers. The price has always been high, for groups can be co-opted only if the system is willing to share its rewards. Yet even though drastic changes have often been made to accommodate the challengers, they have usually been accommodated. Too caught up with the practicalities of industrial and technological achievement, Americans seldom respond to the political philosophy of the ideologues of any era. "There is little ideology in American politics," notes Stephen Hess, who adds, "Trying to identify a Republican or Democratic approach is about as difficult as trying to nail currant jelly to the wall." [2]

Although not united by ideology, American political parties are united by patronage, which uses the machinery of government on all levels (federal, state, and local) to enforce party discipline. A recalcitrant official feels the full weight of the organization. If a legislator defies his party's legislative leadership, his county organization may well give him a primary fight, which is what happened to Assemblyman Albert J. Hausbeck of Buffalo who voted for the Republican-sponsored sales tax and was read out

[2] "Is There a Republican Approach to Government?" *Washington Monthly*, Vol. I, No. 1, February 1969.

of the Erie County Democratic organization by Joseph F. Crangle, the leader. Similarly, a convention delegate who defies his leader can expect not to receive the banking funds, insurance funds, architect's fees, construction contracts, and other favors controlled by the party leaders on all levels of government. Nor is he likely to be named a delegate at future conventions.

In its infinite practicality, co-optation is far more common to American politics than perpetual confrontation, which probably explains why such a wide variety of groups can often operate in direct opposition to each other under the umbrella of the American political system. But since many militants ask no more than to be accepted into the system, the question is whether the system will make accommodations to accept them or, instead, use its discretionary powers—especially its law enforcement powers— to harass and destroy them. Black delegates and reform delegates to the Democratic state convention at Grossinger's, for example, succeeded in persuading Arthur Goldberg, the gubernatorial nominee, and the big-city bosses to place a black State Senator, Basil Paterson, on the state ticket for Lieutenant Governor. This occurred after John Burns, Democratic state chairman who was handpicked by the Kennedys, met with a group of black leaders before the convention and acknowledged the justice of their demands. Against the disgruntled rumblings of many party regulars, Burns told the black caucus that the time was ripe to place a Negro on the ticket.

Historically, ours has been an accommodating society, sufficiently flexible to thwart third-party movements such as those that threatened during the depression years. Perhaps the greatest accommodations—both political and philosophical—were made by the New Deal, which responded to the increasing militancy of the disinherited with Social Security, an Agricultural Adjustment Act for farmers, a Wagner Act for factory workers, a National Labor Relations Act to protect trade unions, a Works Progress Administration to create jobs for adults, and a Civilian Conservation Corps to create jobs for teen-agers. By giving these groups patronage, President Roosevelt also gave them a voice in national policy. In retrospect, these programs were so successful in co-opting the challengers that some of the major beneficiaries—especially the labor unions and the farmers—have now become bastions of the Establishment, and are among the most conservative elements in the nation. Projected as ideological changes, these accommodations produced by the New Deal were also desired by leaders who wished to use their patronage powers to neutralize and incorporate the disaffected groups.

By increasing the federal budget from $4.6 billion in 1932 to $9.5 billion in 1940 (it is $192 billion in 1970), the New Deal also opened up avenues of public spending that benefited groups accustomed to receiving the lion's share of government rewards: contractors, bankers, insurance men, realtors, and businessmen. Cost-plus contracts during the Second World War, while undoubtedly in the national interest, also further benefited these groups, as did the creation of the maze of regulatory agencies vested with broad discretionary powers, which made the federal government the avenue to great personal wealth.[3] Disbursing substantial patronage favors to so

[3] During the FDR years, Representative Lyndon B. Johnson provided a striking example of personal enrichment through favorable rulings by the Federal Communications Commission. After purchasing radio station KTBC in Austin in 1943 for $17,000, Mrs. Johnson quickly won permission from the FCC for unlimited broadcasting hours (KTBC had been limited to the daylight hours), and a thousand watts of transmitting power (four times its previous total). This in turn led to a coveted affiliation with the Columbia Broadcasting System. The radio station became the cornerstone of a fortune in land, banking, and

many diverse groups unquestionably helped President Roosevelt win an unprecedented fourth term at the White House.

If society has been so successful before in accommodating dissatisfied groups, why then is the confrontation today so violent, so continuous, and so hopelessly lacking in any sign of abatement? Instead of accepting society's rewards, groups today demand a change in the process of allocating the rewards. Hidden beneath the rhetoric of violence is the desire for a more rational distribution of favors. The system, structured to meet preordained patronage obligations, is naturally unwilling to abdicate its power. Government still wants to accommodate, but what this really means is that it can disperse to the disenfranchised what is left over after all its other patronage obligations have been met; and this is no longer enough to satisfy the political and economic needs of the disenfranchised.

"The beneficiaries of the system will never change the status quo," said Representative Shirley Chisholm. Don Cox, the Black Panther's Field Marshal, told the guests at Leonard Bernstein's now famous fund-raising party for the Panther defense fund that unless the status quo is changed, black men will never enjoy the same rights as whites. "Like, this is what we want, man," Cox told the affluent guests. "We want the same things as you, we want peace. We want to come home at night and be with the family and turn on the TV . . . and smoke a little weed." [4]

---

cattle. See Rowland Evans and Robert Novak, *Lyndon B. Johnson: The Exercise of Power* (New York: The New American Library, 1966), pp. 31–32.

[4] Tom Wolfe, "Radical Chic," *New York Magazine*, June 8, 1970, p. 48.

Traditional patterns of American democratic pluralism—the co-optation of new groups through patronage favors—no longer work as a method of forestalling revolutionary dissent. Confrontation is no longer the exclusive property of militant extremists; "respected" members of the Establishment have resorted with increasing frequency to confrontation politics, because they believe that society has been unable to accommodate their demands in a genuine way. The postal workers who walked off their jobs and paralyzed the national economy; the air traffic controllers who reported "sick" and jeopardized the safety of air travel; the nurses who walked off the wards; the policemen who undertook "job actions"—all resorted to confrontation as the only viable avenue of genuine accommodation. The Establishment, shaken and jumpy, regarded these confrontations as anarchy.

The demand for system changes, not merely increased patronage favors, was led by the blacks. One Thurgood Marshall on the Supreme Court failed to compensate for the lack of justice to blacks throughout the judicial system. Despite all the rhetoric and the promises, blacks had failed completely to make major inroads into the real bastions of political power. Former Assistant Attorney General Roger Wilkins pointed out that he and Mayor Walter Washington of Washington, D.C., were the only blacks present at the Gridiron Club banquet, an event whose guest list symbolized "the most powerful elements of the nation's daily press and all elements of the nation's government locked in a symbiotic embrace." [5]

In theory and in practice, American politics has never developed a genuine alternative to the patronage system. It has never had to. Developed to correct the worst abuses of patronage, the civil service system has not succeeded in

[5] *I. F. Stone's Bi-Weekly*, Vol. XVIII, No. 7, April 6, 1970, p. 3.

becoming a viable alternative, especially in times of relatively full employment.[6] With a reputation for sluggishness and stagnation, civil service has failed to function well, primarily because it lacks the most basic advantage of the patronage system: clear-cut rewards in return for good service and unquestioned loyalty. Civil service acts instead to augment the patronage system; its jobs have never risen to the status of the ripest fruits guarded by patronage-dispensers. Ironically, critics attribute the failure of civil service to the absence of "threat power"—the power to fire bad workers without going through ceaseless red tape—whereas in truth the drawback to civil service is that the system lacks genuinely substantial built-in rewards, needed to motivate workers toward better performance. When New Jersey's Governor William Cahill, who recognized this problem, publicly called for salary increments for teachers based on performance, he met with overwhelming resistance on the part of entrenched civil service groups.

Not connected politically, civil service is doomed to lag forever behind patronage in the race for rewards. Judges and legislators acquire raises for themselves with ease and regularity, while postal workers are rebuffed by the same Congress and must struggle for the meager salary increases they are able to win.

To preserve their freedom of movement, politicians studiously avoid merit systems, rational planning, and any other good-government "ideas" which might blunt their discretionary power, arguing that ultimately the public will not re-elect them if they abuse this power or if they fail to parcel out their favors to give the impression that

[6] For an excellent presentation of the arguments for and against civil service versus patronage, see Paul T. David and Ross Pollock, *Executives for Government: Central Issues of Federal Personnel Administration* (The Brookings Institution, 1957), Chapter 5.

they are serving the public interest. "Bosses can be beaten," advised the late Bronx County leader Ed Flynn. "They can be beaten when they attempt to go versus what the people want." [7]

Patronage power evades the reformers because its real rewards remain in the shadows of public awareness. As long as they can preserve the judgeship contracts, high-level jobs, subsidies, Model Cities grants, etc., political leaders cannot be too alarmed by the low-level clerks or middle-management bureaucrats that fall under civil service; in fact, many seek out opportunities to publicly support civil service as a means of publicly aligning themselves with the forces of "good government." Presidents Roosevelt and Kennedy greatly enhanced their image by "blanketing in" areas of federal employment previously under the patronage system into the civil service; to them, the gain in image vastly outweighed the meager contributions of money and service that these groups donated to politics. At the same time they extolled civil service, both Presidents quietly and with great skill expanded patronage rewards in areas they knew would pay off, directing favors to those who could return their support to the party. On lower levels, local politicians know how little it matters if city planners work within a civil service system as long as they can still affect zoning patterns by "political contract."

Where it counts, the patronage system is secure. Sound planning almost always takes second place to political necessity; and the real rewards of government fall logically to those with the most "clout." [8] Patronage re-

---

[7] Edward J. Flynn, *You're the Boss* (New York: The Viking Press, 1947).

[8] A word which originated appropriately in Chicago, meaning raw political power.

form, when it does surface, is invariably a phony issue: perhaps this also explains why the young revolutionaries resort to confrontation rather than accept piecemeal reforms offered as accommodations. Reform fails because it comes in an empty vessel. The reformers invariably just want some of the patronage for themselves, and rarely leave in their wake concrete programs (such as: more incentives for civil servants; mandated rational planning for cities; or more stringent competitive bidding procedures for discretionary contracts) to correct the abuses of patronage they fought so hard to remove. When the reformers succeed in gaining some of the patronage for themselves, there remains the nagging question of whether they really represent an improvement over the original patronage-dispensers. Was it really patronage reform to place Cook County Hospital under the jurisdiction of the governor of Illinois who needed the patronage as badly as the mayor of Chicago? Are the bar associations, who want more power over the selection of judges, better judges of judges than local party politicians?

Like civil service, other institutional reforms designed to eliminate patronage often meet with disaster by failing to retain the advantages of the patronage system in the frenetic attempt to avoid its faults. Many cities which have succumbed to nonpartisanship, for example, now find themselves starving for lack of funds, while strong party-connected cities like Mayor Daley's Chicago feed off their political clout. Reforming state and national government by raising the salaries of legislators (another institutional device intended to eliminate the corrupting dangers of patronage obligations) has failed to meet the goal of its protagonists: most congressmen and state legislators have not reduced their law practices, given away their stocks and bonds, or in any way substantially eliminated the numerous potential conflicts of interest traditionally used as an excuse to compensate for low salaries, although minor inroads are being made to check the most flagrant violators.[9]

Since patronage has deep roots in every branch of legitimate American political life, it is unlikely that real changes can be made without accommodating in some degree to its traditions. Patronage is inevitable because of the existence of the two-party system, pressure groups, the vagaries of constitutional government, the human condition, and the financial exigencies of campaigning. Today the politician finds himself even more indebted to the party than were his predecessors fifty years ago; unless he is fortunate enough to be independently wealthy, or endowed with that compelling quality of mass appeal, popularly known as charisma. As his campaign expenses expand along with his constituency, he competes for air time and advertising space with the giants of industry, whose lavish budgets were never intended to compare with political expenditures. Inevitably, political obligations increase proportionately as the need for financial support intensifies, a by-product of changing times. Rarely does anyone question the elected official's right to channel back to his supporters whatever refereeships, jobs, and contracts he has managed to retain within the scope of his discretionary power.

When political obligations overwhelm decisions, the real dangers of the patronage system flare up to challenge

[9] New rules adopted by the House of Representatives on May 26, 1970, now require members, officers, and some employees to report annually the individuals or organizations who pay them more than $300 for speeches, articles, or other services. In addition, they will have to reveal the names of any persons or institutions lending them $10,000 or more for 90 days or longer without any collateral—a response to the revelations that Congressman Halpern of Queens had received more than $100,000 in outstanding bank loans, some of them unsecured. *The New York Times*, May 27, 1970, p. 21.

the public good; and all too often, real community needs
are sacrificed on the altar of political necessity. Dams like
Glen Elder get built in order to get political support in an
intensely competitive market, despite intense resistance by
the farmers who supposedly were to benefit from the dam.
The mayor of New York, faced with the real need to reinforce his support within the hierarchy of the Catholic
Church, advanced a zoning change which threatened to
lower the quality of life in a residential community in his
city. In the awarding of defense contracts, patronage obligations occasionally come to light, as they did in the controversy over the F-111 military plane, which showed how
readily technical considerations could be replaced by political relationships.

Patronage obligations lead to "unplanning" at all levels of government, with most decisions of this kind buried
unless unearthed as a public scandal. Although the reasons for patronage-oriented decisions seem irrational—like
putting a shopping center in the middle of a school district—the rationality centers around the political system
and gives it its coherence. There was no doubt that patronage considerations were paramount when the Department of the Interior finally agreed to put a lake in former
House Speaker Sam Rayburn's district, as Rayburn needed
this piece of "boodle" to keep intact politically. As Speaker
of the House, Rayburn served a vital political function as a
cohesive force in maintaining a well-functioning House of
Representatives. Which rationality ought to take precedence here: the proper distribution of water resources or
political stability?

Politicians fear patronage losses more than any other
political threat, and they spend a goodly chunk of their
time in office developing what patronage resources they
have, while jealously guarding against any incursions into
this power. New York City's county leaders were willing

to risk months of bad publicity, rather than share their judge-making powers with Judge Bernard Botein and his committee, well aware that the public's memory is short, while patronage power serves them indefinitely. At all levels, government helps elected officials remain indispensable as political entrepreneurs. In Chicago, the taxpayer can get a leaky water pipe fixed speedily only by going through his alderman, although the alderman has nothing to do with the legal or functional mechanics of fixing the pipe. In the Brighton Beach section of Brooklyn, Assemblyman Leonard Simon was successful in getting his constituents to identify aid they received from the Medicare and Medicaid programs with Simon himself: no doubt, as they peered through "Simon's eyeglasses," or leaned on "Simon's crutches," they felt duly grateful to their resourceful assemblyman. On the national level, congressmen continuously reinforce the expectation that the citizen can only get justice from the executive branch of government by contacting his congressman first.

Politicians who try, as Assemblyman Simon did, to maximize their patronage power know how closely patronage measures their impact on the system. Regardless of title, the amount of patronage power accorded to political leaders probably serves as the best index of their power over a wide range of government decisions. The patronage powers of the Attorney General, for example, far exceed those of any other Cabinet official; his patronage power, in turn, reinforces his role as a key political adviser of the President's, with functions and influence ranging far beyond his traditional law enforcement powers. In Congress, the extensive patronage power of committee chairmen matches their power dominance over all aspects of the legislative process.

As a major force in the political system, patronage not only reflects the real power structure but determines who enters and who succeeds in politics. Lawyers and businessmen dominate the national and state legislatures, because government's rewards suit the legal and business professions. Delegates from the arts, the sciences, skilled and unskilled labor, the medical profession, or the academic world rarely get elected as political representatives; they are forced by the system and by their own inclinations to influence government one step removed from its inner circles. Allowing lawyers to dominate the legislative process, many argue, has weakened the planning approach to government. Trained professionally to cope with problems on a case-by-case basis, lawyers (and often businessmen) transplanted to government find they must rely more heavily on ad hoc, improvised solutions, and neglect the unfamiliar methods of long-range planning, now regarded as highly desirable as government grows more and more complex.

Political rewards also determine who stays active in politics. Regardless of how he stands on the issues of the day, the congressman who fails to satisfy his district with military installations, dams, post offices, and the like, will have a harder time getting re-elected than his colleagues who have mastered the art of obtaining patronage. Even more certain is the unhappy fate of the elective judge—no matter how brilliant his opinions—who fails to send courthouse patronage back to the clubhouse; he will probably receive poor judicial assignments, meet trouble in processing his cases and obtaining clerical help, and most certainly will never regain his party's renomination.

Patronage seems to have a life of its own, ranging from fairly simple favors—such as being able to call the President on the telephone—to the more complex rewards which emerge from the maze of military and reclamation budgets. Endemic to democracy, where men have relative freedom of action and the ability to expand their opportunities, patronage also presents many dangers. The most potent danger is the impact of patronage on policy, and the exclusion from patronage of those unable to reciprocate political support. This means the exclusion of the poor, who cannot contribute financially to politics and whose election registration lags far behind all other groups, and who therefore don't reciprocate through the ballot box; minority groups, whom custom has excluded from traditional rewards; in short, anyone barred by a political system geared to its own maintenance needs. Parceling out rewards on the basis of a political cost-benefits ratio fails in meeting the demands of these groups, whose arbitrary exclusion from the inner world of political decisions has not eliminated them as a very real part of the political process. These groups have real needs which must be answered by government, despite government's traditional patterns of answering public demands on the basis of patronage obligations or political threat. If it fails, the political system must answer for the ensuing alienation, revolution, and apathy which have characterized American politics for the last two decades with increasingly dangerous momentum.

The real lesson of patronage politics is that those who control patronage invariably control policy. The goal, really, is to harness government's enormous reward powers on behalf of rational planning, and on behalf of the public interest. One simple step in this direction was taken recently by Mayor Lindsay who used his discretionary power to urge the city to use its pension system's $11 million holdings in General Motors stock to pressure the automobile manufacturer to take steps to reduce the pollution generated by its cars.

What would be the effect, for example, if the State of New York used its $4 billion of invested funds to invest only in companies with nondiscriminatory hiring practices; or, conversely, withdraw its funds from corporations that pollute its skies, lands, streams, and rivers? What would be the effect if the federal government denied contracts to polluters, or to companies that discriminated in their hiring? And why aren't these vast reserves of discretionary power used routinely as the rule, not the exception, to solve broad-based social problems?

These utopian thoughts are unlikely to be realized during our lifetime. The best that one can ask is that patronage be employed to advance programs that promote the national interest and aid the rational planning of states and cities. To ensure this, one can hope that a greater cross section of the public will enter the two-party system —where the real allocation of rewards originates. Because patronage is often in the hands of those who have wielded it for generations, it is more often used to promote the status quo. But the status quo is ill served by those who ignore the disenfranchised and disinherited in our midst— be they student militants or construction workers—who then turn to confrontation politics out of a sense of hopelessness and futility. One can still hope that with increased awareness of the real potential of political power, the public will eventually persuade its leaders to use patronage more constructively and more equitably, to accommodate rather than harass those groups worthy of its benefits, and to reflect more truly the pressures and interests upon which our democracy ultimately rests.

APPENDIX A

Members of the Senate Judiciary Committee who passed initial judgment on the fitness of Judge Clement Furman Haynsworth, Jr., to serve on the Supreme Court have applied widely varying ethical standards to their own offices of public trust, the *Congressional Quarterly* reported. Only six members of the committee had made public lists of their stock and other financial holdings, something Haynsworth was required to go into in detail. Seven members of the committee were accused of potential conflicts of interest.

The double standard was criticized by Senator Charles M. Mathias, Maryland Republican, who said, in a letter to constituents: "Having shared his own financial secrets with a locked file, the Senator might then go to a public committee hearing on a nomination for high executive position. There, before the TV cameras and the press, he could interrogate the nominees about the details of his income, stocks and debts. In many cases, Senate committees have gone far beyond requiring disclosure, and have insisted that nominees sell their private holdings or place them in trust before assuming a government post. Clearly, there is a double standard here."

The committee members are Birch Bayh, Indiana Democrat, who made an informal financial disclosure in 1964, according to his office, but no copies were available for immediate inspection; Quentin N. Burdick, North Dakota Democrat, who has voted in favor of financial disclosure by members of Congress, but has not taken the step himself, saying "[I] will be glad to announce what I own when the person who is running against me is required to do the same"; Robert C. Byrd, West Virginia Democrat, who does not disclose his assets, liabilities, or net worth but raised nearly $20,000 from Washington, D.C., business in 1964 to finance an election campaign in West Virginia. Byrd was chairman of the Senate Appropriations Subcommittee for the District of Columbia. Then there is Marlow W. Cook, Kentucky Republican, who has not made a public disclosure of his financial affairs. He is a member of the board of directors of the Bank of Louisville and asked that he not be appointed to the Senate Banking and Currency Committee for this reason. He does not have a policy of abstaining from voting on banking legislation, however. Thomas J. Dodd, Connecticut Democrat, reported his net worth, assets, and liabilities in 1967 during a congressional investigation into whether he had misused political funds. He was censured by the Senate for using funds raised at testimonial dinners for personal purposes. James O. Eastland, Mississippi Democrat, who does not publish financial disclosures, has received more than $100,000 in each of the past three years in agriculture subsidies; Sam J. Ervin, Jr., North Carolina Democrat, has not made public disclosure of financial interests; Hiram L. Fong, Hawaii Republican, a millionaire, published financial statements during the 1959 and 1964 election campaigns, listing road-building firms. In 1967, Fong was accused of conflict of interest because of his position on a Senate committee investigating credit life insurance operations. Robert P. Griffin, Michigan Republican, who has made a partial financial disclosure, was once involved in a dispute with the Post Office Department over alleged misuse of his franking privilege; Philip A. Hart, Michigan Democrat, lists stocks he owns; Roman L. Hruska, Nebraska Republican, makes no financial disclosures, is no longer a partner in a law firm which lists his name in a legal directory with the notation that he is "now serving in the United States Senate." Edward M. Kennedy, Massachusetts Democrat, has never made public disclosures of assets, liabilities, or net worth; Charles M. Mathias, Maryland Republican, has twice published a listing of his assets, liabilities, and net worth, and is "inactive partner" in a law firm; John L. McClellan, Arkansas Democrat, does not make public disclosure, and was criticized in 1966 for owning stock in Midwest Video while heading a committee which was considering copyright laws affecting cable TV firms; Hugh Scott, Pennsylvania Republican, lists stocks and real estate, but not net worth, and receives some income from a law firm for "limited non-federal legal matters." Strom Thurmond, South Carolina Republican, does not list assets. The price paid Thurmond and a partner for land to be used for an interstate highway was criticized as being higher than the amount paid adjacent landowners. Joseph D. Tydings, Maryland Democrat, has listed his net worth at $2.5 million, as well as stocks he holds, but not the extent of his holdings in specific stocks.

Original White House Staff Appointments in the Nixon Administration Related to Campaign Help

NAME	JOB	PREVIOUS CAMPAIGN ACTIVITIES
Martin Anderson	Special Assistant	Campaign aide in 1968.
Roy L. Ash	Special Adviser on Management and Efficiency	Major financial contributor to 1968 campaign.
Patrick J. Buchanan, Jr.	Special Assistant	Drafted most of Nixon's campaign speeches on law and order
Arthur Burns	Counselor to the President	Head of economic task force, 1968 presidential campaign.
Dwight L. Chapin	Special Assistant	Nomination campaign, became personal aide to Nixon in 1967.
Kenneth R. Cole, Jr.	Special Assistant	1968 presidential campaign.

APPENDIX B (*continued*)

NAME	JOB	PREVIOUS CAMPAIGN ACTIVITIES
John S. Davies	Special Assistant	Nixon consultant on communications for the 1962, 1966, and 1968 campaigns.
John D. Ehrlichman	Chief Counsel to the President	Ran 1968 campaign schedule.
Peter M. Flanigan	Assistant to the President	Organized New Yorkers for Nixon in 1959; 1960, organized Volunteers for Nixon-Lodge.
Harry S. Flemming	Special Assistant	1968 campaign; Co-Chairman of the Nixon-Agnew Campaign Committee in Virginia, and special assistant to Republican National Chairman Ray Bliss.
Harry R. Haldeman	Assistant to the the President	Managed Nixon's 1962 campaign for governor; advance man in 1956 for the vice-presidential campaign and chairman of staff for the 1968 campaign.
Bryce N. Harlow	Assistant for Legislative and Congressional Affairs	In 1968 campaign.
James Keogh	Special Assistant	In 1968 campaign.
Herbert G. Klein	Director of Communications	Nixon's press chief for the 1952 and 1956 vice-presidential campaigns, and 1960 presidential race.

APPENDIX B (*continued*)

NAME	JOB	PREVIOUS CAMPAIGN ACTIVITIES
Virginia H. Knauer	Assistant for Consumer Affairs	Vice-Chairman of the Philadelphia Representative Party and founder of the Representative Women's Council. In 1952 worked for Citizens for Eisenhower and Nixon.
Raymond K. Price, Jr.	Special Assistant	Joined the Nixon campaign early in 1967.
William L. Safire	Special Assistant	Speech writer during the 1968 campaign and chief of special projects for Nixon-Lodge Volunteers in 1960.
Ronald L. Ziegler	Special Assistant for press releases	In 1968 campaign and in 1962 Nixon gubernatorial campaign.

APPENDIX C

A Brief History of Patronage
and How It Affected
the Course of Events

Early patronage, the marketing of public offices by bankrupt rulers, predated the Roman Empire, circled the globe, led to the rise and fall of empires, and influenced the development of almost every political institution known today. Patronage began when monarchs in China, Spain, Italy, the Netherlands, and the Ottoman Empire grew tired of relying on noblemen and the clergy for support, and discovered that selling offices was the most convenient way to build up national treasuries.

The ancient Chinese, for example, in response to natural disasters, such as war, flood, and famine, bartered offices in exchange for agricultural produce. As early as 243 B.C., those who gave a certain amount of grain to the state were rewarded with one rank in the official hierarchy. During the Ming Dynasty (1368–1644), the government resorted to selling offices to shore up its resources whenever barbarians from the north threatened to invade the country. Ironically, while China claimed the first known patronage system, she also initiated the first merit system. Mandarin status, the highest in the civil service, could not be bought for any sum of money, and was achieved only by passing a long and difficult examination requiring years of preparation.

Curiously, the Catholic Church was the only institution that sanctioned patronage by law, and references to it in canon law describe the practice as the benevolent exercise of privilege.[1] "Juspatronatus," the sum of privileges according to canon law, was derived from the Roman system, which contained within itself an entire class of free men—not citizens—who attached themselves to "patrons." Translated into canon law, the "patron" was someone who founded a church, that is, financed the building of a church, in return for the privilege of controlling the lives of those involved with the church. This included the occasional right to appoint lower clergy and, more often, to assign candidates who would take part in church ceremonies or enjoy certain of its privileges. After the Middle Ages, the ability of the Church to retain its patronage depended on its power vis-à-vis the monarchy. Thus early in its development, patronage became an index of the power of political institutions.

As patronage bailed out bankrupt governments and brought them to solvency, its excesses grew greater. Rulers discovered the unlimited possibilities patronage held for making money. Patronage politics was an avenue to untold wealth as early as the fourteenth-century Ottoman Empire, when sultans auctioned off the governorships of Egypt and Syria for 60,000 gold ducats apiece, an investment that yielded a return of a million gold ducats in annual tributes. Under the Ottoman emperors, patronage was profitable but fraught with danger, for officeholders who had purchased their power with credit were often tempted to extort, borrow, or steal in order to pay their creditors. When all other attempts to repay their loans failed, governing pashas occasionally resorted to hanging more persistent creditors on the palace door. Creditors with more luck were sometimes paid with influence, just as wealthy party contributors are today; in fact, many Greek

---

[1] The term patronage also was used to describe the transfer of power by the Pope to his natural sons, euphemistically called nephews (hence, nepotism), and to his other relatives.

financiers came along as executive aides to the public officials whose careers they had financed.

The going rate under the English Stuarts for the office of Secretary of State ranged from 6,000 to 10,000 pounds, and by the eighteenth century it had become common practice to purchase seats in Parliament. The practice of patronage, perfected and coined by the French as the *vénalité des offices*, reached its peak in the seventeenth century, and involved the sale of nearly all offices—political, civil, and military. Selling offices without regard to their usefulness created vast bureaucracies laden with what the French called *offices imaginaires*, which only served to drain the economy. Worse, most offices were hereditary, and treated as stock on the open market. Louis XVI, destined to be decapitated in 1793 by an angry public, was saddled with paying the salaries of "wig inspectors" and "inspectors of hogs' tongues," useless jobs which had helped produce revenue for the depleted treasury of his great-grandfather, but no longer helped his own flagging economy.

What happened was that short-sighted monarchs, anxious for solvency and riches, sold offices with abandon, unaware of the drastic consequences soon to change the political structure of the Western world. What they failed to see was that although those who owed their offices to a particular king would remain loyal to him, no guarantee existed that the inheritors of the office would support succeeding governments. By creating a situation in which political power could be purchased, they brought new classes of untitled but moneyed people into government, who were not content to remain on the fringes of power and who began to demand power commensurate with their financial investment. Sir Walter Raleigh was the first to warn the Tudors that their patronage policies would encourage the British masses to revolt against the aristocracy.

By bringing the middle class into the ruling class, European royalty unintentionally signed its own death warrant; bourgeois-led revolutions gripped England, France, and the

Americas. In effect, patronage practices, which were invented with the simple but basic motive of making money, indirectly contributed to the democratization of the Western world by having caused the initial expansion of the ruling class.

No group ever justifies its attempts at revolution by articulating the real reason: the desire for power. Many revolutionaries seized on the abuses of patronage power for their rhetoric, and used this issue as an immediate cause for overthrowing the existing order. Patronage practices under the Stuarts, for example, increased the British public's already intense feelings against them, and led to a civil war. The great jurist, Sir Edward Coke, blamed all the prevailing corruption at the Court of St. James on patronage, which survived a brief reform movement during the Interregnum (1642–1660) but returned in full force with the restoration of the Stuart monarchy.

Perhaps the worst abuses of the patronage system occurred in the British colonies of North America, stirring revolutionary feelings there as they had in Europe. The colonies provided a distorted mirror image of the European patronage system, where no-show officeholders made little pretense of public service, and graft and inefficiency flourished. The practice of selling offices in the colonies of Maryland, Virginia, and North and South Carolina galled the colonists who saw the proceeds from the sale of offices returned to the crown, and the profits of office similarly sent back across the seas.

As distasteful to the colonists as the outflow of capital was their lack of a voice in the selection of their governors. When the citizens of Vera Cruz, Mexico, protested to King Philip of Spain because he had appointed a treasurer and controller without consulting them, Philip shrugged off their complaints with the excuse that he had no choice—he needed the money.

The most basic flaw in the system, and the one most likely to produce revolution, was that those most able to pay for offices were not necessarily the best able to govern. Filling public offices with inept and arbitrary administrators often resulted in rebellion—if not revolution—depending on the relative strength and awareness of the subject populations.

❰ *Patronage in the United States*

Patronage became part of the fabric of the American political system soon after the birth of the republic, despite George Washington's disclaimer that government jobs should be filled by "those who seem to have the greatest fitness for public office." When Thomas Jefferson became President in 1801, he found himself engulfed by Federalists, who dominated the government. President Jefferson replaced enough Federalists with Republicans from his own party, to assure —he said—a more even distribution between the two parties; and he wrote that he would "return with joy to that state of things when the only questions concerning a candidate shall be, 'Is he honest? Is he capable? Is he faithful to the constitution?' "

It was Andrew Jackson, a quarter of a century later, who went on to develop and justify that very system, which allowed victors carte blanche in appointing whomever they wished to political office. Jackson's contribution to patronage was that he was the first to articulate, legitimize, and translate the spoils system into the American experience, although William Learned Marcy, then governor of New York, heralded the era by proclaiming: "To the victor belong the spoils of the enemy."

Ironically, Jackson himself won the presidency largely by accusing his predecessor, John Quincy Adams, of dastardly patronage practices during his administration.[2] Out on

[2] The first time Jackson ran for the presidency against Henry Clay and John Q. Adams (in 1824) the election was stalemated, and thrown into the House of Representatives. Holding the balance of power with only three states in his hand, Clay cast his electoral votes for Adams, who won by the narrow margin of one state. Adams rewarded Clay with the post of Secretary of State, leading Jacksonian Democrats to charge Adams with making a "corrupt bargain."

the hustings, Jackson men charged Adams—a rather dour and straitlaced man—with gross immorality, highly inconsistent with Adams' character, and waxed eloquent on how Adams had purchased "gambling tables and gambling furniture" with public funds. Near the close of the campaign, Adams was even accused of playing pimp to the Emperor of Russia!

Elections are not courts of law; the public too often is satisfied with the accusation, and forgets to ask for the proof. So it was with Adams, who went down to defeat thoroughly disgraced by Jackson's supporters. Thus began what was to become a familiar pattern in American politics: gaining political mileage from equating patronage with political corruption.

The spoils system developed at a time when revenues had to be found to support the increased activities of political parties. With the broadening of suffrage, and the use of elections to choose large numbers of officials, political parties began to assume heavy campaign costs.

With great relish, Jackson insisted on overseeing all patronage appointments personally. Encouraged by the promise that he would see them all, great hordes of men thronged to Washington to demand jobs. One man asked for anything that would yield $300 to $3,000 a year, except for a clerkship because he couldn't write. Jackson did see them all, or nearly all, holding court at his temporary lodging, the tavern Gadsby's.

Patronage, Jackson believed, could give the common man the opportunity to participate in government. He was galled by the fact that one social class—the aristocracy—had monopolized public office for so long. When doling out his Cabinet appointments, Jackson ignored the upper classes, purposely refusing to appoint a New Englander or a Virginian on the grounds that these states fostered exclusiveness in government. Neither of these sections, it might be added, had contributed to his victory.

Jackson changed the structure of government by admitting new classes as participants in it—reminiscent of the way in which patronage in Europe fostered the growth of the bourgeoisie. In Europe, however, the bourgeoisie had wrested power from the upper classes; Jacksonian democracy, more revolutionary in its outlook, professed to have brought the lower classes into government to the shock and dismay of the middle classes who themselves had monopolized power for only a short while.

Despite all the publicity Jackson gave to patronage, in actual fact he removed very few officeholders. No office with judicial functions was touched, and out of 612 executive positions, only 252 were removed. Approximately 600 postmasters out of 8,000 were removed to make way for Jackson appointees. During Jackson's entire tenure of office, it is estimated that only one-tenth to one-third of all federal officeholders were changed, indicating that even then, in matters of patronage, rhetoric bore little resemblance to reality.

Lacking a tradition of professionalism, the spoils system became a battlefield on which several vicious struggles for power were waged. Jackson's administration (which contended with a Whig Senate balanced off against a Democratic House) spent the better part of its time dealing with patronage controversies which barely concealed the political conflicts surging beneath.

Challenging Jackson from the Senate floor were John Tyler, who had lost the position of Secretary of State to Martin Van Buren, and John Calhoun, who was rapidly falling out of presidential favor. Calhoun conducted a formal inquiry into the extent of federal patronage and "the practicability of reducing the same" after leading the battle to refuse confirmation of some of Jackson's appointments. Calhoun's inquiry propounded the theory that patronage made government too big: If this practice continued, he warned, states' rights would be crushed under the force of an ever-expanding federal bureaucracy. His investigation revealed the shocking fact that the 60,294 employees of the federal government, together with their dependents and other pensioners, made up a payroll of more than 100,000 people dependent on the federal treasury. (Today the government employs more than three million people, not including pensioners.) According to Calhoun, this constituted a governmental machine of frightful proportions, and he recommended a drastic reduction of federal patronage as a means of economizing.

Calhoun was the first to recognize and call the public's attention to the scope of federal patronage, going well beyond the appointments power in his revelations. In his recommendations to Congress, Calhoun requested the elimination of the following practices: 1) throwing great amounts of public land on the market to be handled by an army of receivers, registers, and surveyors, all appointees of the President; and 2) giving the President the power to select banks as public depositories, which, Calhoun felt, obligated them to the President.

Needless to say, while the Senate formulated bills to correct these abuses of federal power, the issue really represented an attack on Jackson, for the Whig Senate certainly knew all along that its legislation would be rejected by the lower house. The battles over the spoils system masked the real war, fought between two political parties over parceling out government power. Many felt it was during this period that the two-party system developed into its modern form.

Although Jackson achieved historical notoriety for the spoils system, Lincoln practiced it far more extensively. Lincoln's removal, after his first victory in 1860, of 1,195 out of 1,520 presidential appointees to make room for his own supporters was the most sweeping use of the patronage power to date.

Lincoln showed how necessary patronage was in order to keep together the diverse elements of his party, and to attract the allegiance of those supporting the Union who were outside the party. Patronage was the secret ingredient by which Lincoln secured a power base for a second term, for many federal officeholders participated in the movement to secure Lincoln's renomination. Lincoln was criticized at the time for spending too much of his time on patronage questions; but historians have later admitted that the Union was held together through his clever use of this power.

Patronage grew to full maturity concurrently with the growth of the American political system. By the time Lincoln became President, it was impossible for one man to sit in a tavern and personally take charge of all appointments: [3] gradually congressmen and party leaders were entrusted with some of these powers, and by the time of the Civil War, congressmen had complete charge of post office appointments.

After the Civil War, Presidents Johnson and Grant attempted with considerably less skill to use patronage power as Lincoln had used it. Their ineptitude encouraged a reform movement, composed primarily of dissident Republicans who had not themselves reaped the spoils of victory.

The National Civil Service League, founded in 1881, led a reform movement that succeeded, in 1883, in gaining enactment of the Pendleton Act, which provided for creation of a Civil Service Commission and merit system.

With the spotlight on jobs, American politicians began to exploit the patronage possibilities of other discretionary powers of government. Mark Twain boasted with humor: "I think I can say, and say with pride, that we have legislatures that bring higher prices than any in the world." The legislators earned their fees by voting legislative gifts to railroad, oil, coal, and timber interests. These special franchises were opposed by a handful of men, including Hiram Johnson who ran for governor of California on the platform: "Kick the corporations out of politics." Patronage abuses led to attacks by "muckrakers": Ida M. Tarbell exposed how legislatures were wooed by the Standard Oil Company of New Jersey, and Lincoln Steffens wrote of corrupt municipal governments—Minneapolis, St. Louis, Pittsburgh, Philadelphia, Chicago, and New York. The muckrakers achieved limited success in reforming government, but their writings planted an image on the public mind firmly linking patronage to the shadowy, illegitimate side of government.

[3] In fact, Lincoln dealt with job requests with considerably less relish than Jackson, and when he contracted a slight case of smallpox, he remarked to his secretary: "Tell all the office seekers to come at once, for now I have something I can give to all."

By 1939, all states were compelled to initiate merit systems for employees engaged in programs aided by federal funds. By 1950, 75 percent of all American cities had some type of formal merit system, but only 25 percent of the cities covered all employees. Almost half of the reporting cities with populations of less than 25,000 had no formal civil service system.

Ironically, modern reformers have now begun to question the growth of a civil service system that has allowed the public very little recourse against administrative abuses. They note that under the present civil service system, there is little hope of removing a public servant who, through indolence, ineptitude, or design, sabotages the express wishes of elected officials.

Selected
Bibliography

Books

Adams, Henry. *The Education of Henry Adams*. Cambridge: The Riverside Press, 1918.

Alexander, Herbert. *Financing the 1964 Election*. Princeton: Citizens Research Foundation, 1966.

Altschuler, Alan. *A Report on the Politics of Minneapolis*. Cambridge: Joint Center for Urban Studies, 1959.

American Bar Association. *Canons of Professional and Judicial Ethics*. Martindale-Hubbell, 1908–1965.

Banfield, Edward C., and James Q. Wilson. *City Politics*. Cambridge: Harvard University Press, 1965.

Bendiner, Robert. *Obstacle Course on Capitol Hill*. New York: McGraw-Hill, 1969.

Black's *Law Dictionary*. Revised fourth edition. St. Paul, Minn.: West Publishing Co., 1968.

Bloom, Murray Teigh. *The Trouble with Lawyers*. New York: Simon & Schuster, 1968.

Bolling, Richard. *House Out of Order*. New York: E. P. Dutton & Co., 1964.

Bowers, Claude. *The Party Battles of the Jackson Period*. Boston & New York: Houghton Mifflin Co., 1922.

Carman, Harry J., and Reinhard H. Luthin. *Lincoln and the Patronage*. New York: Columbia University Press, 1943.

Congress and the Nation 1945–1964. Washington, D.C.: Congressional Quarterly Service, 1965.

Congressional Quarterly Almanac. 1960–1969.

Costikyan, Edward. *Behind Closed Doors: Politics in the Public Interest.* New York: Harcourt, Brace & World, 1966.

Dacey, Norman. *How to Avoid Probate.* New York: Crown Publishers, 1965.

David, Paul T., and Ross Pollock. *Executives for Government— Central Issue of Federal Personnel Administration.* Washington: The Brookings Institution, 1957.

Downing, Randall and Richard Watson. *Politics of the Bench and the Bar: Judicial Selection under the Missouri Non-Partian Court Plan.* New York: John Wiley, 1969.

Easton, David. *A Systems Analysis of Political Life.* New York: John Wiley, 1965.

Eulau, Heinz, and John D. Sprague. *Lawyers in Politics.* New York: Bobbs Merrill, 1964.

Farley, James. *Behind the Ballots.* New York: Harcourt, Brace & Co., 1938.

Fenno, Richard. *The President's Cabinet.* Cambridge: Harvard University Press, 1959.

Fenton, John. *Midwest Politics.* New York: Holt, Rinehart and Winston, 1966.

Fenton, John. *People and Parties in Politics.* New York: Scott Foresman & Co., 1966.

Flynn, Edward J. *You're the Boss—The Practice of American Politics.* New York: The Viking Press, 1947.

Grossman, Joel B. *Lawyers and Judges: The ABA and the Politics of Judicial Selection.* New York: John Wiley & Sons, 1965.

Halloran, Matthew. *The Romance of the Merit System.* Limited edition, 1,000 copies. 1929.

Heard, Alexander. *The Costs of Democracy.* Chapel Hill: University of North Carolina Press, 1963.

Hoffman, R. J. S., and P. Levack, eds. *Burke's Politics.* New York: Alfred A. Knopf, 1949.

Hofstadter, Richard. *The Age of Reform.* New York: Alfred A. Knopf, 1955.

Hoogenboom, Ari. *Outlawing the Spoils.* Urbana: University of Illinois Press, 1961.

Jewell, Malcolm. *The State Legislature—Politics and Practice.* New York: Random House, 1962.

Keefe, William J., and Morris S. Ogul. *The American Legislative Process: Congress and the States.* Englewood Cliffs, New Jersey: Prentice-Hall, 1964.

Koenig, Louis, *The Invisible Presidency.* New York: Rinehart & Co., 1960.

Lockard, Duane. *New England State Politics.* Princeton: Princeton University Press, 1959.

Lowi, Theodore. *At the Pleasure of the Mayor—Patronage and Power in New York City 1898–1958.* New York: The Free Press of Glencoe, 1964.

McDonald, Stephen. *Federal Tax Treatment of Income from Oil and Gas.* Washington: The Brookings Institution, 1963.

McNeill, Robert J. *Democratic Campaign Financing in Indiana.* Princeton and Bloomington: Citizens Research Foundation and Institute of Public Administration at Indiana University, 1966.

Makielski, Stanislaw. *The Politics of Zoning.* New York: Columbia University Press, 1966.

Martindale-Hubbell Law Directory, Vol. I, 1969.

Matthews, Donald R. *U.S. Senators and Their World.* Chapel Hill: University of North Carolina, 1960.

Mitgang, Herbert. *The Man Who Rode the Tiger—The Life and Times of Judge Samuel Seabury.* Philadelphia and New York: J. P. Lippincott Co., 1963.

Munger, Frank, ed. *American State Politics.* New York: Thomas Y. Crowell & Co., 1966.

National Forest Products Association. *Directory and Policies.* 1968–1969.

Neustadt, Richard. *Presidential Power.* New York: Signet—New American Library, 1964.

Olson, Mancur. *The Logic of Collective Action.* Cambridge, Mass.: Harvard University Press, 1965.

Pearson, Drew, and Jack Anderson. *The Case Against Congress.* New York: Simon & Schuster, 1968.

Richards, Peter G. *Patronage in British Government.* London: George Allen & Unwin, Ltd., 1963.

Riordan, William L. *Plunkitt of Tammany Hall.* New York: McClure Phillips & Co., 1905.

Sayre, Wallace S., ed. *The Federal Government Service.* Englewood Cliffs, N.J.: Prentice-Hall, 1965.

Sayre, Wallace S., and Herbert Kaufman. *Governing New York City.* New York: Russell Sage Foundation, 1960.

Sidey, Hugh. *John F. Kennedy, President.* New York: Atheneum, 1963.

Silberman, Charles. *Crisis in Black and White.* New York: Random House, 1964.

Stern, Philip. *The Great Treasury Raid.* New York: Random House, 1962.

Swart, Koenrad W. *Sale of Offices in the Seventeenth Century.* The Hague: Martinus Nijhoff, 1949.

Van Riper, Paul. *History of the United States Civil Service.* Evanston, Ill.: Row, Peterson, 1958.

Wilson, James Q. *The Amateur Democrat.* Chicago: University of Chicago Press, 1962.

Wilson, Woodrow. *Congressional Government: A Study in American Politics.* Boston: Houghton Mifflin & Co., 1885.

Wilson, Woodrow. *Constitutional Government.* New York: Columbia University Press, 1921.

Articles, Periodicals, Monographs, Dissertations, and Newspapers

Alexander, Herbert. "The Role of Money in the Political Process," unpublished paper prepared for the National Commission on Law and Law Enforcement and the Prevention of Violence, October 1968.

Alexander, Herbert, and Harold B. Meyers. "The Switch in Campaign Giving," *Fortune*, November 1965. Reprint.

American Judicature Society. "The Extent of Adoption of the Non-Partisan Appointive-Elective Plan for the Selection of Judges," Report # 18, November 1967.

American Judicature Society. "Judicial Selection and Tenure," Report # 7, February 1967.

Albert H. Aronson. "Merit Systems in Grant-in-Aid Programs," *Public Personnel Review*, October 1968, reproduced by the United States Department of Health, Education and Welfare.

Christian Science Monitor (Boston), April 3, 1969.

Cincinnati Enquirer (Cincinnati), June 13, 1959.

Citizens Union. "District Leaders as Judges' Secretaries," Confidential Memorandum from Counsel, November 6, 1957.

Civil Service Leader, Vol. XXVII, No. 11, November 16, 1965.

Congressional Quarterly (Washington). 1950–1970.

Congressional Quarterly. "Fact Sheet," June 5, 1969.

Congressional Quarterly. "Fact Sheet on Federal Patronage Jobs," December 23, 1968, pp. 1–17.

Congressional Quarterly. "Fact Sheet on Model Cities Grants," November 27, 1967.

Congressional Quarterly. "Note to Editors—Tax Reform," July 21, 1969.

Congressional Quarterly Weekly Report. "Campaign Spending in the 1968 Elections," Special Supplement, Vol. XXVII, # 49, pp. 2432–2477, December 5, 1969.

Cooley, Rita W. "The Department of Justice and Judicial Nominations," Vol. 42, *Journal of the American Judicature Society*, 1958, pp. 86–90.

———. "Judicial Appointments in the Eisenhower Administration (January 1952–January 1958), *Social Science*, Vol. XXXIV, No. 1, January 1959, pp. 10–14.

Couturier, Jean J. "Patronage Versus Performance—The Balance Sheet of Civil Service Reform," *Good Government*, Vol. LXXXIV, Fall 1967, pp. 13–16.

Davidson, Bill. "The Worst Jail I've Ever Seen," *Saturday Evening Post*, July 13, 1968.

Daynes, Byron. "The Commission Plan for the Retirement, Discipline and Removal of Judges." Pamphlet, The American Judicature Society, June 1968.

Despres, Leon M. "On the Democratization of the Democratic Party," Remarks of Alderman Leon M. Despres before the McGovern Commission of the Democratic Party at the Sherman Hotel, Chicago, Illinois, June 7, 1969.

Godfrey, Rev. John A. "The Right of Patronage According to the Code of Canon Law." A dissertation submitted to the Faculty of Canon Law of the Catholic University of America, 1924.

Goldman, Sheldon. "Politics, Judges and the Administration of Justice," Ph.D. dissertation, Harvard University, 1965.

Herring, E. Pendleton. "First Session of the Seventy-third Congress," *American Political Science Review*, Vol. 28, February 1934, pp. 82–83.

Highsaw, Robert. "The Southern Governor Challenge to the Strong Executive Theme," in Frank Munger, ed., *American State Politics*. New York: Thomas Y. Crowell Co., 1966.

Katz, Daniel, and Samuel J. Eldersveld. "The Impact of Local Party Activity on the Electorate," *Public Opinion Quarterly*, Volume 25, Spring 1961, pp. 16–17.

Kelley, Stanley. "Patronage and Presidential Legislative Leadership," unpublished paper, Princeton, New Jersey, 1968.

The Knickerbocker News (Albany), 1968.

Kopkind, Andrew, and James Ridgeway, "Law and Power in Washington," *Hard Times*, # 36, June 16–23, 1969, pp. 1–4.

Lindsay, John V. "Address Prepared for Delivery before the Association of the Bar of the City of New York." January 29, 1968.

Lipman, Matthew, and Salvatore Pizzurro. "Charismatic Participation as a Sociopathic Process," *Psychiatry: Journal for the Study of Interpersonal Processes*, Vol. 19, No. 1, February 1956, pp. 11–30.

Maass, Arthur. "Congress and Water Resources," in Alan Altschuler, ed. *The Politics of the Federal Bureaucracy*. New York: Dodd, Mead & Co., 1968.

Mansfield, Harvey. "Political Parties, Patronage and the Federal Government Service," in American Assembly, *The Federal Government Service: Its Character, Prestige and Problems*, 1954, pp. 81–111.

Newsweek (New York), March 10, 1969.

New York Post (New York), January 4, 1968; February 4–6, 1969.

The New Yorker (New York), January 10, 1969; May 30, 1970.

The New York Times (New York), 1950–1970.

Parry, J. H. "The Sale of Public Office in the Spanish Indies under the Hapsburgs," *Ibero-Americana*, No. 37, December 17, 1953. Berkeley: University of California Press, 1953.

Plager, Sheldon, and Joel F. Handler. "The Politics of Planning for Urban Redevelopment: Strategies in the Manipulation of Public Law," *Wisconsin Law Review*, No. 3, Summer 1966, pp. 724–775.

Republican Congressional Committee. "Where the Action is. . . . The President's Club," mimeographed pamphlet. Washington, D.C., 1966.

Sorauf, Frank J. "Patronage and Party," *Midwest Journal of Political Science*, Vol. III, No. 2, May 1959, pp. 115–126.

Sorauf, Frank J. "The Silent Revolution in Patronage," in Edward Banfield, ed. *Urban Government—A Reader in Administration and Politics*. New York: The Free Press of Glencoe, Inc., 1961.

Sorauf, Frank J. "State Patronage in a Rural County," *American Political Science Review*, Volume L, December 1956, pp. 1046–1056.

The Wall Street Journal (New York), December 7, 1967.

Washington Post, November 20, 1969.

Williams, Lynn A. "Intended Remarks of Lynn A. Williams, Democratic Committeeman, New Trier Township, at a meeting of the Central Committee, Cook County Democratic Party on Friday, April 11, 1969, Sherman House, Chicago, Ill."

Williams, Lynn A. "Text of Remarks of Lynn A. Williams at Hearing of the McGovern Commission, Chicago, Illinois, June 7, 1969."

Zoning Procedures Committee. "Planning and Zoning for Fairfax County, Virginia," September 1967.

Public Documents

Central Arizona Project. Report Submitted Together with Minority and Individual Views, submitted by Mr. Hayden, from the Committee on Interior and Insular Affairs, 90th Congress, 1st Session, Senate, Report 408, Calendar No. 395, July 26, 1967.

Citizens Committee on Zoning Practices and Procedures. *A Program to Improve Planning and Zoning in Los Angeles.* First Report to the Mayor and City Council, Los Angeles, California, July 1968.

Colorado River Basin Project. *Hearings before the Subcommittee on Irrigation and Reclamation of the Committee on Interior and Insular Affairs,* House of Representatives, 90th Congress, 1st Session, and H.R. 3000 and Similar Bills to authorize the construction, operation and maintenance of the Colorado River Basin project, and for other purposes: and S. 20 and Similar Bills to provide for a Comprehensive review of national water resource problems and programs . . . March 13, 14, 16, and 17, 1967. Serial No. 90-5.

Colorado River Basin Project. Public Law 90-537, 90th Congress, S. 1004, September 30, 1968.

Committee on the Judiciary, U.S. Senate. Submitted by the Subcommittee on Administrative Practice and Procedure. *Responses to Questionnaire on Citizen Involvement and Responsive Agency Decision-Making.* 91st Congress, 1st Session. Washington, D.C.: U.S. Government Printing Office, 1969.

Department of Defense. *Major Military Installations in the United States.* March 31, 1967.

Marbury v. Madison. 1 CR. 137 (1803).

New York State Bulletin. General Fund Statement of General Fund Operations for the Month of February 1968 and for Eleven Months Ended February 29, 1968 as Required by the State Comptroller by Section 8 of the State Finance Law. Vol. XL, March 15, 1968, # 9.

New York State Constitutional Convention. "Transcript of the Minutes of a Public Hearing of the Judiciary Committee Relating to the Selection of Judges," held in the Senate Chamber, the Capitol, Albany, N.Y., on June 6, 1967.

New York State Constitutional Convention. "Transcript of a Public Hearing of the Judiciary Committee Relating to the Merger of the Courts," held in the Senate Chamber, Albany, New York, 1967.

Office of the Secretary of Defense, Directorate for Statistical Services. *U.S. Military Prime Contract Awards by Region, State and Commodity Category.* Fiscal Years 1962–1967.

Office of the Secretary of Defense. Directorate for Statistical Services. *Department of Defense Prime Contract Awards by State*, March 1968.

President's Commission on Law Enforcement and Administration of Justice. *Task Force Report: The Courts.* Washington, D.C.: U.S. Government Printing Office, 1967.

United States Department of Health, Education and Welfare. Office of State Merit Systems. *Directory of State Merit Systems.* October 1968.

United States Department of Health, Education and Welfare, United States Department of Defense, and United States Department of Labor. *Progress in Intergovernmental Personnel Relations.* Report of the Advisory Committee on Merit System Standards. December 30, 1968.

INDEX

339

About the Authors

MARTIN TOLCHIN is City Hall Bureau Chief for the *New York Times* and an Associate in Journalism at the Columbia University School of Journalism. He was educated at the University of Utah and received a law degree from New York Law School.

SUSAN TOLCHIN, his wife, is Visiting Assistant Professor of Political Science at the Graduate School of Brooklyn College and a Democratic County Committeewoman in Montclair, New Jersey. She is a graduate of Bryn Mawr College, the University of Chicago, and New York University, from which she received her Ph.D.

The Tolchins live in Montclair, New Jersey. They have two children.

WITHDRAWN